Mary McLeod Bethune the Pan-Africanist

UNIVERSITY PRESS OF FLORIDA

Florida A&M University, Tallahassee
Florida Atlantic University, Boca Raton
Florida Gulf Coast University, Ft. Myers
Florida International University, Miami
Florida State University, Tallahassee
New College of Florida, Sarasota
University of Central Florida, Orlando
University of Florida, Gainesville
University of North Florida, Jacksonville
University of South Florida, Tampa
University of West Florida, Pensacola

Mary McLeod Bethune the Pan-Africanist

ASHLEY ROBERTSON PRESTON

University Press of Florida
Gainesville · Tallahassee · Tampa · Boca Raton
Pensacola · Orlando · Miami · Jacksonville · Ft. Myers · Sarasota

Publication of this work was made possible by a Sustaining the Humanities through the American Rescue Plan grant from the National Endowment for the Humanities.

Copyright 2023 by Ashley Robertson Preston
All rights reserved
Published in the United States of America.

28　27　26　25　24　23　　6　5　4　3　2　1

Library of Congress Cataloging-in-Publication Data
Names: Preston, Ashley Robertson, author.
Title: Mary McLeod Bethune the Pan-Africanist / Ashley Robertson Preston.
Description: First. | Gainesville : University Press of Florida, [2023] |
 Includes bibliographical references and index. | Summary: "Broadening
 the familiar view of Mary McLeod Bethune as an advocate for racial and
 gender equality within the United States, this book highlights Bethune's
 global activism and her connections throughout the African diaspora"—
 Provided by publisher.
Identifiers: LCCN 2022051284 (print) | LCCN 2022051285 (ebook) | ISBN
 9780813069654 (cloth) | ISBN 9780813068923 (paperback) | ISBN
 9780813070421 (pdf) | ISBN 9780813072807 (ebook)
Subjects: LCSH: Bethune, Mary McLeod, 1875–1955. | African American women
 teachers—United States—20th century—Biography. | African American
 philanthropists—United States—20th century—Biography. | Civil rights
 workers—United States—20th century—Biography. | BISAC: HISTORY /
 African American & Black | SOCIAL SCIENCE / Black Studies (Global)
Classification: LCC E185.97.B34 P74 2023 (print) | LCC E185.97.B34
 (ebook) | DDC 370.92 [B]—dc23/eng/20221107
LC record available at https://lccn.loc.gov/2022051284
LC ebook record available at https://lccn.loc.gov/2022051285

The University Press of Florida is the scholarly publishing agency for the State University System of Florida, comprising Florida A&M University, Florida Atlantic University, Florida Gulf Coast University, Florida International University, Florida State University, New College of Florida, University of Central Florida, University of Florida, University of North Florida, University of South Florida, and University of West Florida.

University Press of Florida
2046 NE Waldo Road
Suite 2100
Gainesville, FL 32609
http://upress.ufl.edu

This book is dedicated to my guys. Marcellas, I could not do any of this without you, my love. Carter G., you are Mommy's favorite little boy in the whole wide world. You two are my reason, and I love you beyond words.

Contents

List of Illustrations ix

Acknowledgments xi

Introduction: Honoring the Africa within Her 1

1. Southern Roots and Evolving African Identity in Bethune's Early Life 10
2. Global Citizenship and the Influence of the Black Clubwomen's Movement 22
3. The Founding and Internationalizing of the National Council of Negro Women 37
4. World War II and the Challenge of Decolonization 65
5. National Council of Negro Women's Postwar Leadership Abroad 88
6. Bethune Advances Her Global Agenda beyond Retirement 108
7. The Legacy Continues 129

Conclusion 140

Notes 143

Bibliography 173

Index 189

Illustrations

Illustrations follow page 54.

1. Bethune with Liberian vice president and Liberian official, 1945
2. Bethune with W. E. B. Du Bois and Walter White, 1945
3. Delegates from India attending NCNW Annual Convention, 1947
4. Bethune and fellow delegate representing India at the NCNW Annual Convention, 1947
5. Reception at the NCNW Headquarters honoring Ambassador Charles of Haiti and Minister King of Liberia, 1948
6. Bethune at intercultural party for foreign students, 1948
7. Retirement dinner for Bethune at US Department of the Interior, 1949
8. President Harry Truman, Madame Pandit, and Ralph Bunche at Bethune's final meeting as NCNW president, 1949
9. Bethune signing a document for Liberian secretary of state Momolu Dukuly, 1952
10. Liberian president William V. S. Tubman with Bethune, 1952
11. Bethune rushing to plane being held for her at LaGuardia Airport, 1952
12. Bethune at inauguration event for Liberian president William V. S. Tubman, 1952
13. Bethune at inauguration event for Liberian president William V. S. Tubman, 1952
14. Bethune alongside fellow attendees of Emancipation Day Celebration events in Windsor, Ontario, 1954
15. Members of the Hour-a-day Study Club alongside Bethune in Windsor, Ontario, 1954

16. A letter from Bethune to David P. Botsford, 1954
17. Bethune with Madame Pandit of India, 1950s
18. African women looking at international flag during visit to Council House in Washington, DC, date unknown

Acknowledgments

This book has been the ultimate labor of love, and there are so many people who have been a blessing to me throughout this journey.

I always tell my students that "Great sources are what make a great paper!" Whether in-person or online, the archives that I visited played a significant role in my ability to produce a thoroughly researched monograph. Special thanks to Kenneth Chandler at the National Archives for Black Women's History and staff at Moorland-Spingarn Research Center; Schomburg Center for Research in Black Culture; University of Massachusetts Amherst Libraries; and the Indiana University Digital Library. To my Canadian colleagues Kaitlyn and the ladies of the Hour-a-Day Study Club—Preston Chase, Sue Fader at the University of Windsor, and Mary-Katherin Whelan at the Amherst Freedom Museum—thank you so much for providing me with such incredible resources that detailed Mrs. Bethune's travels to your country. Ms. Elise Harding-Davis, I truly appreciate your willingness to speak with me and the wealth of knowledge that you shared.

Writing can be a very lonely process, but having a village of women scholars encouraging you makes all the difference. Dr. Kimberly Brown Pellum, every time I call, you always answer, and I can never repay you for your wise counsel and scholarly advice on this book. Thank you so much, sis! Dr. Ana Araujo, I cannot put into words how much of a blessing you have been to me. I could not have finished this project without your encouragement, and for that I say thanks! Dr. Nikki Taylor, thank you for your support as the Chair of the Howard University History Department and for being an advocate and a friend. Mrs. Jada Wright-Greene, your encouragement and support has truly been my saving grace.

More than a decade ago I started this book, and my colleagues have been with me every step of the way, pushing me and challenging me to dig deeper. Thank you, Dr. Elizabeth Clark-Lewis and Dr. Joy Kinard, for encouraging me to examine the international aspect of Mrs. Bethune's work.

Dr. Stephanie Evans, your advice opened my eyes to the depth of this work. Thank you! My fellow Bethunite Ranger John Fowler, if it wasn't for you, I would have never known how much of an impact Mrs. Bethune had on this nation! Thanks, friend! Thank you for the creation of the Momma Musings Writing Group, Dr. Arlisha Norwood Austin! The feedback from the group really helped me to reframe my thoughts on this book. Thanks to you and Jessica Wick. Dr. Ida Jones, thank you for giving me space to write at a time when I needed it most.

Prayer is what I always ask for, and it is what my family and friends always provide. Thank you so much! Mommy, Auntie M, Auntie Carolyn, Cassandra, Tanya, Pastor Dove and Lady Dove, I love you all! Princess, Jerilyn, Nerissa, Cliffordette, Selma, April, Carolynn, Renee and Aja, thank you for your support. Special thanks to those who help us take care of Carter. I truly appreciate you, Nurse Esther, Nurse Godfrey, and Hannah.

This book would not be possible without my husband, Marcellas Preston. He created an environment that allowed me to write by going above and beyond as my partner while I committed myself to this project. You are my coauthor to the book of life, and I love you so much, babe. Carter G., now that this book is complete, Mommy promises to take you to the zoo. I love you so much, kiddo.

Introduction

Honoring the Africa within Her

> Well Mrs. Bethune was a person that everyone knew, and she had a deep sense of identification with her people. It's amusing to me to hear people talk today about black being beautiful, because Mrs. Bethune was one of the chief exponents of that idea, perhaps twenty-five or thirty years ago. I remember many of her speeches, in which she would stand up and say yes, I'm black and I'm beautiful. And I never sensed any disagreement on anybody's part, with Mrs. Bethune. She was a queenly woman in appearance and there were so many things about her life which showed her sense of identification.
>
> —Clarence Mitchell

A proud descendant of Africans long before she gained the title First Lady of Negro America, Mary McLeod Bethune had a strong sense of where she came from and who she was.[1] She embraced her heritage, her dark skin, and the entirety of her story. She once wrote: "I have not let my color handicap me. Despite many crushing burdens and handicaps, I have risen from the cotton fields of South Carolina."[2] Rather than being ashamed of her illiterate parents, her rural upbringing, and her founding of a school with just $1.50, Bethune found confidence in these aspects of her life, realizing that these were the things that shaped her identity.[3] Her life was complex, with layers that have yet to be revealed. Throughout the course of her life she would work with presidents and world leaders, putting the issues of people of African descent at the forefront of her concerns, using her influence to address diversity in the military, decolonization, suffrage, and imperialism.

Often Bethune and many other women were not thought of as Pan-Africanist unless they associated themselves with organizations led by men. They were in the shadows of those men and validated primarily by their work with them.[4] Women like Anna Julia Cooper and Fannie Barrier Williams are vaguely remembered as a part of the Pan-African struggle largely because of their attendance at Henry Sylvester Williams's Pan African Conference (held in London in 1900).[5] Amy Ashwood Garvey and Amy Jacques Garvey are largely known for their activism in the United Negro Improvement Association (UNIA), but their individual Pan-African activism is often overshadowed by their relationships with Marcus Garvey. Bethune neither attended the conferences nor was a member of UNIA, but she was, in fact, a Pan-Africanist. Mary McLeod Bethune was a Pan-Africanist who internationalized the scope of Black women's organizations to accomplish her agenda to create solidarity among Africans throughout the Diaspora.[6] This is the first full-length book that frames Bethune as a Pan-Africanist. This examination of the life and legacy of this trailblazer takes into consideration her anticolonialist, sociopolitical leanings as well as her belief that Africans throughout the Diaspora have shared experiences of oppression.

Bethune once said: "For I am my mother's daughter, and the drums of Africa still beat in my heart. They will not let me rest while there is a single Negro boy or girl without a chance to prove his worth."[7] For Bethune the drum, a powerful instrument among people of African descent, symbolized her connection with the continent as the daughter of a direct descendant of Africa. Her activism as a Pan-Africanist is seen through her efforts to bring liberation to Africa, create solidarity among Africans throughout the Diaspora, and bring attention to the plight of Africans outside of the United States. According to P. Olisanwuche Esedebe's text *Pan-Africanism*: "Pan Africanism is a political and cultural phenomenon which regards Africa, Africans and African descendants abroad as a unit. It seeks to regenerate and unify Africa and promote a feeling of oneness among the people of the African world. It glorifies the African past and inculcates pride in African values."[8] Esedebe's definition is the one I use in identifying Bethune as a Pan-Africanist.

Born in the rural South to formerly enslaved parents, she had none of the privileges that many of those around her at the height of her career enjoyed, but her faith and pride in knowing who she was kept her from seeing herself as being less than anyone. In fact, being born into a place where African heritage and traditions were celebrated and remembered and having a personal connection to Africa and Africans throughout the Diaspora are what influenced her to advocate for the rights of Black people throughout the world. Whether she was visiting Europe to meet with Lady Astor, writing in the *Chicago Defender*, or speaking at the founding of the United Nations, she used every opportunity to address issues impacting Africans throughout the Diaspora. She called for voting rights for Haitian women, criticized

America for neglecting the issue of decolonization, and persistently fought for the inclusion of Black women in World War II. Bethune saw herself as a voice of the oppressed.

Paul Robeson, W. E. B. Du Bois, Walter White, and Booker T. Washington were some of the well-known men whom Bethune worked with during the twentieth century. However, within their writings, they often disregard her significance. In fact, she is left out of the male-dominated conversations on Pan-Africanism although her actions and philosophies warrant acknowledgment within this space. For example, how is it that Du Bois's Pan-African congresses are recognized as having "established the idea of Pan-Africanism" and that he is often called the "Father of Pan-Africanism"?[9] There is no doubt that congress meetings were significant spaces, but the women of the International Council of Women of the Darker Races (ICWDR), of which Bethune was a founding member, also brought women from Haiti, Liberia, Cuba, and India together to take a stance against the occupation of Haiti and to promote race pride, as an organization of women standing in solidarity from around the world. Although it was founded first, just a few years before ICWDR, the Congress tends to dominate the historical record. Alongside Du Bois at the San Francisco Conference, which led to the founding of the United Nations, Bethune took a bold stance against the colonization of Africa, yet she is often relegated to being only a national leader. Unlike her male contemporaries, she had to work within the confines of being a Black woman in a racist and sexist society. Carefully planning her steps and using her networks among women to build solidarity throughout the Diaspora, Bethune's Pan-Africanist work has been under the radar until now.

From her early years Bethune learned about the glorious past of Africa, the place from which her ancestors descended, and she remembered her mother as being a beautiful dark woman who "came down from one of the great royalties of Africa."[10] Bethune was born in a place that once included the largest port of entry of enslaved Africans into the United States and a coastal area where the Gullah people preserved African culture. It was also where Africans gathered and united on the banks of the Stono River to oppose slavery. Resistance to white supremacy and resistance to the erasure of African culture were part of the South Carolina experience, and Bethune's life embodied both. In her youth, as her family history was passed down to her, she came to understand that she was a part of the African Diaspora. Bethune declared that when she finally visited the continent in 1952, "I was thrilled to set foot in this soil of Africa which I have so long dreamed of visiting—of returning to my homeland."[11] The acknowledgment of Africa being home is significant to her understanding of her connectedness to the continent and its people, and it is a clear demonstration of Pan-African activity, which is defined as "attempts of some people in the diaspora to make contact with the ancestral homeland, either to return there to stay, to visit temporarily, to take back to it what they assume are some of the benefits they have secured."[12] Bethune visited schools and met with women's organizations during her trip to Liberia, to share her insight and knowledge as an educator and global leader. Noted Pan-Africanist Marcus Garvey called for people of African descent to return to Africa in the early twentieth century, but just a few decades later Bethune urged readers of the popular Black newspaper the *Chicago Defender* to consider making a home in Liberia.[13] Following the visit, she encouraged her readers to seek out opportunities to aid Liberia by visiting or considering moving to the country, in the hope that they could bring innovative ideas to help advance the country.

At the age of twenty she attempted to go to Africa as a missionary, but it was not until she was seventy-six that she finally was able to go. In the five decades between, Bethune focused on unifying descendants of Africa through the leadership of women's organizations, starting with the founding of her school. "Fostering solidarity between all Black people everywhere" is a distinct characteristic of Pan-Africanism, and Bethune understood the limitations that came with being a woman in a male-dominated society. For her, though, connecting with women was the access point.[14] She welcomed women from Haiti, Liberia, the Bahamas, Cuba, and beyond to join her organization, and she traveled to their countries to hear their concerns and foster relationships. Bethune surrounded herself with globally minded individuals and organizations to gain insight into the issues she sought to understand. Sue Bailey Thurman, Mary Church Terrell, Madame Vijaya Pandit, Addie Hunton—these were all women with whom she connected. She didn't necessarily need formal conferences and congresses as a way to demonstrate her Pan-African ideals because for her it was the foundation of the work that she did.

* * *

I fell in love with Mrs. Bethune's story when I was a graduate student at Howard University. I was encouraged to volunteer at the Mary McLeod Bethune Council House National Historic Site by my professor (now colleague) Dr. Elizabeth Clark-Lewis. It was there that I met Dr. Joy Kinard, and immediately I was intrigued. I wondered how Mrs. Bethune's story could be so overlooked when she was one of the most influential women of her time. She was, in fact, the Oprah of the 1940s and 1950s. As I listened to the stories of her life from Mrs. Margaret Miles and Ranger John Fowler, I realized how much of her story resonated with mine, with both of us being from a small Carolina town and understanding the power of education. The Council House itself was a powerful space that had welcomed people such as Madame Vijaya Pandit, Mary Church Terrell, Ralph Bunche, and Liberian ambassador Charles D. B. King.

The archives became my home away from home, and I was offered a position as an archives technician. The job never felt like work because every day I was there I learned more about Mrs. Bethune and the women whom she mentored and was mentored by. The National Archives for Black Women's History is the only archive in the United States dedicated solely to the preservation of Black women's history, and it was the starting point for my research.

After completing my doctoral degree, I was offered a job at Bethune-Cookman University to be the director of the Mary McLeod Bethune Foundation National Historic Site. In the five years that I was there running her home I learned so much about her life from the people I met in the community who knew her. My first book, *Mary McLeod Bethune in Florida*, was inspired by her grandson (who was also her legally adopted son) Mr. Albert McLeod Bethune Jr. The book features interviews with her student Mr. Harold Lucas, her former colleague Dr. Cleo Higgins, and her last secretary, Mrs. Senorita Locklear. In the Bethune-Cookman University archives I thumbed through documents that revealed the depth of her leadership abilities as a college president and a world leader. In Daytona I became engrossed in community work, leading projects including the placing of historical markers at Bethune Beach, the home of Dr. Howard Thurman, and the Harold V. Lucas Foundation. In the early years, when Florida was considering Mrs. Bethune for Statuary Hall, I was the only Bethune scholar to speak to the Ad Hoc Committee of Great Floridians, presenting a speech on the contributions that she made to the state throughout her five-decade residency. In 2022 she replaced Confederate general Edmund Kirby, making her the first African American to have a state-commissioned statue.

This book is the culmination of more a decade of research and my experience as the director of the Daytona home that she lived in for more than four decades, oral interviews with those who knew her, working in the Mary McLeod Bethune Council House and archives in Washington, DC, where she conducted the business of the National Council of Negro Women and my tenure as an assistant professor of history at the university she founded. Working in two of her homes has given me insight into her life that goes beyond the depths of research, making this work very personal to me. My quest to tell the story of this multidimensional woman led me to archives including the Library of Congress, Schomburg Center for Research in Black Culture, Moorland-Spingarn Research Center, National Archives for Black Women's History, and the State Archives of Florida. I was fortunate to be able to visit the online archives of the University of Massachusetts Amherst Libraries for the collection of W. E. B. Du Bois and the Indiana University Archives for William V. S. Tubman Papers. Canadian archives including the Amherstburg Freedom Museum and the University of Windsor Archive and Special Collections were especially helpful. When writing this book, I consulted multiple archives and relied heavily on primary source material for a thorough examination of the international aspect of Mrs. Bethune's life.

You will note that I sometimes call her Mrs. Bethune, and there is a story behind this. At an event she attended the announcer asked, "Mary, do you wish to come to the platform?" She stood up, with her cane in hand (a gift from President Franklin D. Roosevelt), and corrected the announcer, saying, "My name is Mrs. Bethune!"[15] Within the world of scholarly writing it is standard to refer to someone using their last name only, but I will always think of her as Mrs. Bethune!

* * *

Chapter 1 examines Bethune's early years, the significance of her experiences in South Carolina, and her early understanding of Africa. As a child growing up in the small town of Mayesville, she was very much aware of her African lineage, and she took great pride in this throughout her life. It became her life goal to journey to Africa as a missionary after hearing a speech at church, but she was denied the opportunity. The idea of returning to the home from which her ancestors came played an important role in why young Bethune wanted to become a missionary, but she found that as an educator she could still make an invaluable impact on African Americans and beyond. Chapter 2 examines how Bethune's involvement in ICWDR and National Association of Colored Women (NACW) gave her a new sense of international awareness and renewed her desire to connect with the African Diaspora. Rising through the ranks of NACW presented her with opportunities to be mentored by women including the internationally known activist Mary Church Terrell. As a founding member of the

ICWDR, Bethune met women from Haiti, India, and Africa, arming her with knowledge of the issues faced by people of color, far from the United States. The experience that she gained working with NACW and ICWDR clarified the vision for the type of global agenda she wanted to create for her own organization.

Chapter 3 discusses the 1935 founding of the National Council of Negro Women (NCNW) as the culmination of Bethune's activism as a clubwoman and an emerging national leader. While simultaneously serving as director of the Division of Negro Affairs for the Franklin D. Roosevelt administration, she called attention to the plight of Black America and forged relationships throughout the African Diaspora. As president of NCNW, she created a network of women who studied global affairs, and she gave them space to internationalize the work of the US-based organization. Sue Bailey Thurman, Dorothy Porter, and Eunice Hunton were a few of the women whom Bethune relied on to implement her vision of solidifying bonds between African descendants. The *Aframerican Woman's Journal*, the official magazine of NCNW, became an important part of its global agenda, and it was distributed widely in Latin America, India, the Philippines, and Haiti. NCNW members traveled to Cuba to learn more about the history and current challenges of Afro-Cubans, shared cultural exchanges with Ethiopian women who visited the United States, and wrote letters to women in Liberia in the hope of meeting them. Chapter 4 examines how Bethune and the NCNW navigate the challenges of World War II and their response to decolonization efforts. Advocating for Black women's involvement in war efforts, Bethune saw the opportunity as a vital step toward the world recognizing Black women as being participants in world affairs. As the war sought to defeat fascism, decolonization efforts intensified and Bethune became a part of the movement. As a supporter of the Council on African Affairs, she aligned herself with one of the leading anticolonial organizations of its time. In 1945 Bethune served as an associate consultant for the founding charter of the United Nations, alongside W. E. B. Du Bois and Walter White, and the trio took a bold stance against colonization, speaking for oppressed people of color around the world. This was a pivotal point in her activism because her voice would now be heard among world leaders, and being in that space unlocked access to people whom she would not have met otherwise, including Vijaya Lakshmi Pandit.

World War II sparked a fire in African Americans that laid the foundation of the modern civil rights movement and a fire in Africans that ultimately led to decolonization across the continent. Chapter 5 examines NCNW's post–World War II activism as they strengthened coalitions with women around the world to address issues that were plaguing their communities. With the creation of the International Relations Committee, NCNW worked closely with Howard University scholars including Margaret Wormly, Dorothy Porter Wesley, and Merze Tate to gain insight on issues that would become a part of the organization's global agenda. Located in Washington, DC, NCNW headquarters became a safe haven for international travelers of color, where they could have open discussions and cultural exchange. Expanding their presence on the international front, NCNW members traveled to Trinidad to join women from Jamaica, Barbados, and British Guiana to deepen their understanding of the issues faced by women in these respective areas, gaining firsthand insight through workshops and conversations. In the years following the war, Bethune continued to work to solidify her position as an international leader and as a recipient of the Haitian Medal of Honor and Merit, she was finally recognized as such by her peers. For years to come she would continue to reflect on that moment of recognition and her time spent in Haiti.

After fourteen years as president of NCNW, Bethune retired from the organization that she founded, but in many ways her work had just begun. As detailed in chapter 6, she looked beyond leading formal organizations as a means of creating solidarity with Africans throughout the Diaspora. In her travels Bethune consistently made an effort to engage meaningfully with local people so that she could better understand how to use her platform to advocate for them. Ultimately, Bethune sought to create solidarity among people of African descent through "Small p" Pan-Africanist methods. St. Clair Drake defines these methods as those that have "ends that are not political and [are] part of a people-to-people approach to transatlantic relations among black people."[16] In the years following her retirement from NCNW she became an advisor to women's organizations around the world. She was called upon by the women of the Bahamas, who were in the early years of their struggle for suffrage, to share her insight and mentorship on how to move toward obtaining true citizenship and equality. She was also sought after for advice on the issue of education, and on each international visit she included talks with educators. Ultimately, she fulfilled her dream of visiting Africa on her 1952 trip to Liberia, but she brought much more to the continent than she would have in her earlier years, in terms of her ability to advocate for resources and change. Throughout the years that Bethune led NCNW she mentored the women around her, giving them the tools to continue the work of the organization. Chapter 7 examines how NCNW presidents after Bethune interpreted and implemented the international agenda of the organization.

Throughout all of this book's chapters—from Bethune's early years in a space in which African heritage was embraced, to her final years in which she traveled extensively throughout the African Diaspora—we see the manifestation of her role as a Pan-Africanist. Her understanding of the tenets of the ideology was not based on her attendance at Pan-African conferences or events because she embraced Pan-Africanism as a way of life, all of her life. From her work with women's organizations, to the formation of National Council of Negro Women, her focus on issues impacting people of African descent, her love for Africa, and feeling of connectivity to the continent shapes her role as an activist. Within the various organizations and relationships described throughout this work Bethune consistently implemented her goal of unifying people of African descent, and as she recognized herself as a daughter of Africa, she used her voice to advocate for its people around the world.

1

Southern Roots and Evolving African Identity in Bethune's Early Life

With the ending of the positive gains made during Reconstruction, the emergence of the European colonization of Africa, and the formal establishment of Jim Crow through the US Supreme Court's *Plessy v. Ferguson* decision, the late nineteenth century was a precarious time for people of African descent. In many ways the promise of freedom was broken by racism, yet young Mary was determined to overcome it. Although she had never left her small town of Mayesville, South Carolina, as a youth she had a keen sense of her familial connection to Africa, and it was a present force in her life. Excavating Bethune's early years presents important insight into the factors that influenced her Pan-Africanist leanings and her understanding of the African Diaspora. This chapter examines how Bethune's environment, which fostered historical memory of Africa and an understanding of religion as a tool of liberation, played a critical role in shaping how she perceived herself and her role within the struggle of African people. She grew up in a space where African people were able to maintain their connection to the continent unashamedly, and in the McLeod household Mary and her siblings were taught that their family history did not start with slavery but with the lives their forebears lived as free people who were taken from Africa. It was in her home state that she was introduced to the idea of traveling to Africa as a missionary, a role that she saw as a fulfillment of her desire to serve. Although she was unable to do so, not going to Africa was a turning point in which she realized that as a part of the African Diaspora her ability to serve her people was not limited by location. When presented with the opportunity to educate herself, Bethune saw it as the path to liberation, not just for herself but for those whom she encountered. Ultimately, she merged ideas of religion and educational training to found a college where she would educate the masses, to fulfill her promise to serve her people. No matter where she went, she went with the understanding that she was a daughter of Africa with African blood running through her veins, and it was her early years of life that grounded her and gave her a sense of identity.

Early Education of Africa

On July 10, 1875, Mary Jane McLeod arrived, making her the fifteenth of seventeen children born to her formerly enslaved parents, Patsy (McIntosh) and Samuel McLeod. Being the first child to be born free to a family that had lived through the horrors of slavery held much promise for little Mary. According to the 1880 United States Federal Census, Bethune's father, Samuel, was fifty years old, living in Lynchburg, Sumter County, South Carolina, and working as a farmer. Her mother, Patsy, was listed as forty-seven years old and occupied as a housekeeper.[1] The children in the home were Mary Jane (four years old), and her siblings Beauregord (nineteen years old), Julia (seventeen years old), Kissie (seventeen years old), and William T. McLeod (ten years old).[2] The census also revealed that neither parent could read or write, Beauregord could both read and write, Julia and Kissie could read, William T. could read and write and had attended school in 1880, and Mary Jane could read and write and had not yet attended school.

Before Mary Jane could read, she was once ridiculed by a white child for not being able to do so. During a trip to the home of her mother's former enslaver, where her mother was working, Mary Jane picked up a book, and the child took the book out of Bethune's hands, telling her that she could not read, showing her pictures instead. From this moment she became determined to gain an education, understanding that it was a powerful tool that had been withheld from her because she was Black. Just as many formerly enslaved people saw gaining an education as being an important part of their newfound freedom, Bethune began to see that it would be a necessary step in her lifetime also and that it would open doors for her. It was not until she was about ten years old that Bethune was able to attend Trinity Presbyterian Mission School. This required a major sacrifice for her farming family, as they depended on her to join them in the fields, but they allowed her to formally begin her education.

Although Bethune's entire family may not have had the opportunity to attend school, the family's knowledge of their history and the fact that their origins were in Africa was strong. Although the sources of the information are unclear, Emma Gelders Sterne's text *Mary McLeod Bethune* revealed that Bethune's great-grandmother was born in Guinea and was said to have been the daughter of a West African ruler who was captured, taken to America, and sold into slavery.[3] In a 1940 interview with Charles S. Johnson, Bethune stated about her mother: "My mother had a great philosophy of life. She came down from one of the great royalties of Africa. She could not be discouraged."[4] Although her mother could not read, Bethune was proud of her strong will and how she had been able to keep their family together, speaking very highly of her at all times. She often reflected on her mother's faith and leadership abilities, attributing them to her African lineage. In many ways Bethune saw these characteristics as something that was passed down to her from her mother as a unique characteristic of African identity. During the 1800s there were those who minimized the contributions of Africa to the world, calling it a "Dark Continent" in order to justify the colonization and the pillaging of resources that started with the Atlantic slave trade and continued with European colonialism.[5] German philosopher Georg Hegel stated that Africa was "no historical part of the world," characterizing its people as "undeveloped," with the understanding that it was a place unworthy of inclusion in world history.[6] Stereotypes about Africans being savages who needed civilization were widespread, yet in the McLeod household they remembered Africa as their homeland, the place in which their lineage had begun. This early understanding would shape her thoughts on the importance of knowledge of self and one's history.

In her youth, Bethune not only knew of her African ancestry, but she heard stories about African Americans going to Africa as missionaries spreading the gospel of Christianity:

> We found that Dr. Bowen was to speak at the Methodist church. I got with Sister and went over to hear him. As I heard him tell about African people and the need of missionaries, there grew in my soul the determination to go some day and it has never ceased, and I sent up a prayer to God to give me the light—to show me the way that I, in turn, might show others. And for years I just had a yearning to go to Africa and thought that when I was through with my education I could be sent—but instead, I found my way into the deep South.[7]

After learning how to read, write, and count in school, Bethune used her skills to teach other children their letters, she read the Bible to her illiterate parents, and she was often called on in the cotton fields to assist with counting. Hearing about Africa as a place where she could impact others' lives positively was music to young Bethune's ears. She had been using her education to serve her local community, but Bowen's address showed her that there was a place for her to do so in Africa also, and that became her motivation. She did not give Dr. Bowen's full name, but knowing that he was a Methodist minister encouraging missionary work in Africa in the late 1800s makes it plausible that she was speaking of John Wesley Edward Bowen. In her 1941 interview with Charles Johnson, she mentions working as an educator alongside her friend Irene Smallwood, who would later marry and become Mrs. John Wesley Edward Bowen.[8]

This connection opens an important conversation on Bowen's work, particularly his role as host of the Congress on Africa, held in Atlanta, Georgia, in 1895. After making history as the first African American to earn a PhD from Boston University, Bowen rose through the ranks of the Methodist Episcopal Church as a pastor and educator. In his position at Gammon Theological Seminary he became the first full-time African American professor, and he served as the secretary of the Stewart Missionary Foundation for Africa.[9] The Stewart Missionary Foundation hosted the Congress that has been described as "the First Pan-African Christian Church Conference, which brought together African and African American Christian scholars and church leaders."[10] Congress participants presented on topics including "Religious Beliefs of the Yoruba People," "The American Negro and His Fatherland," and "The Outlook for African Missions in the Twentieth Century."[11] Thomas E. Smith notes that "Bowen's Africa for the Africans sentiment emphasizes an emigration theme that was another strand of Pan-African thought."[12] It is very likely that during his travels to promote mission work Bowen transmitted these same Pan-Africanist ideals to a young Mary McLeod Bethune. In Bethune's words, Bowen's speech was a turning point in her life: it was the key influence on her decision to go to Africa, reflecting on the weight of the message that the minister shared. Being in the small town of Mayesville with the understanding that she was very much a global citizen of African descent gave Bethune insight into a greater world that she was determined to understand more about. What a profound impact being raised by a mother who carried the spirit of Africa and meeting a religious leader who showed her the importance of serving and returning to Africa must have had on young Mary.

South Carolina as an African Space

Bethune's early understanding of Africa and her lineage was heavily impacted by her geographic location. Being born in the South, particularly South Carolina, which was the home to Charleston, the largest port of disembarkation of enslaved Africans in the United States, shaped her early years. The 1880 census revealed that South Carolina, followed by Georgia, Louisiana, and Alabama, had the largest number of children born to African parents.[13] Mrs. Patsy McLeod would have been included in this number as it was her side of the family that Bethune recalled as being of direct African descent. Although slavery had ended a decade before Bethune was born, and the abolition of the African slave trade occurred in 1807, many African-born men and women were alive to tell the story of the Middle Passage. Historical memory transmitted by those who had experienced the beauty of life in Africa before being forcibly removed from it presented a powerful picture to those who had never stepped foot on the continent. Bethune benefited from the memories of her family, which had been kept alive, giving her a sense of belonging.

Economically, South Carolina also became one of the richest states in the South during slavery. With its subtropical climate and swampy coastal regions, the state was the ideal place to raise rice. By the eighteenth century, South Carolina's economy was heavily concentrated in the production of rice. In the Georgetown District alone "no other region of the South Atlantic Coast was rice-planting more predominantly the major economic interest; in none was the volume of production greater."[14] To keep the production of rice consistent and profitable, more Africans were brought into South Carolina, and by the end of the slave trade there were more Africans than Europeans in the state. According to Voyages: The Trans-Atlantic Slave Trade Database, an estimated 210,478 Africans disembarked in the Carolinas/Georgia between 1710 and 1858, and the four major regions of embarkation were West Central Africa and St. Helena (60,191); Senegambia and offshore Atlantic (44,682); Sierra Leone (35,042); and Gold Coast (31,387).[15] As early as the 1450s Portuguese travelers observed rice cultivation in West Africa from Senegal to Liberia, and scholar Judith Carney suggests that cultivation in South Carolina can be credited to the agricultural knowledge of West African women, who deeply impacted food culture in the Americas with this skill set alone.[16] In the mid-1700s, indigo also became a major cash crop for South Carolina. Although indigo was a different plant, it grew in the same swamplike conditions as rice, and its season was opposite of the rice-growing season. Because of the two economies existing in South Carolina, the demand to bring more enslaved people from Africa was constant and great. According to the 1860 census South Carolina had the fifth-largest population of enslaved people in the nation, accounting for 57.2 percent of the state's total population.[17]

The Gullah community is an important example of the retention of memory and culture among Africans. The Gullah Coast is located nearly one hundred miles from Mayesville, South Carolina, and it is widely recognized as an area heavily influenced by African culture. Much of its distinct culture and dialect can be traced to West African roots. In 2006, Congress deemed the coastlines of North Carolina, South Carolina, Georgia, and Florida to be the Gullah/Geechee Cultural Heritage Corridor. This area includes the "Gullah/Geechee who settled in the coastal counties of Florida (Duval and Nassau), Georgia (Bryan, Camden, Chatham, Glynn, Liberty and McIntosh), North Carolina (Brunswick and New Hanover) and South Carolina (Beaufort, Charleston, Colleton, Georgetown, Horry, Jasper and parts of Berkeley and Dorchester)."[18]

Lorenzo Dow Turner, a linguist and one of the leading scholars of Gullah studies, was one of the first people to identify and thoroughly research the Gullah people's unique dialect and culture in the areas of South Carolina, Georgia, and Florida. Turner's book *Africanisms in the Gullah Dialect* was published in 1949.[19] In it, Turner argued that the Gullah language, commonly referred to as "baby talk" or "broken English," had phonetic origins in Africa. He examined specific Gullah words and their African origins, debunking E. Franklin Frazier's notion that Africans did not retain their African past throughout the course of slavery.[20] His work essentially showed that although Africans were far from home and experiencing horrific living and working conditions, they did not forget where they came from. Their lives in North America retained their rich African traditions.

Dow's study of the Gullah affirms historian Patrick Manning's "homeland plus" model in which he argues that studying Africa as the place of origin must be understood for proper analysis of the Diaspora.[21] This model also speaks to Melville J. Herskovits's argument that people of African descent retained Africanisms throughout slavery and that African culture and ethnicity must be understood to fully analyze the African retention throughout the Diaspora.[22] Throughout the work of scholar Michael Gomez, he provides a clear definition of the African Diaspora while also exemplifying the study of the African Diaspora as a homeland-plus model. Gomez defines African Diaspora as African descendants whose African "cultural, social and political forms" continue to manifest as a major influence even outside of their homeland although they may be modified.[23] Understanding Bethune's home as a space in which African people, herself included, were able to maintain their connection to the continent, deepens our understanding of the importance of the location in which she grew up and its impact on the person that she would become. Having access to historical memory of Africa through elders who passed this knowledge while also retaining culture would later shape Bethune's interactions with the African Diaspora. She did not have to physically go to Africa to get to know it as her homeland because it was ingrained in her by her family at an early age.

The Drums of Africa

After hearing Bowen speak of the need for more African American missionaries to go to Africa, Bethune says that she "had a yearning to go to Africa."[24] Some African Americans felt that it was their duty to uplift Africa, and religion became a way in which they could do so while also connecting with their heritage.[25] Black women in particular saw missionary work as a way to have a positive impact on African women and children while spreading the Gospel.[26] In pursuit of the opportunity, Bethune continued to further her education. She attended Scotia Seminary in North Carolina (graduating in 1894) and Moody Bible Institute in Chicago (completing her studies in 1895). It was at Moody that she took her final steps toward becoming a missionary, only to have her dreams crushed. When she applied to become a missionary with the Presbyterian Board of Missions, she was denied: "When I completed my work at Scotia, I was sent to the Moody School in Chicago, Illinois. I studied there two years, applying myself. I applied to the Mission Board in New York for a chance to go to Africa. They informed me that no openings were available where they could place Negro missionaries, so they sent me to Augusta, Georgia to work with Lucy Laney."[27]

It is likely that Bethune was among many other African Americans who were not permitted to go to Africa, and, in fact, although large numbers of white missionaries crisscrossed the continent, only a small percentage of total missionaries were Black.[28] The number of African American missionaries sharply declined in the early 1900s, which may have impacted the board's decision to not allow Bethune to go to Africa just a few years before the turn of the century. With the Berlin Conference (1884–85), which resulted in the colonization of most of Africa, occurring as newly freed African Americans were increasingly concerned about the state of affairs on the continent, this presented a possible threat to European colonial powers.[29] Radical ideas of African Americans promoting Pan-Africanism or the philosophies of the New Negro could possibly weaken the hold of Europeans by empowering Africans; therefore, some were prohibited from going altogether.

In her determination to become a missionary, Bethune was not only motivated by religion but also by familial connection to Africa. According to P. Olisanwuche Esedebe, a key component of Pan-Africanism is recognizing "Africa as the homeland of Africans and persons of African origin."[30] Throughout her life she constantly acknowledged and affirmed her African lineage, and she continued to try to extend her reach to Africa. Bethune once said: "For I am my mother's daughter, and the drums of Africa still beat in my heart. They will not let me rest while there is a single Negro boy or girl without a chance to prove his worth."[31] The drum was more than an instrument for people of African descent; it also was a powerful tool that they used to express their feelings, bring about unity, and, often, as a part of healing rituals.[32] For Bethune the drums symbolized the bond she had with Africa. In her essay "A Yearning and Longing Appeased," acknowledging her membership in a matriarchal society, Bethune also professed her African ancestry, saying, "My mother was a direct descendant of a ruling family in West Africa, where even to the present time succession and kinship are reckoned through the mother."[33] Although she was born in South Carolina, Bethune was clear on where her family descended from, and she made others aware of this in her writings and speeches. These very short yet important statements demonstrate Bethune's pride as a woman of African descent and her feeling of connectedness with the continent.

Bethune's desire to spread the Gospel as a missionary has often been overlooked, but we must not underestimate the significance of her actions as a part of her Pan-Africanist agenda. Had she been able to go to Africa with her understanding not only as a Christian but as a daughter of Africa returning to her homeland, perhaps her life would have been much different. For further insight on how mission work converged with Pan-Africanism, it is important to understand the life of Henry McNeal Turner. A noted bishop in the African Methodist Episcopal (AME) Church, Turner made several trips to West Africa (1891, 1893, 1895) to expand the reach of the denomination by establishing churches in Liberia, Sierra Leone, and South Africa.[34] He was a proponent of emigration who believed that as African Americans were returning to Africa, spreading Christianity was an important part of their mission. In a 1894 address he stated that the reasoning for the existence of slavery had been so that "they might come in contact with Christian civilization, and by intercourse with the powerful white race they might fit themselves to go back to their own land [in Africa] and make of that land what the white man had made of Europe and of America."[35] Although his ideals are problematic in that they assume that Africans need civilization, he sees religion as a tool that can be used to empower, and he feels that it is the responsibility of the AME Church to be a part of this mission. Due to his emigrationist efforts, Bishop Turner is considered to have been a forerunner to noted Pan-Africanist Marcus Garvey and his "Back to Africa" movement, which encouraged people of African descent throughout the Diaspora to return to the continent.[36] Turner's religious-based emigrationist work is mentioned as part of the foundations of what would become known as Pan-Africanism, and in later years his rhetoric was mirrored by Garvey.[37] Turner was also among religious leaders who attended the 1893 Chicago Conference on Africa, who were noted as those who "captured the spirit of Pan-Africanism that would serve as a driving force in later movements."[38]

Examining the significance of missionary work and its centrality as the vehicle by which Bishop Turner was able to reach Africa gives us a sense of how important Bethune's attempt to become a missionary was. Bethune's desire to spread the Gospel, though through a different denomination in which she did not have the high ranking of bishop, is very similar. She saw missionary work as the way to connect with Africans and the way in which she would be able to reach the land of her ancestors. Unlike Turner, who had the support of the Black church (AME) in a leadership position that gave him an incredible amount of access to resources, Bethune's fate was determined by a white-affiliated institution that made a decision for her. Given her leadership abilities and organizing efforts in the United States, who knows what she may have been able to accomplish in Africa?

After the upset of not becoming a missionary, Bethune was still determined to continue the work of not only spreading the Gospel of Christianity but also sharing the value of education and hard work. Lucy Craft Laney, an educator and founder of Haines Normal and Industrial School in Augusta, Georgia, offered her a position as a teacher. During Bethune's short but impactful tenure (1896–97), she adopted the idea of starting her own school. Bethune received valuable mentorship from Laney, from whom she learned "Africans in America need Christ and school as much as they do in Africa."[39] She would carry this idea of the necessity of Christ and school as she continued her work as an educator, as it allowed her to continue her missionary journey within the confines of the United States. After completing her work with Laney, she returned to her home state of South

Carolina to teach at Kendall Institute. While working at Kendall she fell in love with a fellow teacher, a young man named Albertus Bethune. In just a few months the pair married and nine months later became parents, when Albert McLeod Bethune was born on February 3, 1899.

Over the next few years there would be much transition for Bethune as a new wife and mother. The family moved to Savannah, Georgia, for a short period before relocating to Palatka, Florida, where she ran a mission school. The newly incorporated town of Daytona was just over thirty years old, making it a ripe place for change and the place where Bethune decided to start her school. On October 3, 1904, she opened the Daytona Literary and Industrial School for the Training of Negro Girls. In later interviews she recalled how she started the school with very humble beginnings: "When I got to Daytona I had only one dollar and a half left in cash. I got a little rented house ... I couldn't pay the rent. The house belonged to a Negro man named John Williams, he rented the house to me for eleven dollars a month. I told him I had no money—but he said he would trust me. I had no furniture. I begged dry goods boxes and made benches and stools; begged a basin and other things I needed and in 1904 five little girls here started school."[40] She not only welcomed her students, but the school became a pillar in the Black community as it opened McLeod Hospital to address the challenges of healthcare disparity. Bethune opened the school doors to host community meetings while also opening the library for local children.[41]

Bethune gave Daytona the service, commitment, and dedication that she would have given Africa, with the mindset that improving the plight of Black people was invaluable work in any part of the Diaspora. Daytona was where she fulfilled her dreams of sharing knowledge to better those around her and where she began to emerge as a rising leader. After the ratification of the Nineteenth Amendment, which gave US women the right to vote, Bethune used her influence to lead Black voters to the polls in the upcoming 1920 election. Her autonomy as the principal allowed her to host night classes to teach people how to pass literacy tests; it also made her a target of the Ku Klux Klan.[42] The night before the election the Klan circled the school, but Bethune was not deterred. She continued to be a vital part of the Daytona Beach community while becoming even more politically engaged on the national level in the years following the incident. It was through hard work and determination that Bethune was able to raise the status of her school from a rented house, which she started with "1.50, faith in God and five little girls," to what, by 1923, became known as Bethune-Cookman College.[43]

Before becoming an educator, Bethune saw religion as the primary medium to equality, but she was forced to reimagine these ideals when she was unable to go to Africa. Education with a religious underpinning became the powerful tool that Bethune brought to the Black community as a means to liberate those who faced limitations in a Jim Crow society. The disappointment of her past did not overshadow her desire to serve, and she was reenergized by young people who depended on her to help shape their futures. The knowledge of her heritage and the pride that she felt was something she wanted her students to feel also, because she understood the impact of it. Stephanie Evans explains that "in her thought and work, Bethune was aware of the complex and central role that cultural identity played in one's educational attainment. Bethune asserted that, in addition to critiquing the dominant culture, African Americans must cultivate knowledge of their own heritage."[44] As an educator Bethune was a fierce advocate of teaching history as a way to empower her students. She believed that knowledge of the past was essential to pride in oneself, and she was especially vocal about the inclusion of African history. Growing up in a home where she knew of her family history had a profound impact on Bethune, shaping her understanding of Africa's greatness. In later years, in an address at the twenty-second annual meeting of the Association for the Study of Negro Life and History, she stated:

> When they learn the fairy tales of mythical king and queen and princess, we must let them hear, too, of the Pharaohs and African kings and the brilliant pageantry of the Valley of the Nile; when they learn of Caesar and his legions, we must teach them of Hannibal and his Africans; when they learn of Shakespeare and Goethe, we must teach them of Pushkin and Dumas. When they read of Columbus, we must introduce the Africans who touched the shores of America before Europeans emerged from savagery.[45]

For Bethune it was important that Black children understood that they did not come from slavery, and that they, too, were descended from people who impacted the world in positive ways. Teaching about Africa as a place of significance and glory, correcting the narrative of it being a dark continent, was an important part of Bethune's work. Becoming an educator was the way in which she would cultivate knowledge of self to empower the next generation. She poured herself into her school, making it successful and impactful in changing the world she saw around her. She was fulfilled by the opportunity to serve, and eventually it would launch her into a position to empower and engage on an even larger scale.

    The pride that was instilled in her during her early years gave Bethune the courage to step out on faith to build an institution to educate African Americans although she had few resources to do so. The mission to serve her people despite the setbacks and obstacles that had been placed before her drove her to be useful to the uplift of the race, deciding that wherever she was, she would use education and religion as tools of liberation. In many ways Bethune's school would help establish her as an influential figure, giving her a voice to become a part of a larger cadre of Black leaders who would impact the world. Attending the all-girls' school Scotia Seminary, founding a girls' school, and the transformative mentorship that she received from Black women allowed Bethune to witness the power of organizing and leading among women. As she sought to continue to build bridges among people of African descent beyond Florida, she saw Black women as her most powerful allies, and she began to cultivate those relationships.

2

Global Citizenship and the Influence of the Black Clubwomen's Movement

As the Black clubwomen's movement began to emerge in the late nineteenth century, its influence was felt not only in the United States but throughout the world. Club members traveled widely, kept themselves abreast of foreign affairs, and used their privileged positions to take a stand against issues such as the colonization of Africa and, later, the occupation of Haiti. Seeing themselves as global citizens who were living in the United States, the women sought to be included in international conversations. Bethune began her journey as a clubwoman seeking to be a part of a larger network in which she could further expand her ideals of building solidarity among African descendants through involvement in these organizations. She began to engage with the NACW and ICWDR, which further expanded her reach globally and helped her to meet women who were involved in international activism. Both organizations gave her the opportunity to glean knowledge and ideals that furthered her understanding of Pan-Africanism and the Diaspora.[1] Ultimately, she accepted that missionary work was not the only path to serving, and within her new role as a clubwoman she would channel her energy into creating change for Africans throughout the Diaspora.

As the founder and principal of her school, Bethune often traveled to raise money, and it was during one of her trips that she met Mary Church Terrell. The mentor/mentee relationship that she developed with Terrell had a profound impact on Bethune's emergence in the club movement, particularly her international involvement. According to Paula Giddings, a speech Bethune made at the National Association of Colored Women's conference wowed the organization, causing Terrell to predict that she would someday be the organization's president: "Bethune asked for permission to address the group, and if she felt self-conscious about coming from a less privileged background than most of the delegates, or by her dark skin and Negroid features, she certainly didn't show it. Bethune spoke with such impassioned eloquence that at the end of her speech Margaret Murray Washington offered to take up a collection for the school."[2] Unlike many of the women to whom she was speaking, Bethune did not come from a privileged background nor was she fair-skinned, but she did not consider either fact to be a hindrance to her. Many may have been surprised that someone of her color who was relatively unknown would have the courage to speak with such boldness among women who were much wealthier and influential than she was. For Bethune, her mother's dark skin, which she inherited, was a reminder of her African heritage, which filled her with pride and allowed her to thrive in a space where she often stood out from others because of her physical appearance. Although her parents had been enslaved just a few years before she was born, they taught Bethune to stand tall, knowing that no matter what her present situation was, she came from royalty. The confidence that she exuded would allow her to speak to anyone whom she thought would be beneficial to her cause, no matter their race or socioeconomic status. As a descendant of African royalty whose skin was the gift of her ancestry, she wrote: "I have never been sensitive about my complexion. My color has never destroyed my self-respect nor has it ever caused me to conduct myself in such a manner as to merit the disrespect of any person. I have not let my color handicap me."[3] Her color, not just being African American but being dark-skinned, could have very well handicapped Bethune. Having lighter skin often provided privileges that were not available to people of her color, but she refused to accept this mindset. Bethune saw herself as a daughter of Africa who was intimately connected to the struggle of its descendants, giving her the courage to approach the women of NACW and to ultimately join them.

As a member of a premier organization, she joined the ranks of Black women who were using their resources and influence to impact women around the world. She was able to support the work of African educators, serve on committees that discussed foreign relations, and network with women who lived and worked abroad, allowing her to expand her knowledge of international affairs as she rose through the ranks of NACW. As a founding member of the ICWDR, Bethune joined an organization whose mission was to instill pride in people of color, forging relationships with women from places including Liberia, South Africa, the Philippines, Brazil, and Haiti. Her experience as a member of ICWDR further enlightened her to the challenges faced by people of color, particularly those who lived under colonial rule, and the importance of women unifying to create change. When Bethune became the national president of NACW, she encouraged the women to take a more active role in the struggle for liberation among people of color, moving beyond their past efforts.

National Association of Colored Women

At the time that Bethune gave her impassioned speech that captured the attention of Terrell, the National Association of Colored Women was one of the leading Black women's organizations in the nation. It was founded on July 21, 1896, at the Nineteenth Street Baptist Church in Washington, DC, when the Colored Women's League of Washington, DC (CWL), and the National Federation of Afro-American Women (NFAAW) merged to form the NACW. The two women's organizations came together following a letter written by the president of the Missouri Press Association, James W. Jacks, in which he said of Black women, "[they] were prostitutes and all were thieves and liars."[4] The immorality of Black women was a constant theme in speeches and publications. The periodical the *Independent* wrote that Black women were said to have "brains of a child, the passions of a woman."[5] In a 1902 edition of the periodical one writer asserted that he could not conceive of a virtuous Negro woman. Fictional works such as *Three Lives*, written in 1909, also featured promiscuous African Americans further advocating immorality. Mary Jane Paterson, Mary Church Terrell, and Anna Julia Cooper "called on a united black womanhood to solve the race's problems" when they created CWL in 1892.[6] NFAAW was founded in 1895 by St. Pierre Ruffin, and the organization's first elected president was Margaret Murray Washington, the wife of Booker T. Washington and the dean of women at Tuskegee.[7] Under the motto "Lifting as We Climb," NACW not only protested Jack's letter, but they set out to strengthen Black womanhood. Some of the key founders of the organization were antilynching activist and journalist Ida B. Wells, civil rights activist Josephine Silone Yates, and abolitionist/poet Frances Harper.[8]

As a self-help organization, NACW brought together hundreds of clubs from across the nation including the Harriet Tubman Club of Boston; the Woman's Musical and Literary Club in Springfield, Missouri; the Semper Fidelis Club of Birmingham, Alabama; and Tuskegee Women's Clubs. Local clubs were led by state federations, which were all under the aegis of the NACW. By 1914 the organization had nearly one hundred thousand members, and its departments included rescue work, mothers' meetings, kindergartens, professional women, businesswomen, and temperance.[9] As the national organization set the goals and mission of the organization, local chapters were responsible for implementing the objectives through action. Some of the objectives included eradicating illiteracy, supporting alcohol prohibition, ending the lynching of Blacks, and gaining full citizenship. *National Notes*, the organization's official publication, "served as an instrument to unite the women and to educate them in the sciences and techniques of reform."[10]

Bethune's initial attendance at the national NACW conference was transformative because it marked the moment that she would begin to surround herself with powerful Black women who would become an important part of her network of change agents. For years she wrote letters to try to connect with influential leaders, including Booker T. Washington, in the hope that they would give her advice or assistance with her school. She understood that alone she could not reach national or global power brokers, but with the help of Black women she could. She found a mentor in Mary Church Terrell, and it was through that relationship that Bethune saw the power of using one's voice internationally to bring attention to the plight of people of African descent. Over the years the relationship between the two women would become one of mutual respect and collaboration.

Mary Church Terrell was born in Memphis, Tennessee, in 1863 during the bloody Civil War and the year of the issuing of the Emancipation Proclamation. Although it is unclear if her parents were enslaved at the time of her birth, they had been enslaved, and after the ending of slavery both became wealthy business owners. Terrell attended Oberlin College and was one of the first Black women to graduate from the university with an undergraduate and a graduate degree. She was one of the founding members of NACW and its first president and one of the founding members of the National Association for the Advancement of Colored People. Terrell was heavily involved in organizations centered in Washington, DC. However, her international activism was also a significant part of her work, which focused on "the understanding that race and gender are inseparable factors in Black women's lives and oppression."[11]

Attending international conferences provided often challenging yet important moments where Black women were able to engage with audiences beyond the realms of the United States, making their plight known globally.[12] When Mary Church Terrell was invited to deliver an address at the 1904 International Congress of Women Congress in Berlin, Germany, she did not hesitate. Traveling abroad during segregation presented its own set of challenges, but she availed herself nevertheless. Her presence alone drew the attention of the other attendees, as she was the only Black woman at the conference, speaking on behalf of Black women throughout the African Diaspora. Terrell felt the pressure and the significance of this moment, stating: "I wanted to place the colored women of the United States in the most favorable light possible. I represented, not only the colored women of my own country but, since I was the only taking part in the International Congress who had a drop of African blood in her veins, I represented the whole continent of Africa as well."[13] She rose to the occasion, giving her speech in English and German. In the address she discussed the challenge of being handicapped by both race and sex, as well as the achievements of Black women in the business, education, finance, and volunteer work.[14] She did not shy away from calling out labor federations for excluding African Americans while she praised Black women for what they had been able to accomplish despite being just a few decades out of slavery.[15] The speech was well received by attendees, not only because of the content but because of her impressive delivery in German. In her autobiography Terrell recounted how the speech aroused interest on the "Race Problem of the United States" among her attendees and that requests for more information on the issue came from Germany, France, Austria, and Norway.[16]

As a delegate to the Quinquennial International Peace Conference in Zurich in 1919, Terrell also used the occasion to bring international attention to the unequal treatment of African Americans. Of her experience, she wrote: "I appealed for justice and fair play for all the dark races of the earth. 'You may talk about permanent peace till doomsday,' I predicted, 'but the world will never have it till the dark races are given a square deal.'"[17] At a time when African Americans were living under the thumb of Jim Crow laws and experiencing lynchings, disfranchisement, and discrimination in every aspect of daily life, it was essential to alert the world to these conditions. America was becoming a global power, but it had failed to live up to the promises that it made to every one of its citizens, particularly African Americans. Terrell understood that meetings with global audiences were significant events in which her words could transform the plight of Black people everywhere. Terrell's international addresses made a very important contribution to the legacy of African American women's internationalism, paving the way for others to continue to bring global awareness to their struggle, and ultimately Bethune would become an heir of that legacy.

Although the women came from different socioeconomic backgrounds and at times they did not agree, Bethune was influenced by Terrell's visionary leadership and activism. She often referred to her in her writings and speeches, naming her in a 1926 essay as one of the nation's "beacon lights."[18] When Bethune later organized the National Council of Negro Women, Terrell was present, and she reluctantly supported its founding.[19] Bethune saw her as someone who affirmed the work that she was doing, and in many ways she modeled Terrell's leadership. Terrell used her platform to speak against injustice internationally, and she was well traveled and very much a global citizen; Bethune would go on to model this part of her vision.

Rising up the Ranks

Despite the incredible responsibility of running a school (which became a college in 1923, making her a college president), Bethune began to put just as much work into becoming a clubwoman, specifically a NACW member. First, she became involved on the local level in her state, working her way through the ranks to become president of the Florida Federation of Colored Women in 1917. The Florida Federation consisted of various local clubs such as the Civil Improvement Club, Sojourner Truth Club, Amanda Smith Club, Woman Development Club, and Women's Literary Art and Social Club.[20] Although there is little information on Bethune's involvement with NACW before her national presidency, we do know that during her tenure as the president of the Florida Federation of Colored Women, she founded the Delinquent Home for Colored Girls in Ocala, Florida, as the organization worked with the mission to "lend a helping hand to the unfortunate girl."[21] In 1920 she was elected as president of the Southeastern Federation of Colored Women's Clubs, which consisted of state federations from Alabama, Florida, Georgia, North Carolina, South Carolina, Tennessee, Mississippi, and Virginia.[22] During her tenure some of the projects of significance included "get out the vote" activities, interracial programs, and social welfare services.[23]

On the national level, Bethune was vice president of NACW from 1922 to 1924, while also serving on the organization's advisory board. With each appointment, Bethune's network grew, allowing her to forge relationships with influential women who had spent years furthering causes that impacted the Black community. National conferences provided the perfect opportunity for her to meet and connect with women who could assist with her work. During the Thirteenth Biennial Convention of NACW, held in Richmond, Virginia, August 6–12, 1922, the organization created a Peace and Foreign Relations Department, which was led by Addie Hunton. Hunton had served as a YMCA worker in France during World War I assisting Black troops, and in 1920, she released the book *Two Colored Women with the American Expeditionary Forces,* cowritten by Kathryn Magnolia Johnson.[24] In it Hunton shared vivid details of the trials and triumphs of African American soldiers during World War I, and the experiences of being in France. Hunton was also a suffragette, a field worker for the National Association for the Advancement of Colored People (NAACP), and she traveled extensively during her lifetime. Her work abroad and her leadership in NACW would draw Bethune to invite her to become a part of her organization (National Council of Negro Women) almost a decade later. During her tenure with NACW, Bethune understood that making connections with women like Hunton would prepare her for the work that she would do.

The NACW conventions often invited speakers from throughout the Diaspora, while members who traveled would share intimate details of their trips as a part of the convention itinerary. During the Thirteenth Biennial Convention, Madam Casely Hayford, better known as Adelaide Smith Casely Hayford, spoke with NACW members about African culture. Hayford was married to Pan-Africanist, lawyer, educator, and author J. E. Casely Hayford, and during her time in America she spoke with several African American organizations, educating them on Africa.[25] Born in Sierra Leone to an elite Freetown Creole family, Hayford spent much of her youth in England before returning home. In Freetown she headed the United Negro Improvement Association's Ladies Division of the Freetown branch and founded the Girls' Vocation School.[26] In 1920 she arrived in the United States, hoping to raise funds for her school by educating various groups about Africa and sharing her cultural philosophies. During her talk with NACW, Hayford discussed the importance of community and cooperation in Africa, African aesthetics, and experiences of motherhood in Africa.[27]

Instilling African pride was one of Hayford's main tenets during her talks to African Americans, and she often wore African attire in an attempt to "instill into us some form of racial pride and . . . foster a national spirit."[28] She would also often display artwork during her talks, as she believed it to be "Africa's greatest contribution to world civilization."[29] In support of

Hayford's mission to develop young girls socially and educationally, NACW raised nearly $150 after her presentation to assist in her work in Sierra Leone. As the sole founder of a school that was started with $1.50, if there was any member of NACW who understood Hayford's situation and the importance of supporting the work, it was Bethune. NACW was particularly concerned about raising up a race of respectable women, and Hayford's Girls' Vocation School fit the mold of the work they were doing. Having access to women like Hayford was an important connection for Bethune because it gave her insight into the concerns of Africans, allowing her to better prepare herself to meet those needs as a rising leader.

In 1924 the vision that Mary Church Terrell had years earlier came to fruition when Mary McLeod Bethune was elected as the eighth president of NACW. She was stepping into a position that had been filled by the most influential women in Black America. She was preceded by her mentor, Mary Church Terrell, and other leading women including Josephine Silone Yates, Lucy Thurman, Elizabeth Carter Brooks, Margaret Murray Washington, Mary B. Talbert, and Hallie Q. Brown. During the 1926 Fifteenth Biennial Convention held in Oakland, California, Bethune announced plans to build a national headquarters by the next convention as a means to stabilize and centralize NACW's activities. In her address she expressed ideals about the significance of the headquarters, stating: "We want unborn generations of Negro youth to map the national home of this federation a shrine to which they will make pilgrimages for inspiration. There they will find their ground for home in the carefully kept records and history of our people."[30] Bethune saw the headquarters as essential to the building of the organization's legacy, and she put all of her efforts into fundraising to ensure that it was completed by the end of her tenure as president. It was not only a historical moment for the organization and a major accomplishment for President Bethune, but it would become an important aspect of the preservation of its history.

According to the convention notes, there also was much discussion of conditions in Africa during the Fifteenth Biennial. NACW member Helen Curtis spoke to members about the years that she spent in Liberia. Curtis was the wife of James L. Curtis, who served as a minister resident and consul general to Liberia after the two relocated to Liberia in 1915. Following his 1917 death, Curtis continued to support Liberia and "returned to Liberia for nearly a decade to conduct missionary work and teach in the capital of Monrovia."[31] She shared her experiences as a teacher in the public school system in Monrovia, the necessity of mission schools, and the need for more attention to Africa. In support of Curtis's mission work, NACW members called upon each other to send barrels of flour, clothing, and bandages, and $116.40 was raised.[32] In keeping with its motto "Lifting as We Climb," NACW was determined to do its part in lifting the social and educational status of Africans.

In Bethune's convention speech she used her position as president to encourage NACW members to continue to not only see themselves as global citizens but to work to address issues faced by "colored" people around the world:

> Colored people's difficulties are political and economic throughout the world. Through wise politics and statesmanship, they must liberate themselves. Through far-sighted economic leadership, they must master the business of taking care of themselves like other races. Bred, born and living here under the American Flag, we nevertheless bear a relation to others of our blood. Their problems are ours and vice versa. All our wisdom, energy and foresight should be dedicated to the great task of achieving freedom and independence which are the highest goals for human striving. We must make this national body of colored women not merely a national influence, but a significant link between peoples of color throughout the world.[33]

Much of the focus of NACW's work was within the United States, but Bethune challenged the members to think beyond the confines of the nation and to unify themselves with "colored" people around the world. Traditionally, as in the case of Hayford and Curtis, the organization financially supported mission efforts in Africa, but in her speech Bethune calls for greater involvement and concern, challenging the women to move beyond what had already been done. She wanted them to understand that, although they were worlds apart, there was commonality in their struggles. The mention of "others of our blood" speaks to the belief that she saw herself and other Black people throughout the Diaspora as being one unit. Her discussion of the need for freedom and liberation gives the sense that she is expressing concern about the issue of the colonization of Africa. As the leader of the influential organization, Bethune sought to not only bring attention to issues impacting people of African descent around the world but to become unified with them and to use their resources and privilege as American citizens to aid in securing their freedom.

Bethune continued to challenge NACW members to expand their network globally when she announced the "Good Will and Investigation Tour" to Europe for the summer of 1927. Members of NACW often traveled abroad individually, but it was her desire to make united travel a part of the organization. It was not enough to discuss international affairs at conferences; she wanted them to visit the places and meet the people for themselves as a collective. She stated, "If Ethiopia is to stretch forth her hands, then those hands must belt the seas, and to belt the seas, it is fitting that the women of the N.A.C.W. should know from actual observation and touch, how to go about their work."[34] Her biblical reference to Ethiopia stretching forth its hands has historically been used by people of African descent including Maria W. Stewart, Martin Delany, W. E. B. Du Bois, and Marcus Garvey as a call for liberation.[35] At a time when much of Africa was colonized by European forces, Bethune was calling for the women to study and understand imperialism by traveling to the place from which it stemmed. It was not enough to study international affairs from the comfort of the United States; she was interested in them having a firsthand experience. She proposed that the trip would be one in which the organization would "observe and study" the industrial centers, caste problems, educational systems, and governments of Europe.[36] With her mentor and friend Terrell in mind, she noted that she knew it would be pleasing to Terrell to know that the organization was traveling internationally.[37]

Although Bethune urged NACW to travel to Europe, records do not indicate that members other than herself attended. Led by Dr. A. Wilberforce Williams, Bethune represented NACW among a group of fourteen, which included several physicians.[38] In June the group set sail for a two-month trip to destinations including England, Italy, Germany, and France. They had dinner with officials including the lord mayor of London and lord provost of Edinburgh, while they also visited children's hospitals, churches, colleges, and museums.[39] Bethune personally arranged for the women in the group to have tea with Lady Edith MacLeod, the daughter-in-law of the founder of the Church of Scotland. Using her connection as a member of the International Council of Women of the World to set up the meeting, she led an "intelligent discussion of the women of America of color."[40] Overall, Bethune saw the trip as further expanding the network of NACW to connect with people of influence. Her organizing of the tea with Lady MacLeod to discuss issues pertaining to Black women demonstrates her attempt to foster a relationship that could possibly benefit the women whom she represented. Just as she gave her NACW speech in 1909 to draw the attention of the members to the work of her school, this was a similar opportunity but from a global perspective.

International Council of the Women of Darker Races

As a national leader in NACW, Bethune was able to meet leaders from Africa and women who traveled and studied abroad. The national convenings encouraged members to become more culturally aware and to financially support mission and education efforts in Africa, but Bethune sought more opportunities to address issues faced by people of color. Stepping outside of NACW, members including Mary Church Terrell, Mary McLeod Bethune, Addie Hunton, and Nannie Helen Burroughs founded the ICWDR. Margaret Murray Washington, wife of Booker T. Washington, led the charge to create the organization, and she was elected as its first national president. Bethune and Washington knew each other not only through their clubwomen's activism with NACW and ICWDR, but they were dear friends. Bethune referred to her as her "big sister" who would provide invaluable mentoring over the years.[41]

The organization was founded in Richmond, Virginia, at the closing of the NACW national meeting; however, its first organizing meeting did not take place until August 1922 in Washington, DC, at Nannie Helen Burroughs School.[42] Margaret Murray Washington was elected as president; Mary Church Terrell as first vice president; Addie W. Hunton as second vice president; and many other women including Charlotte Hawkins Brown, Addie Dickerson, Mary Talbert and Adelaide Casely Hayford accepted leadership positions.[43] Bethune joined the organization as a member during the first meeting. According to the August 26, 1922, *Chicago Defender*, during its first meeting women from as far as Africa, Haiti, the West Indies, and Ceylon (Sri Lanka) were in attendance.[44] The organizers described the group's founding principles: "Our object is the dissemination of knowledge of peoples of color the world over, in order that there may be a larger appreciation of their history and accomplishments and so that they themselves may have a greater degree of race pride for their own achievements and touch a greater pride in themselves."[45] At the time the term *colored* was generally used for people of African descent, a usage dating back to the nineteenth century, when it was created to reject colonization efforts. At the time when discussions to send free Africans back to Africa were happening, there were many who did not want to be forced to uproot themselves, so they referred to themselves as colored rather than African.[46] Overall, in the United States the term was used to describe people of African descent, but its use was expanded to include darker-complexioned people around the world who found themselves being oppressed by Europeans. By the first meeting ICWDR had begun to correspond and exchange ideas with women from Liberia, South Africa, the Philippines, Brazil, and Haiti.[47] Under the leadership of Washington, the organization was intentional about uniting people of color, and Sheena Harris notes that, with the founding of ICWDR, "She became, in her own way, a Pan-Africanist."[48]

ICWDR presented Bethune with an opportunity to forge relationships with women of color from around the world while also delving into the issues they faced. Although the organization was inclusive, it did not accept white members. Murray wrote, "The Anglo-Saxon race [is] barred because of [its] racial antagonism to darker women—not being defamed like women of color, hence [it] would not have the interest and could add nothing to the determined purpose to ameliorate conditions for darker races throughout the world."[49] The phrase "darker race" was used by W. E. B. Du Bois in *Souls of Black Folk*, where he states, "the problem of the twentieth century is the problem of the color line—the relation of the darker to the lighter races of men in Asia and Africa, in America and the islands of the sea."[50] In his 1903 book, Du Bois saw the oppression faced at the hands of whites as the commonality among "darker races" wherever they were in the world. Color was a factor in their experience, and it could not be denied. Several decades later, during the mid-twentieth century, Asians and Africans of the darker races would come together for the Bandung Conference, where they would resolve to work together to "promote goodwill and cooperation among the nations of Asia and Africa."[51] Noted author Richard Wright attended the conference, and in his analysis of it he stated, "This meeting of the rejected was in itself a kind of judgment upon that Western world!"[52] Before Bandung there was ICWDR, working to strategize and bring women together to solve their own problems without the help of whites. Washington and members felt that because whites had not faced oppression and could not relate to the experiences of being of the "darker races," they could be of no assistance.

In a September 15, 1922, letter to Lugenia Hope, Washington wrote that ICWDR's first task was "to get into every school, private, public or otherwise Negro Literature and History."[53] Taking it a step further, the women formed a committee to create a curriculum for studying Black literature and history. It was not until 1926 that Carter G. Woodson launched Negro History Week. In 1920, however, Omega Psi Phi Fraternity started to celebrate "Negro History and Literature Week" after Woodson advised the men to begin to promote Black history.[54] ICWDR called on Woodson to assist with their initiative, as he had already established the Association for the

Study of Negro Life and History, and he was leading the charge to popularize Black history.[55] However, many of the educators who were a part of ICWDR were already including Black history in their school curriculum, including Bethune. According to Sheila Flemming, as early as 1915 courses including "history of the Negro" and a study of Booker T. Washington's *Up from Slavery* were included in the curriculum of Bethune's school.[56] However, what Washington was calling for was not just a study of Black History but the history of the African Diaspora through the study groups, which would be initiated by members. The groups would help the women become more knowledgeable about international affairs by honing in on specific places where "darker races" resided. Michelle Rief notes: "The popularity of the study clubs indicates the strong desire of ICWDR members to learn more about various parts of the world. Equally significant, they encouraged women in their local communities to learn more about international issues and hence see their day-to-day struggles in a larger global context."[57]

In August 1923, the ICWDR gathered in Washington, DC, on the campus of Nannie Helen Burroughs National Training School, and the following elections were made: Mrs. Booker T. Washington, president; Addie Hunton Floyd, first vice president; Mary Church Terrell. second vice president; and Miss Elizabeth C. Carter, recording secretary.[58] Bethune was elected to be a part of the executive committee, which was headed by Nannie H. Burroughs. In her new position Bethune was responsible for the planning of annual meetings, receiving potential members' information, and the overall decision-making process for issues that arose in between meetings.[59] With its membership including women from around the world, the executive committee played an important part in ensuring that the work of ICWDR continued once everyone returned to their homes and that they were as organized as possible. Three committees were created during the 1923 convention: International Relations; Social and Economic Conditions; and Education.[60] Resolutions were also adopted to continue to disseminate information about "darker races" and to generate race pride through historical appreciation. Some of the adopted recommendations to be carried out by the organization included a study on "the history and literature of the darker races of the world"; the publishing of "the result of our study of the condition of women and children in Haiti"; and "a special study of conditions of women and girls in all parts of Africa."[61] Ultimately ICWDR sought to use their influence to publish information that addressed the plight of women and children around the world, so that others could join them in their efforts. This information was not just for the organization, but there was a plan in place to educate those around them also. One of the first international service projects that the organization initiated shortly before their meeting was an "investigation of the conditions of the women and children of Haiti."[62] The occupation of Haiti was in its eighth year, and overall the Black community was concerned about the treatment of its people. In many ways African Americans held the "First Black Republic" in high regard because of its inspiring defeat of slavery.[63] Over the years Haiti would continue to have a presence on the ICWDR agenda, particularly because the occupation would last almost two decades. The organization was interested in ways that they could support the women of the country, and for them it was imperative to have one of their own to see the conditions faced by Haitians by traveling there.

After 1925, much of the scholarship and many of the records of ICWDR are scattered. The sudden death of president Margaret Murray Washington on June 4, 1925, created some instability within the organization. But despite the loss of the founder, over the years, the study of African American history and literature continued to be a part of the ICWDR agenda, as well as problems affecting colored people across the globe. In 1925 the organization joined forces with the Women's International League for Peace and Freedom (WILPF), an interracial organization that supported women's rights and peace from war abroad. Addie Hunton, who was president at the time, represented ICWDR as a part of WILPF's program to investigate US occupation of Haiti, and in "February 1926 the delegation traveled to Haiti to observe and evaluate U.S. rule there."[64] Again, Haiti continued to be a major focus for the organization, as the Black community called for the United States to leave Haiti. Continuing their international engagement through travel, Addie Dickerson later became the president of ICWDR, and on behalf of the organization in 1930 she traveled to Europe to "study the attitudes of many of the women of the darker races."[65]

As Bethune simultaneously worked to expand her college while building a national headquarters for NACW, she was busier than ever, and it is unclear whether she remained a part of the ICWDR past the 1920s. However, what is clear is that her involvement in NACW and ICWDR played a crucial role in her understanding of the African Diaspora. In every leadership position that she held after her involvement with the organization, she used it as a platform to not only bring attention to issues impacting Africans in America but also within the Diaspora. Through her participation in the ICWDR she studied international affairs, supported an investigation of conditions faced by women and children in Haiti, and she took part in intimate conversations with women from countries who felt the impact of colonization firsthand. This was very much a training ground for Bethune, and it prepared her to be able to speak for people of African descent with clarity and true understanding. Armed with the knowledge from the ICWDR once she became the president of NACW, she sought to use her position to create change. NACW shows an embrace of African people and culture, but Bethune challenged the women to also use their resources and positions of privilege and power to be a part of the liberation struggle for people of African descent. She made a call for the women to go beyond the work that they had previously done. As Bethune's influence grew, NACW and ICWDR allowed her to hone her craft as an international leader preparing for her next step of creating her own organization.

3

The Founding and Internationalizing of the National Council of Negro Women

Having served as the president of one of the leading Black women's organizations of the era, Mary McLeod Bethune was becoming a powerful voice throughout the nation. Just ten years after its founding she became an honorary member of Delta Sigma Theta Sorority in 1923, joining the ranks of influential Black women including Hallie Q. Brown, Sadie T. M. Alexander, Vashti Turley Murphy, and Mary Church Terrell. In 1930 journalist Ida M. Tarbell named her as one of fifty most influential American women, alongside Jane Addams, Helen Keller, and Margaret Sanger.[1] Bethune singlehandedly founded a school with a $1.50, and because of her hard work and dedication, it was now a thriving college, making her an expert in the field of education. Bethune had become a recognized national leader, but she sought to expand her influence globally. Following in the steps of her mentor, Mary Church Terrell, she worked to create a new Black women's organization with the intention to build international relationships with women. She would call on women including Sue Bailey Thurman to lead the newly formed National Council of Negro Women (NCNW) on a trip to Cuba to meet the country's most influential women while also forming the *Aframerican Woman's Journal*, publishing articles in English, French, and Spanish and distributed globally. As she simultaneously led the Black division of the National Youth Administration (NYA) and NCNW, she leveraged relationships to bring council members to the White House to discuss with government officials the issues faced by African Americans. Her influence grew both nationally and internationally, and she was honored when she became a member of the Society of Afro-Cuban Studies. Having experienced discrimination during an earlier trip to Cuba, her admission into the Society was a testament to her ability to connect with Africans despite attempts to prohibit her from doing so. As the leader of NCNW, she welcomed African women to collaborate and join the organization, expressing interest in visiting their countries through her communication to Liberia and Ethiopia.

Although Bethune could work with anyone, her ability to successfully wield power among Black women was unmatched. Bethune was a visionary who saw herself as someone who could unify the masses beyond the United States, and she would do so by joining forces with other women; however, she did not limit herself to women-led spaces. In 1930 she was received by the government of Bermuda to conduct an educational survey of the island, an indication of her growing international influence.[2] In her overall analysis of the visit, she promoted race consciousness and self-leadership among Bermudians to overcome the challenges they face as a colonized territory.[3] Bethune also called for more cooperation between African Americans and Bahamians, stating, "I believe, for the darker races of the world to aim at and strive for a closer relationship among themselves, with the great object in view—self development."[4] Her words to the people of Bermuda were no different from her message to NACW when she encouraged the women to look across the sea to understand and unify with other people of African descent. The message of building coalitions and mutual understanding among Black people was Bethune's primary desire, and she would be most effective at doing so through the creation of her own women's organization.

Founding of NCNW

The year 1935 would mark a leap in Bethune's career trajectory as she became the second woman to receive the coveted Spingarn Award from the NAACP. The award was instituted in 1914 and issued annually "for the highest or noblest achievement by an American Negro during the preceding year or years." Spingarn winners prior to Bethune included former NACW president Mary Talbert; author and *Crisis* magazine editor W. E. B. Du Bois; scientist and inventor George Washington Carver; and historian Carter G. Woodson.[5] Recognition from such a prestigious organization, one of the premier advocates for civil rights, was a major success for Bethune and an indication of her prominence and influence. The success that she wielded as a leader was the catalyst for the founding of her organization.

The National Council of Negro Women was founded on December 5, 1935, at the 137th Street branch of the Young Women's Christian Association

(YWCA) in New York City. The thirty African American women who attended the first organizational meeting represented a broad array of organizations. The who's who of women included Addie Hunton (Alpha Kappa Alpha Sorority); Charlotte Hawkins Brown (Palmer Memorial Institute); Mabel Keaton Staupers (National Association of Colored Graduate Nurses); Irene E. Maxwell (Women's Auxiliary of the National Baptist Convention); and Daisy Lampkin (NAACP).[6] It was on this day Bethune announced her desire to create a council of colored women that would "make a stronger appeal for putting over big projects."[7]

During her tenure with the NACW she encountered the predominantly white National Council of Women, and it was there that Bethune began to envision a similar organization for Black women. While brainstorming, she stated, "This council would function among colored women somewhat as the National Council of Women functions among white women largely."[8] As she gained more understanding of the inner workings of the political climate in Washington, DC, Bethune realized that what was needed was "a super organization [that] would have greater access to federal dispensation of funds."[9] Bethune founded NCNW to bring unity among African American women's organizations relating to public opinion and to have more cooperation as a whole among existing African American women's organizations. As great an idea as this may have been, the organization was not created without some resistance. With women already heavily involved in the NAACP and other male-led organizations and in light of the Great Depression, some felt that it was an inauspicious time to create an organization. The NACW was almost forty years old and was already an influential force among Black women, with members across the nation. NACW founder and former president, Mary Church Terrell, was resistant to the idea, stating, "I cannot see any reason how this group can do any more than others, but I think it worthwhile."[10] Although there were a few initial objections from women who did not understand the point of "another organization," a unanimous vote from the women at the meeting supported the idea, and Bethune was voted to become the first president of the organization.[11] It was not until April 29, 1936, that permanent officers were elected and the constitution was adopted.[12]

president—Mrs. Mary McLeod Bethune
first vice president—Dr. Charlotte Hawkins Brown
second vice president—Mrs. Christine Smith
third vice president—Dr. Eudora Ashburn

fourth vice president—Mrs. Mary Church Terrell
recording secretary—Mrs. Florence K. Williamson
executive secretary—Dean Lucy D. Slowe
treasurer—Mrs. Addie W. Dickerson[13]

What would set the organization apart from others was its structure and accessibility, which allowed women from all walks of life, from college and professional women to religious organizations, to join as members of current organizations or as individuals.[14]

Terrell's hesitancy about NCNW could also have been due to the timing of its inception. The United States was in the midst of the Great Depression, and although the nation was devastated by its effects, African American communities were hit especially hard. In urban areas specifically, the unemployment rates for African American women were double and sometimes quadruple that of white women.[15] Internationally, people of African descent rallied around Ethiopia as the Italians invaded one of only two African nations that remained untarnished by European colonialism. The lynching of African Americans had gained national attention, and in 1935 Black leaders attempted to get President Franklin D. Roosevelt to support the Costigan-Wagner Anti-Lynching Bill; to their disappointment he refused to support it. For people of color, 1935 had been a year of ultimate highs and lows.

It was an incredible feat to start an organization in the midst of economic and social crisis while simultaneously accepting a historic position that would provide invaluable opportunities for her and the women that she led. She had become an authoritative voice on issues impacting African Americans, particularly youth, and her 1936 appointment as the National Youth Administration's (NYA) director of the Division of Negro Affairs confirmed Bethune's position as one of the most influential women in the nation. The previous year President Franklin D. Roosevelt appointed her as a part of the NYA advisory board, but in her new position she made history by becoming the first Black woman to head a federal agency. The NYA was one of several New Deal programs Roosevelt created in response to the impacts of the Great Depression, which left the country in an economic downturn. Focusing on "work relief" and "student aid" for youth between the ages of sixteen and twenty-five, NYA provided invaluable funding at a time when it was desperately needed.[16] It was also in this role that Bethune would become the unofficial leader of the Black Cabinet, a group of Black federal employees who came together to "channel their individual campaigns against discrimination and transform them into an unofficial lobby for African American concerns."[17] Bethune was honored to accept the role of leading the agency, as it allowed her to advocate for and assist African American youth across the nation, building upon her work as an educator. During its seven-year tenure the organization would create job opportunities for more than three hundred thousand Black youth, provide training programs for librarians and teachers in rural Mississippi, and provide critical medical exams for more than twenty-six thousand Black children.[18] As she worked to establish NCNW as a nationally and internationally known organization, Bethune's role as the director of the Division of Negro Affairs would provide access to resources and networks that would help expand the organization's influence.

From its inception NCNW had a clear vision and purpose. One of the core principles of the organization was to bring unification to national organizations, particularly those that concerned African American women. Serving as an umbrella to more than twenty-five organizations, NCNW was able to implement calls to action in which each individual organization played a unique role. Many of the women who were a part of the formation of NCNW were leaders in their communities, national civil rights organizations, and the women's club movement who embodied the organization's goal to further the progression of the race educationally, economically, and politically. The organization was also intended to be a voice "to provide articulation for the millions of Negro women of this country in their struggle for opportunity and equality."[19] Raising cultural awareness while also informing women on the issues concerning them was also at the center of the organization's purpose. This commitment to inform was implemented by the founding of newsletters, journals, and community events. Although the bulk of NCNW's work was grounded in the United States, its purpose was to go beyond the domestic domain, and it was committed to affiliating "with international organizations of women in order to promote world peace through cooperation and friendship."[20] In the midst of building international relationships based solely on issues affecting women, NCNW built cross-cultural bridges between women of color throughout the Caribbean and Africa.

For the first few years of her presidency, Bethune employed her high-ranking position with the National Youth Administration to gain access to federal resources, often giving members opportunities that otherwise would not have existed. In 1938 the women were received by First Lady Eleanor Roosevelt in a meeting at the White House to discuss the status of women's participation in federal programs. Members including Eunice H. Carter,

Sadie T. M. Alexander, Addie Hunton, and Arenia Mallory gave short talks on issues affecting women, while they also sought answers as to why there was limited participation in programs including Unemployment Compensation, Housing and Vocational Rehabilitation, and Child Welfare Services.[21] As she sought opportunities for Black women overall, Bethune brought influential, well-respected women to represent the race. Working alongside her mother, Addie Hunton, Eunice Hunton Carter came from a family that was deeply engaged in social justice work. Her father, William Alphaeus Hunton Sr., broke barriers as one of the first Black YMCA administrators, and her mother, Addie, worked abroad for the YMCA assisting Black troops in France during World War I.[22] Eunice a successful lawyer at a time when the field was primarily dominated by men and one of the first Black women to pass the New York State Bar.[23] Sadie T. M. Alexander was a lawyer and the first graduate of the University of Pennsylvania Law School and the first African American to earn a doctorate in economics.[24] Her organizational experience prior to NCNW included serving as the first national president of Delta Sigma Theta sorority. Starting as the head of the Church of God in Christ–backed Saints Academy, Arenia Mallory grew the small school to become a junior college, similar to Bethune, making her one of few women to serve as college presidents during her time.[25] Over the years she worked closely with the organization, raising money and serving as the director of Region IV (Mississippi, Louisiana, Arkansas, and Tennessee).[26]

Bethune's relationship with First Lady Eleanor Roosevelt allowed NCNW to voice their concerns among audiences and leaders who were connected to the president. They were able to host conferences at the Department of Labor, members were invited to tea with the First Lady, and ambassadors and members of Congress attended their meetings.[27] Bethune did not see her NYA position as separate from NCNW; instead, she embraced both roles and worked to create greater collaboration between the women and the federal government. The organization used every meeting and every connection as an opportunity to address the concerns of Black women across the nation. Establishing herself as an advocate for equality for Black America, Bethune created a solid foundation within the United States. In the years that followed, as she sought to build bridges between Africans throughout the Diaspora, the work of the "First Lady of Negro America" gave her credibility, and African descendants around the world looked to her for her wise counsel and advice.

The Influence of Sue Bailey Thurman

An important aspect of NCNW was its desire to engage women from different backgrounds and organizations; this included an impressive group of women who were well versed on international affairs. Bethune came to rely on her colleagues to help her to reach beyond the United States, seeking women who had experience with traveling and researching. During the November 1939 Annual Meeting in New York Bethune appointed Sue Bailey Thurman as the editor in chief of the organization's new quarterly magazine.[28] She was the wife of the revered theologian Howard Thurman, who was serving as dean of Andrew Rankin Chapel at Howard University. Thurman had deep admiration for Bethune, having grown up in Daytona Beach, where the success of her school made her a larger-than-life figure. Before meeting her husband, Sue Bailey Thurman traveled extensively, lecturing in Europe and leading the charge to create the World Fellowship Committee, during her tenure as secretary for the YWCA.[29] In 1936 the pair led an all-Black "Pilgrimage of Friendship" to India, Burma, and Ceylon (now Sri Lanka). It was during this trip that they met Mahatma Gandhi. As a delegate she gave lectures and presentations to audiences of as many as four thousand people on topics including: "Negro Women," "Women's Organizations," and "Internationalism through Music."[30] During their brief conversation with Gandhi, Sue Bailey Thurman brought the issue of lynching in America to his attention while she also asked why he excluded native Africans from his satyagraha campaigns in South Africa.[31] Although she aimed to make the influential leader aware of the plight of African Americans, she was unafraid to challenge his position in areas where her opinion may have differed from his. Gandhi's nonviolent resistance movement in South Africa took a bold stance against the oppressive nature of British rule, yet he saw the Indian struggle as separate from native Africans, who were equally, if not more oppressed. Upon her return she gave lectures at a number of historically Black colleges and universities, including Bethune-Cookman College, using it as a chance to encourage attendees to travel to broaden their horizons.[32]

Impressed by her international experience, Bethune envisioned Thurman as someone who would help take the organization to greater heights in her quest to connect with people of African descent around the world. As president of NACW, Bethune encouraged the women to travel more widely as a united front because she envisioned the clubwomen's movement as being a part of a global struggle for freedom. Although the organization embraced conversations about issues around the world, while they also supported various causes in Africa, they did not share her vision to further internationalize their efforts as a collective. Experiences with ICWDR and NACW allowed Bethune to hone her skills as a leader, almost as a training ground for what she would create. She was intentional about expanding her reach abroad, and now she would do so with the organization that she founded. She sought the expertise of women like Thurman to make her vision a reality. A major part of her goal was to lead an organization that was "not merely a national influence, but a significant link between peoples of color throughout the world" was fulfilled in August 1940, when NCNW took part in a seminar in Cuba spearheaded by Thurman.[33] During the trip members were hosted by the Afro-Cuban feminist organization Asociación Cultural Femenina (ACF Women's Cultural Association), allowing them to learn more about an organization that did similar work. Founded in 1935 by Ana Echegoyen and Consuela Serro, its membership consisted of prominent Afro-Cuban women who supported "the civil and cultural betterment of women" through its activities.[34] Their community work included leading literacy campaigns and providing nurseries for working mothers, while they also hosted exclusive dances and fashion expositions for the elite.[35] Takara Brunson writes that "ACF members built relations with African American women as part of their internationalist approach to achieving reform," further explaining why the trip was beneficial not only to NCNW but also to the women of Cuba.[36]

Bethune was unable to participate in the trip to Cuba, but she oversaw important details of the trip and entrusted most of the planning to her former student and close friend Henry Grillo.[37] Just a few months before Bethune was hospitalized at Johns Hopkins Hospital in Baltimore, Maryland, for six weeks. In a June 1, 1940, letter to the *Baltimore Afro-American* she reported that she was "on the road to recovery" after undergoing surgery for bronchitis.[38] She spent much of the summer in Daytona Beach, away from the public. However, she did not let this stop her from fulfilling her role as president of NCNW; she continued her work from the hospital, home, and wherever she was, writing letters with her direct orders to be carried out by the organization. It was during this time that she leaned on the expertise and knowledge of the women around her to ensure that NCNW reached its goals, despite her absence. The trip to Cuba was designed to be a learning experience and cultural exchange for NCNW, so that the members could be better informed on the plight of Afro-Cubans. NCNW brought organizational information translated into Spanish with the idea of educating the woman on the experience of Black women in America; in return, they received Cuban flags and greetings. The exchanges that occurred exemplified Bethune and NCNW's desire to explore the linkages between women of African descent in the African Diaspora and the United States. Through her organization Bethune sought to create solidarity among women of African descent through "Small p" Pan-Africanist methods, as St. Clair Drake affirmed.[39]

Led by Sylvia Grillo, Jose Grinan, and Ana Echegoyen, a professor at the University of Havana, the seminars were "a comprehensive program of study consisting of nine conferences to be given during the Seminar period."[40] The seminars focused heavily on educating NCNW on Afro-Cuban history and achievements. Ana Echegoyen's presentation on "Cuban Social Life and the Negro Woman" raised issues of racial prejudice in Cuba, the importance of women's organizations, and the lack of unity among Cubans. In her presentation she expressed her views on racial prejudice and discussed "Cuba's Negro Problem," which she suggested had started with the arrival of enslaved Blacks and the lasting view of them as "a negative element in that rising nationality."[41] Echegoyen also felt that in order for the "Cuban Negro Problem" to be solved, the country would have to ensure that Black people had their rightful place in society, being seen not as slaves but as people.

The "Negro Problem" was a familiar discussion topic for the women of NCNW, with Bethune having led two national conferences, in 1937 and 1939, focused on "Problems of the Negro and Negro Youth." Upon the conclusion of the second conference, Bethune submitted a report to President Franklin D. Roosevelt with recommendations for the executive and legislative branches of the government on how to improve conditions for African Americans.[42] The report highlighted problems in areas including social and economic security, health and housing, and civil liberties. Ultimately both Echegoyen and Bethune were seeking equality for people of African descent in their quests to solve the Negro problem. Although it is unclear what conversations were had regarding the comparison and contrasting of the situation of African Americans and Afro-Cubans, Echegoyen's accounts of racism must have resonated with the women due to their similarities to the Black experience in segregated America. Gaining awareness of these similarities was a first step toward unifying to change them. The seminar was featured in the *Aframerican Woman's Journal* to share with NCNW members across the United States and beyond. At a time when African Americans were fighting for basic civil rights, the women learned firsthand that Afro-Cubans were waging the same battle.

The seminar also included a lecture by Angel C. Pinto on "The Negro in the Cuban Political Order," which was also printed in *Aframerican*. Pinto was an internationally known sociologist and writer whose research looked at social problems of people of African descent in Mexico, Venezuela, Brazil, and Cuba.[43] The lecture focused on the Cuban Blacks' history of protest and resistance as runaways forming their own "Cimarron" communities, as organizers of the Aponte Rebellion in 1812, and as leaders in Cuba's push for freedom from the Spanish. Utilizing numerous historical examples, Pinto argued that the Black "in his struggles against the slave masters ha[s] not always employed the same tactics. . . . [H]e has continuously modified throughout, his struggles, his tactics, and technics of battle, according to the demands of each epoch, and the particular circumstances of each historic moment."[44] Starting with the resistance of the enslaved and chronologically discussing ways in which Blacks resisted oppression as free people, Pinto deemed the race to be a revolutionary people who always have sought and always will seek liberation. Speaking to African American women, many of whom were of the lineage of formerly enslaved Africans, helped them to see their connection to the Black radical tradition. Pinto urged the seminar attendees to share and draw from the greatness of history of the past to find solutions about how to solve current issues.

During the visit and seminars, members of ACF also took part in the sessions, giving the women the chance to discuss issues common to Afro-Cubans and African Americans. They met Cuban government officials and Governor Dr. Valdes Astolfi, and during the reception he was presented with a copy of the *Aframerican* as a gift from NCNW. Dr. Echegoyen also presented NCNW with copies of her Spanish children's book, to distribute to youth. Editor Portuondo Cala announced the women's arrival in the August 22, 1940, edition of his column "El Pais" in the *Havana Daily*. Cala felt that the trip had been a necessary exchange between the women of Cuba and NCNW. He also noted that it showed that African Americans "send their delegations abroad to observe the development of groups to which they are closely drawn ethnically, so that they can observe and learn from whatever they may have advantage for their culture and economy."[45] The time that NCNW spent in Cuba was recognized by the writer as one in which they would learn from the people of Cuba, people to whom they were already connected. The women also congregated in the homes of members of ACF and visited various sites and social gatherings. Spending time in the country learning about the plight of its Afro-Cubans while also sharing their own stories as Americans living in a country plagued by Jim Crow allowed the women to connect and create linkages through shared experiences.

Aframerican Woman's Journal

Most of the Cuba trip was captured in the 1940 summer-fall issue of the *Aframerican Woman's Journal*, which featured several articles translated into Spanish.[46] The journal also featured a short biography of Dr. Ana Echegoyen. The seminars introduced NCNW members to the issues of discrimination faced by Afro-Cubans, their culture, way of life, and history. In traveling and studying the situation, the organization was able to take the information back to its members to educate them. Also by visiting the homes and social functions of La Asociación Cultural Femenina, one of Cuba's most influential feminist organizations, NCNW was able to discuss social, economic, and political issues informally and formally through the lectures. The exchange of ideas and knowledge was the basis of building the relationship between the two organizations. NCNW spent a little over a week committing themselves to a "study of the cultural, economic, political, and social conditions of the Cuban people—especially of the Negro race."[47]

Bethune valued Thurman's expertise, and she saw a publication as being the medium that would document NCNW's activities while sharing the achievements of Black women. The magazine would disseminate the ideals of the organization globally, and to do so effectively it was published in three languages.[48] *Aframerican Woman's Journal* published its first issue in the spring of 1940, and within the first few pages Bethune set the tone for her international agenda. In her column "From the President," she wrote that the journal would travel "to far away countries where we, ourselves, may never travel," indicating her hope for the journal to be a voice of African American women to be heard throughout the world.[49] She understood the significance of a publication that would share the progress and the challenges of Black women with the world; it was an opportunity to speak for themselves and share their firsthand experiences. With the creation of the journal, Bethune and Thurman gave Black women an important space to share their unfiltered truth around the world.

The issue also contained NCNW's resume, which summarized the five-year history of the organization, its objectives, and its five-year plan in English, Spanish, and French. On the international front the plan included "the establishment of new relations with women of the East, especially India (the All-India Women's Congress) and with Latin America, through tours, seminars and exchange of literature and fraternal delegates."[50] The All-India Women's Congress (AIWC) was an organization created in 1927 by the women of India with the major focus being the eradication of child marriages (particularly for young girls), empowering women through education, and improving the welfare and treatment of women and children. Recognized by many as a profeminist organization, AIWC was instrumental in the fight for women's rights during the India's colonial period.[51] The ideals of NCNW, particularly those that called for equal rights for women, coincided with the ideals of AIWC, and the organization sought to be an ally in the global fight for women's rights.

Highlighting the international successes of Black women, the summer-fall 1940 issue featured the article "The Fifteenth Hubert Herring Seminar in Mexico," in which NCNW member Virginia Simmons chronicled her trip to Mexico to attend the Hubert Herring Seminar. Herring spent years traveling the Americas, and he would later author the text *A History of Latin America from the Beginnings to the Present*. The seminar covered topics such as "The Status of Women in Mexico," "The History of Education in Mexico," and "Economic Life of Mexico." After spending days hearing lectures on the state of Mexico, visiting cathedrals and local shops, and meeting the local people, Simmons summarized her trip by saying, "As I enjoyed a sense of companionship with other citizens of the United States traveling in Mexico, I felt brother-sister to Latin Americans."[52] Members of NCNW educated themselves while building bridges cross-culturally during their travels. The journal provided an opportunity for members to share the information they learned abroad while also encouraging others to visit these places.

In the 1941 issue, the journal recapped the events of the NCNW Conference, held October 24–26 with the theme "Women Facing New Frontiers." In Bethune's feature, she urged the Council to support the antilynching efforts.[53] This was a concern that she continuously pressed President Roosevelt on in her private conversations.[54] The issue also featured Sue Bailey Thurman's conference address titled "The International Program of Negro Women," which highlighted NCNW's seminars in Cuba. According to the issue on the concluding day of the conference, Cape Verdean concert pianist and composer Ethel Ramos Harris provided music for the conference, and J. Borden Harriman, United States minister to Norway, addressed the organization, discussing how Norwegians had been impacted by the Nazi invasion. The minister of Haiti and First Lady Madame Elie Lescot also attended the conference as delegates for Haiti.[55]

The conference reports gave *Aframerican* readers insight into how NCNW was beginning to expand its international reach through networking and traveling. The journal reached those who may not have been able to physically be a part of NCNW activities but were still interested in supporting and learning more about their efforts. The organization also challenged its members to engage in further study of world relations so that they could gain a great understanding of international affairs. In Chairman Mary L. McCrorey's report of the international committee (featured in the journal), she suggested that members and member organizations study periodicals written by the Council on Foreign Relations of New York. McCrorey also suggested that the journal be disseminated "throughout other countries, with emphasis on closer cooperation between Latin America and countries having a large Negro citizenship" and to International Houses on college campuses.[56] Ultimately McCrorey challenged NCNW to raise their international awareness and their efforts to build relationships abroad. It is also significant that she was intentional about the journal getting to "Negro citizenship" in other countries, which demonstrates the significance of the journal as a tool by which NCNW sought to connect with other people of African descent.

Bethune stated that "some of the most brilliant work in promoting the international program through sponsorship of the Seminar of Goodwill to Cuba, and the unprecedented Women's Archives Exhibit at the Chicago Exposition was accomplished by the journal."[57] Dorothy Porter, a librarian at Howard University, led efforts to develop the exhibit for the 1940 American Negro Exposition in Chicago. Bethune entrusted Sue Bailey Thurman with expanding the scope of the work of the organization, and the results were outstanding. In celebration of its second anniversary, the *Aframerican* received applause from the Women's National Press Club, Smith College, and the Division of Cultural Relations for the Department of State.[58] By 1942 the journal was disseminated to "twenty Latin American Republics, India, China and the Philippines," and in 1943 foreign correspondents joined the staff to "report on women's war activities and programs in Cuba, Haiti, the Virgin Islands and Puerto Rico."[59] Just as UNIA founder Marcus Garvey distributed his *Negro World* newspaper to people of African descent in the West Indies, South America, Europe, and Africa, NCNW took a similar approach.[60] Bethune understood the power of the pen and its ability to spread the message of NCNW to those who were worlds away. *Aframerican* was not simply the voice of NCNW; its attempts to seek foreign correspondents show that it sought to connect with women around the world while becoming a leading voice among them. As editor, Thurman created a platform for both NCNW women and women abroad; she served until 1944 and later became an honorary editor.

Bethune's Growing Global Influence: Cuba, Liberia, and Ethiopia

In May 1943, Bethune received the distinction of becoming an honorary member of the Society of Afro-Cuban Studies. Based in Havana, Cuba, under the leadership of Fernando Ortiz, the organization selected Bethune to be a part of its work due to her achievements as an intellectual. The Society of Afro-Cuban Studies' objectives were "to study with critical purpose the phenomena: demographic, economic, legal, religious, literary, artistic, linguistic and social produced in Cuba by the existence of two distinct races, white and black, in order to obtain the knowledge of actual facts."[61] In the context of Cuba's understanding of itself as a "raceless" nation, the organization sought to understand the unique history of Afro-Cubans as having a past that differed from that of white Cubans.[62] Having served as the president and founder of Bethune-Cookman College and as the president of the Association for the Study of Negro Life and History from 1936 to 1951, Bethune's work as an educator coincided with that of the Society. She was thrilled to accept the membership, and in a letter to President Ortiz she wrote, "I consider it an honor and a privilege to be affiliated with your distinguished body."[63] National newspapers such as the *Chicago Defender* celebrated Bethune's admission into the organization.[64]

Membership into the Society of Afro-Cuban Studies and the success of NCNW's trip to Cuba marked a significant turning point in Bethune's status as a global leader. Just a decade before the NCNW seminars in Cuba, Bethune faced racism during her trip to the country. Upon arriving in Havana in August 1930 along with her grandson Albert Bethune Jr. and president of Bluefield Institute, Dr. R. P. Sims and his daughter, Bethune was not allowed to proceed past a checkpoint.[65] Prior to arrival she was told by a ticket agent in Miami, "We do not encourage Negroes to go to Cuba," and was not allowed to purchase a round-trip ticket from Miami.[66] Although both Bethune and Sims were people of color, his lighter skin allowed him to pass through the checkpoint with ease whereas immigration officers held Bethune and threatened to send her to Tiscornia, a detention center in Cuba. After hours of waiting in the sun along with Sims, who decided to stay, Bethune and her young grandson were allowed to pass, but the officer withheld their departure tickets.[67]

It seemed that racism was inescapable for Bethune, demonstrating how, even in the "raceless" nation of Cuba, discrimination still existed. During Cuba's struggle for independence, a multiracial group came together to drive the Spanish out of the country for complete liberation. On May 20, 1902, Cuba emerged as an independent nation that saw "no whites nor blacks, but only Cubans."[68] Less than three decades later, when Bethune met the new nation, color was very much an issue along with race. In response to the racism Bethune and other African Americans experienced in Cuba, NAACP field secretary William Pickens wrote Secretary of State Henry Stimson a letter condemning the actions of the Cubans and asking that the United States take action on the matter.[69] A few months prior to Bethune's trip, writer Langston Hughes was denied a ticket to travel to Cuba and was told that "Negroes" were not allowed to visit the country.[70] The *Chicago Defender* also highlighted Bethune's incident in a September 30, 1930, article, "Cuba Seeks to Stop American Tourists," in which it recapped the situation. The article also revealed the responses of both parties, stating, "The Cuban and American officials accuse each other for discouraging our people from coming here."[71] Gustavo Urrutia, a Cuban writer and editor of the weekly column "Ideals de una raza" (Ideals of a race), also covered the incident by printing Pickens's letter to Stimson in the September 7, 1930, issue of the column in Spanish.[72] Urrutia often took on issues of race relations in Cuba in his work, and he advocated for self-determination for Afro-Cubans, urging them to adopt the mindset of the "New Negro" in his writings.[73] He saw Bethune's mistreatment as another example of Cuba's overall attitude toward its darker citizens and anyone who resembled them.

Although the incident was unfortunate for Bethune, she did not allow it to deter her from building a relationship with the people of Cuba. Upon her return to the United States, she wrote Urrutia expressing frustration about the injustice she experienced while visiting the "beautiful city and the wonderful spirit of the Cuban people."[74] She also recounted the event and blamed both the American and Cuban governments for attempting to humiliate Blacks. In closing, a determined Bethune promised to return to Havana while also encouraging "well-trained, right-thinking Negroes of this country to go to Cuba."[75] Overall the twelve-day visit was positive, and Bethune continued to foster and develop relationships with the people of Cuba. Acceptance into the Society of Afro-Cubans was significant because it demonstrated her growing influence in a place where she was once rejected. Being awarded this honor was very much a vindication for a woman who had risen in stature, and in some ways it corrected the wrong that was done.

This shows that the connection between people of African descent could not be broken by those who oppress them and that the government's viewpoint did not necessarily determine how Afro-Cubans saw Bethune. Throughout the years, as she led NCNW, the members welcomed Afro-Cuban visitors to meet with them in their headquarters in Washington, DC, just as the organization had been welcomed during their visit.[76] Bethune and NCNW's trips and their hosting of Cubans were important steps toward creating solidarity by simply sharing their experiences with one another and increasing understanding.

As Bethune emerged as a global leader, opportunities began to open for her to connect with Africa as prominent visitors came to the United States. On May 26, 1943, President Edwin Barclay of Liberia arrived in Washington, DC, along with Vice President William Tubman as guests of the US government. At the White House, Barclay was honored with a state dinner hosted by President Roosevelt, and accommodations were made for his stay at the historic Blair House, a space generally used to entertain foreign dignitaries. Southerners were in uproar about the extravagant treatment of a "Negro," and the *Chicago Defender* reported, "The only other time when this country has been honored by the visit of a Negro chief of state was in August 1919 when C.D.V. King [sic], the then president of Liberia, headed a mission here," making Barclay's trip a historic event.[77] Since Liberia did not have an embassy in Washington, DC, local African American men headed by Emmett J. Scott, along with men such as Ralph Bunche, Oscar De Priest, William Leo Hansberry, Rayford Logan, and others held an all-men's luncheon at Howard University on Saturday May 29, 1943. Scott served as a longtime aide to Booker T. Washington and "the highest ranked African American in Woodrow Wilson's Administration," and he presided over the program and gave remarks to honor Barclay.[78] Although Bethune could not attend the luncheon, she realized that it was an opportune time to connect with the women of Liberia. In a May 28, 1943, letter to "The Women of the Republic of Liberia," she expressed greetings and a desire to make a "pilgrimage" to Liberia to "solidify the efforts of women everywhere who are working to secure a durable and lasting peace."[79] She also expressed interest in having the women of Liberia visit NCNW in America, along with the hope that a "sisterly relationship" would evolve among the women.[80]

On June 11, 1943, "Citizens of New York City," led by committee members Mayor Fiorello H. LaGuardia, Honorable Nicholas Murray Butler, Dr. Mary McLeod Bethune, Dr. Channing H. Tobias, and Commissioner Samuel J. Battle hosted a testimonial dinner for President Barclay. Barclay was unable to attend due to being hospitalized, but more than eight hundred guests were present, and Vice President Tubman attended on his behalf. The address was provided by the mayor of New York City, the Honorable Fiorello H. LaGuardia. The Reverend A. Clayton Powell Jr., Anson Phelps Stokes, Max Yergan, and Bethune brought greetings. Also in attendance was Paul Robeson, who provided a selection for the event, and an "official welcome and presentation of the keys of the city" were made.[81] The event was a success and demonstrated cooperation between African Americans and whites in honoring the African leader, while for Bethune, it allowed her to network and to show goodwill toward Africa. She seized every opportunity to build a bridge between herself, as the leader of NCNW, and other leaders of color as a starting point toward future collaboration.

With NCNW being strategically located in the nation's capital, members were often able to meet international leaders who visited the White House, particularly during the time that Bethune worked for the Roosevelt administration. The NCNW headquarters became an important place for people of African descent who visited because of the limitations that segregation presented to people of color at the time. In many ways Bethune and the members became ambassadors who represented African Americans overall when they welcomed foreign visitors, and they did not shirk from this role. In March 1944 members of NCNW met with Getahoun Tesemma, the first secretary of the Ethiopian Legation in Washington, DC. During the meeting, hosted by Tesemma, the women were educated on the state of the country, and they began to think about ways to continue their relationship beyond the meeting. In a letter from NCNW executive director Jeanetta Welch Brown to Tesemma, who also attended the meeting, she discussed the significance of the meeting and wrote, "we desire to know more about our brothers and sisters in Ethiopia."[82] Brown requested information about Ethiopian children and contact information for women's organizations in the hope of creating cultural exchange between the two, while she also requested pictures to feature Ethiopia in the *Aframerican Woman's Journal*. In exchange, Tesemma was given issues of the journal and information about NCNW.

In a follow-up to the request, Tesemma provided contact information for NCNW to reach out to Princess Tenagnework, the daughter of Haile Selassie.[83] At the time the princess was the president of the Women's Work Association based in Addis Ababa, Ethiopia.[84] Bethune followed up with a letter to the princess extending membership into NCNW in April 1944 and stating that she was interested in "having a closer cooperation with you in the work that women are doing and must do in order to make this a better world in which to live" on behalf of herself and NCNW.[85] Copies of *Aframerican Woman's Journal* were also issued to Princess Tenagnework. Although it is unclear if Tenagnework responded, Bethune and NCNW expressed interest in cultural exchanges with Ethiopia through Tesemma and Tenagnework. The conversations during meetings and letter exchanges provided an invaluable chance for NCNW to gain better understanding of the plight of Ethiopian women while also helping them to understand the challenges faced by Black women.

NCNW firmly established itself as an organization building solidarity among women as demonstrated by their travels to Cuba, cultural exchanges with Ethiopian women, and their flourishing magazine, which was now disseminated across Latin America and to China and the Philippines. Bethune's sought-after presence among foreign dignitaries and leaders reaffirmed her place as a global leader whose voice was important and necessary. She continued to look for ways to press for NCNW to be a linkage between people of color, using her influence to strengthen the organization's network. She did not take her position as an international leader for granted, and she realized that her voice could be used effectively to bring attention to the causes of those who were oppressed. World War II would present itself as a time for Bethune to take her activism to even greater heights.

Figure 1. Mary McLeod Bethune with Vice President Clarence L. Simpson (*left*) of Liberia and Lemuel Gibson, chairman of the Liberian Senate Foreign Relations Committee (*right*), at the San Francisco Conference, May 18, 1945. Photo by E. F. Joseph Studios Oakland, CA; courtesy of Mary McLeod Bethune Council House National Historic Site, National Archives for Black Women's History.

Figure 2. Mrs. Bethune with W. E. B. Du Bois (*left*) and Walter White (*right*) in San Francisco at the United Nations Conference on International Organization, 1945. Photographer unknown; courtesy of Mary McLeod Bethune Council House National Historic Site, National Archives for Black Women's History.

Figure 3. Delegates from India attending the National Council of Negro Women Annual Convention, 1947. Photo by Fred Harris; courtesy of Mary McLeod Bethune Council House National Historic Site, National Archives for Black Women's History.

Figure 4. Mary McLeod Bethune and fellow delegate representing India at the NCNW Annual Convention, 1947. Photo by Fred Harris; courtesy of Mary McLeod Bethune Council House National Historic Site, National Archives for Black Women's History.

Figure 5. Reception at the National Council of Negro Women Headquarters honoring Ambassador Joseph Charles of Haiti and Minister of Liberia Charles D. B. King, February 15, 1948. Photo by Fred Harris; courtesy of Mary McLeod Bethune Council House National Historic Site, National Archives for Black Women's History.

Figure 6. Mrs. Bethune at intercultural party for foreign students, June 1948. Photo by Riley; courtesy of Mary McLeod Bethune Council House National Historic Site, National Archives for Black Women's History.

Figure 7. Retirement dinner for Mrs. Bethune at the US Department of the Interior, 1949. Mrs. Bethune, wearing the Haitian Medal of Honor and Merit, with Daisy Lampkin, Vivian Carter Mason, Arenia Mallory, Dorothy Ferebee, and Dorothy Height. Photo by Fred Harris; courtesy of Mary McLeod Bethune Council House National Historic Site, National Archives for Black Women's History.

Figure 8. President Harry Truman, Madame Pandit, and Ralph Bunche at Mrs. Bethune's final meeting as NCNW president, 1949. Bethune is wearing the Haitian Medal of Honor and Merit. Photo by Fred Harris for the *Washington Post*; courtesy of Mary McLeod Bethune Council House National Historic Site, National Archives for Black Women's History.

Figure 9. Mary Jane McLeod Bethune signing a document for Liberian secretary of state Momolu Dukuly during a 1952 event honoring President V. S. Tubman's inauguration in Monrovia, Liberia. Photo by Leon M. Jordan; courtesy of Indiana University Libraries.

Figure 10. Liberian president William V. S. Tubman shakes hands with Mary McLeod Bethune while Liberian vice president Clarence Lorenzo Simpson and First Lady Antoinette Tubman look on during Bethune's 1952 trip to Liberia. Photo by R. S. Scurlock; courtesy of Indiana University Libraries.

Figure 11. Mrs. Bethune rushing to a plane that was held for her at LaGuardia Airport when she was late for departure to Paris on her way to Monrovia, Liberia, to attend the inauguration of President Tubman at the request of President Truman, January 3, 1952. Photo by James C. Campbell; courtesy of Mary McLeod Bethune Council House National Historic Site, National Archives for Black Women's History.

Figure 12. Mary McLeod Bethune converses with guests during an event honoring William V. S. Tubman's inauguration as president in Monrovia, Liberia, 1952. Photo by Leon M. Jordan; courtesy of Indiana University Libraries.

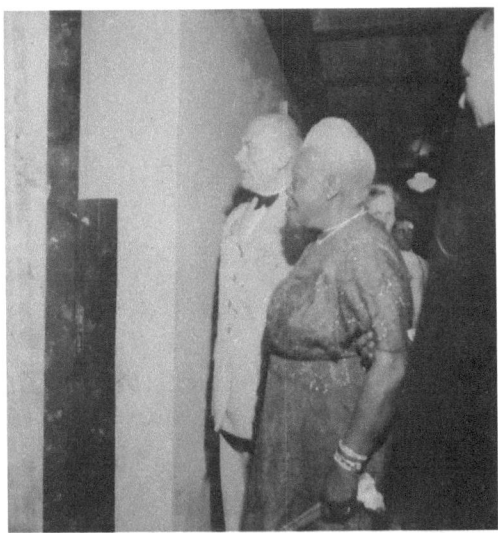

Figure 13. Mary McLeod Bethune at an event honoring President William V. S. Tubman's inauguration in Monrovia, Liberia, 1952. Photo by Leon M. Jordan; courtesy of Indiana University Libraries.

Figure 14. Mrs. Mary McLeod Bethune alongside fellow attendees of Emancipation Day celebration events in Windsor, Ontario, 1954. Amherstburg Freedom Museum Collection P.84.53.02A.

Figure 15. Members of the Hour-a-Day Study Club alongside Mrs. Mary McLeod Bethune in Windsor, Ontario, during her 1954 trip, where she served as the guest speaker for the Emancipation Day celebration. Amherstburg Freedom Museum Collection P.84.53.02B.

CS-12

Mary McLeod Bethune Foundation
Incorporated

OFFICERS AND TRUSTEES
Mary McLeod Bethune, *President*
Roy S. McWilliams, *Vice-President*
Julius Davidson, *Treasurer*
Paul W. Harvey, *Legal Advisor*
Maxwell W. Saxon, *Curator*
Bertha L. Mitchell, *Secretary*
Albert M. Bethune, Sr.,
Marjorie S. Joyner
Richard V. Moore
John Sengstacke

631 Pearl Street
Daytona Beach, Florida

TELEPHONE 2-3519

August 31, 1954

Mr. David P. Botsford, Custodian
Fort Malden National Historic Park
Amherstburg, Ontario
Canada

My dear Mr. Botsford:

May I thank you for the copies of material relating to slavery and fugitives from slavery which interested me greatly as I visited the historic site, so wonderfully explained to me and our friends during our short stay in Amherstburg.

It occurred to me that the files of the Foundation should certainly carry references like these which I consider real monuments to freedom - not for one nation alone but for all who love freedom and truth and justice.

Some day, we hope, that the Mary McLeod Bethune Foundation, located here in our beloved Florida, will offer just the same kind of inspiration and fulfillment as I was able to acknowledge when we visited Fort Malden.

May I commend you and your co-workers for the historic services you are rendering and for the beautiful spirit in which you work and share yourself and your findings with others.

It is my hope that you and your friends will come to Florida one day and see our work here. It shall be our pleasure to receive you and help to make your visit as interesting as you have made ours.

I am exceedingly grateful to you and Mrs. Oakley the Museum Assistant for this kindness to me and for this contribution to the files of our Foundation.

Sincerely yours,
Mary McLeod Bethune

MMB/fs

Figure 16. A letter from Mrs. Mary McLeod Bethune sent to David P. Botsford on August 31, 1954. David P. Botsford was the curator/"custodian" at the Fort Malden National Historic Park, which is now the Malden National Historic Site in Amherstburg, Ontario, Canada). Amherstburg Freedom Museum Collection 2016.25.52 CS-12.

Figure 17. Mrs. Bethune with Madame Pandit of India, 1950s. Photographer unknown; courtesy of Mary McLeod Bethune Council House National Historic Site, National Archives for Black Women's History.

Figure 18. African women looking at international flag during visit to Council House in Washington, DC, date unknown. Photographer unknown; courtesy of Mary McLeod Bethune Council House National Historic Site, National Archives for Black Women's History.

4

World War II and the Challenge of Decolonization

In a 1943 *Free World* article, Bethune called for America to decide how it would use its powers in regard to colonized countries: "Hundreds of millions of people in colonies, dependences, and economically exploited nations demand basic economic and political changes. Either the American people are determined to exercise their strength in the coming years for every democratic step or that strength will be misused—misused for destructive economic and political repression."[1] In this statement, Bethune calls on the United States to choose whether it will operate on the side of the exploited and colonized countries or allow itself to be a part of that exploitation. Urging the country to use its power and influence for the good of those who were oppressed, she saw herself as a voice for the voiceless. Nearly two years before the signing of the United Nations Charter, Bethune was foreshadowing one of the key agenda items for African Americans who would participate in San Francisco. She had been a leading voice among women, but asserting herself in the male-dominated global arena would present challenges.

When European forces gathered for the Berlin Conference in 1884, Mary McLeod Bethune was just nine years old, so for most of her life colonization existed throughout the continent of Africa. The Africa of her ancestors had not yet been partitioned by outsiders and stripped of its natural resources and autonomy. Bethune's understanding of precolonial Africa and her reverence and feeling of connectedness to the continent were the underpinnings of her decolonization efforts. As a well-known leader in the Black community, Bethune addresses issues impacting those around her with the understanding that she is a citizen of the African Diaspora, and when given the opportunity she spoke on behalf of Africans around the world.

World War II changed the course of history for Africans in the United States and on the continent. Although its aims focused on gaining victory against fascism, those who were under the thumb of colonization saw it as a step in the direction of freedom. Bethune saw the war as a means by which African Americans could be active participants in securing the promise of democracy for all, including people of African descent. She created space for Black women to serve, and she put her organization at the forefront of war efforts, rallying women across the United States. As peacetime efforts began, she sought inclusion in the founding of the United Nations because she understood the importance of having a seat at the table among international power brokers and leaders. It was her chance to insert the conversation of freedom, just as Africans had done for hundreds of years.

As an active supporter of the Council on African Affairs (CAA), Bethune became more engaged in humanitarian efforts to support Africa and events to call attention to the conditions of colonized Africans. Younger CAA activists like Paul Robeson challenged Bethune to use her influence to become more vocal about the issue of colonization. She supported their efforts financially, with her writings, and through participation in events hosted by the organization. As a consultant at the founding of the UN, Bethune voiced the concerns of Black America while also making a call for the liberation of colonized people, rising to the challenge of Robeson and his peers. Ultimately, she was able to use her federal connections as leverage to access global leaders to voice the concerns of Black America and Africans throughout the Diaspora in San Francisco.

Victory Abroad, Victory at Home

As agents of their liberation, Africans fought valiantly for freedom from European colonization just as African Americans had resisted slavery since their arrival. John. H. Morrow writes: "These soldiers shed their blood for the right to equal treatment under their respective colonial regimes and, later, for the independence of their respective African nations from the colonial yoke. Their struggle, in fact, paralleled that of the African-American soldiers who fought in both world wars to prove that black Americans merited the equality that white Americans denied them."[2] Freedom was never gifted but, rather, was the result of agitation, struggle, and consistency, and

Africans throughout the Diaspora understood this. More than a million Africans fought in World War II on behalf of European countries with the hope that the end of the war would bring an end to colonization. In 1941, many believed that the Atlantic Charter's promise—the restoration of self-government—would restore African colonies to sovereignty, but this was not the case. The African National Congress responded to the exclusion of continental Africans from the promise of autonomy by drafting a response with the publishing of "Africans' Claims in South Africa." In the document the organization called for the peace, freedom, equality, and justice that the Atlantic Charter granted also be applied to Africans and other oppressed people.[3] Realizing the significance of the global war between the Axis and Allied powers, Africans inserted their freedom into the conversation, just as they had during the American Revolution and the Civil War.

Although the war had been in progress for almost two years and the United States had provided support for the Allies, it was not until the Japanese attacked Pearl Harbor on December 7, 1941, that the United States formally declared its entrance into the war. African American soldier Doris "Dorie" Miller fought during the attack on Pearl Harbor, manning a machine gun while he also saved the lives of his fellow troops by taking them to safety.[4] Shortly after, he was awarded the Navy Cross for his bravery as he proved that African American soldiers were not only necessary, but they were dedicated to the protection of the United States. When the United States entered the war, troops served in France, Great Britain, and Tunisia, risking their lives far from home. As African Americans fought to end the terrorist fascist reign of Adolf Hitler, they also committed themselves to end the reign of terror known as Jim Crow. From the beginning, Bethune reminded African Americans of their roles in past wars, encouraging participation while also linking the fate of democracy to the winning of the war. She was hopeful that this time would be different and that true change would come.

On January 31, 1942, cafeteria worker James G. Thompson wrote a letter to the editor of the *Pittsburgh Courier* on the subject of the war and asked the question, "Should I sacrifice my life to live half American?"[5] Like many African American men, Thompson was concerned about both the possibility of being drafted and how his sacrifice would affect the community. Facing prejudice, segregation, and disenfranchisement at home, many Black Americans found fighting abroad for the freedom of unknown citizens of fascist countries illogical. In his letter, Thomas questioned whether or not democracy would come to African Americans as a result of the war. The

Allied forces had taken on the motto "V for Victory," using the letter *V* to represent victory against the enemies. In keeping with the understood victory symbol, Thompson called for a "Double V" campaign for African Americans: "The first V for victory over our enemies from without, the second V for victory over our enemies within."[6] Thompson linked African American participation in the war as a war on two fronts, hoping that if they proved their loyalty by fighting for the United States, then, in turn, the country would honor the sacrifice of its soldiers by committing to equality and democracy.

As the war continued, the African American press, particularly the *Chicago Defender* and *Pittsburgh Courier,* promoted the ideals of the Double V campaign and criticized the United States for its hypocritical stance against fascism. The press was so influential in rallying African Americans that FBI head J. Edgar Hoover "believed that elements of the Double V campaign were seditious and therefore violated the Espionage and Smith acts."[7] In response, an agreement was made between African American newspapers and the government to lessen the combativeness of the articles, but the campaign continued. Throughout World War II, African Americans strategically linked the need to eliminate the evils of Jim Crow with the need to end fascism across the world, confirming their role as international activists.

As John Thompson's call for "Double Victory" was popularized throughout African American newspapers and the media, African Americans also became involved in the war on the front line as soldiers, and they took on defense-related jobs. Bethune fully supported America's position in World War II and encouraged African Americans to get involved in war efforts. As the Double V campaign persisted, some, including W. E. B. Du Bois, were skeptical about how the war would actually help African Americans. In a speech to the local Chicago community, he stated, "The popular notion that World War II was a fight to the finish between democracy and fascism is false."[8] During World War I he encouraged African Americans to "close ranks" and join the fight for democracy.[9] After serving and risking their lives abroad, many African Americans returned and found that their participation in the war effort had changed little for them at home. The summer of 1919, deemed "Red Summer" by James Weldon Johnson, was filled with racial violence against African Americans. In the *Crisis* magazine essay "Returning Soldiers," penned by Du Bois, he wrote: "We return from fighting. We return fighting."[10] Realizing that war involvement had not ended lynchings, disfranchisement, or discrimination, it is no wonder that he was skeptical about African American participation in World War II. In the speech

"What Are We Fighting For?" Bethune acknowledged the "hindrances" that kept African Americans from fully participating but urged them to continue to fight because "full democracy hinges upon the outcome of this war."[11] She also reminded white America that they too had the duty of "removing obstacles" to ensure that African Americans could fully participate in the war.

At a time when men were going off to war by the thousands, opportunities also opened for women. Representative Edith Nourse Rogers of Massachusetts introduced a bill to Congress to create the Women's Army Auxiliary Corps (WAAC) in 1941. The corps would "create a voluntary enrollment program for women to join the U.S. Army in a noncombat capacity" in positions such as clerical workers, cooks, phone operators, and medical-related jobs.[12] Doing so would allow more men to be on the front line and free from noncombat positions. One year later, on May 15, 1942, President Franklin D. Roosevelt signed the bill into law, making Oveta Culp Hobby the first director. Behind the scenes Bethune fought for the inclusion of African American women as WAAC members. In her 2011 memoir, *Justice Older Than the Law*, former WAAC officer Dovey Roundtree Johnson recalled watching Bethune meet with First Lady Roosevelt in attempts to get "her girls" involved in the war. Roosevelt was apprehensive about having African American women serve alongside white women, but Bethune did not back down. Johnson wrote, "Watching Dr. Bethune fight so hard over so many months for a place for black women in the military, I came to the conclusion that for all my reservations and fears, I couldn't turn away from her challenge."[13] It was due to Bethune's continued persistence that, when the first class of officers for the WAAC began their July 1942 training in Des Moines, Iowa, approximately thirty-nine African American female officers were among their number. Roughly 10 percent of the WAAC's members were intended to be African American women, and in its early phase Bethune saw to it that the number was fulfilled.[14]

Bethune became a special assistant to Secretary of War Harry L. Stimson and was responsible for handpicking the first forty members of WAAC. In choosing the members, she selected women who were college educated whom she felt would best represent the race. She went throughout the United States recruiting on college campuses to find women to serve. On the first day of training, Bethune met the women in Des Moines and checked out the facilities to ensure that the women were in livable conditions.[15] Remembering the sobering effect of Bethune's visit, Roundtree wrote, "She gathered her 'girls' about her . . . and reminded us of our place in history."[16]

She also wrote, "Dr. Bethune transformed the atmosphere of those uneasy hours with a few carefully chosen words."[17] Bethune didn't just throw the women into action; she paid a personal visit to ensure their safety and to give them a boost of confidence. Over the years she would be a supporter of the women and a confidante whom they could call on.

The first thirty-nine African American women in the Corps were the first women to serve in the army in roles other than nurses. For the women it was a scary, yet historic time. In Roundtree's text she recalled explaining her desire to enlist in WAAC, despite the doubts of her grandmother and mother, who "regarded the military with fear."[18] WAAC's members and their families did not know what to expect. As a recruiter and advisor, Bethune utilized her organization to calm the fears of African Americans. In the 1942 anniversary preconference issue of *Aframerican Woman's Journal*, NCNW featured the WAAC. In the article "The W.A.A.C.—The Girl Who Wouldn't Be Left Behind," the journal emphasized the historical significance of the Corps, featured information about Director Oveta Culp Hobby, and provided an outline of the typical daily requirements for a WAAC.[19] The article also featured the names and contact information for the women who graduated from the officer's training school. The journal updated the community on the conditions of the women of the Corps.

Bethune was also concerned about the general welfare of soldiers abroad and pushed for NCNW to be on the advisory council on soldiers' welfare. In a letter to Stimson published in the *Atlanta Daily World*, she advised the general, "We still seek this end and urge upon you that Negro representation be included in this advisory until and in all future plans."[20] In Bethune's protest she also reiterated the connections between inclusion of African Americans and democracy. She often told the government that African Americans receiving equal treatment and equal opportunities were a vital extension of American democracy. By 1943, NCNW was represented by Dorothy Porter as a member of the Advisory Council for the Women's Interests Section.[21] The organization was created to inform women about the welfare of soldiers and distributed information about soldiers' health, available recreational activities, and how women could contribute to the war.[22]

As the president of NCNW, Bethune fully involved the organization in war efforts. On June 3, 1945, the SS *Harriet Tubman* was launched and became the first Liberty ship named after an African American woman. Previous Liberty ships had been named after African American men including Frederick Douglass and Booker T. Washington. For Bethune and NCNW, the ship made a vital statement to the United States and to the world that

African American women were willing to work to be included in the war and also that they wanted to be recognized as equals. Funds to revamp the ship were raised solely by members of NCNW. By September 1944, the organization had passed a fundraising goal of selling $2 million in war bonds, and "A total of $3,452,361.75 bond purchases were credited to the drive."[23] Over the course of the year, the organization called on its member organizations, including sororities and professional organizations, to assist in selling United States War Bonds. By August 1944, the Los Angeles chapter of NCNW had surpassed their goal of $10,000 by $7,500 by selling bonds, and all across the United States local organizations were doing the same.[24] The organization also used the *Aframerican Woman's Journal* to advertise the sale of bonds as a way to communicate to members about the significance of the ship.

During the launch of the ship, Tubman's family members, including her great-niece, attended the event. The women had accomplished a historic feat. The SS *Harriet Tubman* made history for African American women, not only as the first ship to be named after an African American woman but as the only ship to be named after an African American woman during World War II. Only 17 Liberty ships were named after African Americans out of the 2,751 built during the war.[25] Liberty ships were used to take vital goods and cargo to soldiers fighting abroad. For NCNW it was befitting to name the ship that would assist in liberation from fascism and racism after a woman who had brought hundreds of enslaved people to freedom. The SS *Harriet Tubman* was one of the ways in which NCNW ensured that the participation of Black women during World War II was recognized and that the world understood their historic contributions.

As a fierce advocate for the inclusion of Black women during the war, Bethune affirmed both their roles and hers as powerful voices in the worldwide struggle for freedom. She expounded upon the meaning of the "Double V" by carving out a place for Black women so that they, too, would have a chance at fighting for their rights. Just as she had done with the founding of an all-girls school and NCNW, she organized women for change because it was among women that she often was able to make a difference. With the selling of war bonds and the raising of funds for the SS *Harriet Tubman*, Bethune, along with NCNW, honored a courageous ancestor so that her name would reach an international audience. By raising the SS *Harriet Tubman*, a ship that would be sent thousands of miles across the Atlantic, they shared the rich legacy of a woman who represented the African American quest for freedom. Although for some, the war was strictly about the Allied versus Axis forces; for Bethune, it was about African Americans establishing themselves as global citizens who would make their voices heard on international affairs.

Council on African Affairs (CAA)

During the same time that Bethune and NCNW took an active role in World War II, securing positions for Black women in the military, Bethune began to become more engaged in decolonization efforts through her work with the Council on African Affairs. Founded in 1937 as the International Committee on African Affairs, the CAA was one of the preeminent authorities on the issues of colonization and throughout its existence it called for liberation and solidarity with Africans. With its primary focus being self-determination for Africans, the Council embodied the main ideals of Pan Africanism.[26] Serving as a liaison between African Americans and Africa, the organization addressed issues, such as famine in Africa and the Italian invasion of Ethiopia, and advocated for the Indian Independence movement. The CAA also became a vital communication line to disseminate accurate information about Africa from Africa, informing both Africans and Americans.[27] The organization's widely distributed monthly bulletin, *New Africa* (which would later become *Spotlight on Africa*), included "coverage of and support of the Mau Mau movement in Kenya[,] . . . support for indigenous African leaders, the call for arming Africans during World War II, and the cry for Western leaders to uphold resolutions of the Atlantic Charter for self-determination for all colonized people after the war."[28] Initially the organization was led by Executive Director Max Yergan. William Alphaeus Hunton Jr. would join as educational director in 1943 and later become the executive director.[29] Paul Robeson, who was also one of the organization's founders, served as its chairman throughout its existence.

Bethune was an avid supporter of the CAA, and she often sponsored and attended major events held by the organization. The August 1943 issue of *New Africa* includes articles that addressed the forced use of African labor support during World War II, an address from Ethiopian leader Haile Selassie, and a review of the text *Africa: Facts and Forecasts*.[30] The editorial (by W. A. Hunton) challenged the United States to ensure that the freedoms that were outlined in the Atlantic Charter were applied to the colonized people of Africa. Bethune contributed a quote, alongside several other leaders including Ferdinand D. Smith, Dr. Harold Moody, and F. Nwia Kofi Nkrumah, in support of Africa: "Innately, I am deeply interested in Africa. We realize that progress in one country should stimulate progress in another. The world is fast becoming a melting pot for races. It is therefore, vitally important that some constructive action and thought be employed through which the people of Africa have a chance for self-improvement made possible by a closer relationship with us here in America."[31] This statement is significant because at the time Bethune was an internationally recognized leader of NCNW and NYA who was intentional about the causes that she supported or attached herself to. She chose to lend her voice to the Pan-Africanist organization while making a call for unity between Africans and African Americans. Bethune was fond of both Paul Robeson and Max Yergan, and she supported the work of CAA for several years. It was during this time that she also became more vocal about colonialism, particularly during the years that she partnered with the organization. In more relaxed settings, she attended Robeson's forty-sixth birthday party, hosted by Yergan and the Council, and gave an address honoring his work.[32] During Bethune's seventieth birthday party, hosted by the National Negro Youth Congress, both men attended, and upon the discovery that it was also Yergan's birthday, he and Bethune were both presented with cakes.[33] The work of the Council was the prominent connection, but they also developed friendships outside of their work.

Although she was their elder, Bethune learned a lot from the well-traveled pair, and in many ways they impacted her anticolonial leanings. Yergan, a fellow Carolinian (from North Carolina) had spent many years abroad in South Africa working for the YMCA. Just as Bethune had once wanted to travel to Africa to be a missionary, Yergan's formerly enslaved grandfather had the same wish for one of his progeny, and this heavily influenced his decision to go abroad.[34] Robeson grew up in a segregated community in New Jersey and attended both Rutgers University and Columbia Law School before leaving for England. He and his wife, Eslanda, spent over a decade there during his rise to fame as an actor and singer, in his role as Othello, while they also began to travel extensively to Africa and throughout Europe.[35] Again, Bethune was building connections with those who had knowledge and resources about Africa that would allow her to learn more through these relationships. While she was lending her support to CAA, she was also able to glean information that she would utilize to strengthen her global agenda and expand her scope.

On April 14, 1944, the organization hosted its "Conference on Africa—New Perspectives" to discuss the future of colonized Africans after the war. The three main topics were how to increase Africa's contribution to victory over fascism, solving jurisdictional and territorial problems in Africa, and establishing principles upon plans for the social, economic, and political advancement of the African people.[36] Nearly 150 attendees came from all over the Diaspora, and guests included Amy Ashwood Garvey, Kwame Nkrumah, and Ferdinand Smith.[37] Bethune and Eunice Hunton-Carter attended and represented NCNW, and the organization served as one of the official sponsors of the conference.[38] During this monumental event anticolonialism was at the core of the conversation, and the participants discussed how to bring the issue to the attention of African Americans in leadership. Directly impacting the United Nations Charter, the conference also called for equal representation for Liberia and Ethiopia, as it related to European colonies. It also encouraged the "unification of people who have been arbitrarily divided and separated by colonial boundaries and other barriers."[39]

The CAA encouraged Bethune to use her relationship with President Roosevelt to support the cause of decolonization. November 1944, Max Yergan and Paul Robeson wrote to Bethune asking for assistance in "bringing to the attention of our government and the American public the importance of supporting the incorporation of certain basic principles and objectives for the advancement and liberation of the African people."[40] The letter also encouraged Bethune to take individual action in raising the issue of colonialism through other means. Although it is unclear whether she responded, she does begin to become more visible as a supporter of the CAA, particularly their humanitarian efforts. In 1945 one of the worst droughts on record occurred in South Africa, and the CAA provided vital resources to the region. CAA found that the "non-white population of South Africa, being the last element to receive consideration from the government, must depend largely upon outside aid for support," and in response Paul Robeson created "Help Africa Day" as a way to collect needed goods to send to South Africa.[41] In February 1946, the Council held a kickoff mass meeting at Abyssinian Baptist Church and collected several hundred dollars and vital canned good items donated by everyone from schoolchildren to local civic leaders.[42] After collecting donations at the church and throughout the local New York community, CAA was able to send $1,000 and more than fifty boxes of food to the African Food Fund in Cape Town, South Africa.[43] Bethune was a part of the sponsoring committee, which had supported the campaign along with leaders such as Marian Anderson, W. E. B. Du Bois, Lena Horne, and Arthur Spingarn. The humanitarian efforts of CAA and the African American community undermined colonial forces by ensuring that Africans were able to eat despite the government's decision to unfairly distribute resources. African Americans embraced ideas of self-help and collective action as a way to obstruct the oppressive nature of colonialism.

One of the most well-known and -supported events hosted by the CAA was its June 6, 1946, "Big Three Unity for Colonial Freedom" rally held at Madison Square Garden. More than nineteen thousand people attended the event as the organization's leaders, Yergan and Robeson, brought together African American leaders from around the country to speak out against colonialism in Africa. Among the speakers were "W. E. B. Du Bois and Mary McLeod Bethune; William Haynes, president of the New England Baptist Convention; and Michael Quill, head of the Transport Workers Union."[44] Entertainers such as Katherine Dunham and Mary Lou Williams also attended and performed. Yergan, executive director of CAA, in his speech served notice to colonial forces that "Colonial imperialism stands indicted before the bar of world opinion" and he also criticized the "plunderers of Africa."[45] CAA chairman Robeson denounced those who sought to exploit Africa, stating, "There is a category of Americans, quite few in number, but extremely powerful, who are interested in Africa for the wealth they can extract from it and from the labor of the people there," and concluding with, "You can be sure their ideas for the future of Africa do not include freedom."[46] The resolutions announced during the rally called on President Harry Truman and the State Department to use their resources to implement the ideals of self-determination that were put forth by the United Nations to make democracy and liberation a reality for colonized people. They adopted a "Charter for African Freedom" that called for recognition of Ethiopia's territorial claims, for African countries that were colonized by Spain and Portugal to be brought under UN supervision, an end to the exploitation of African labor and resources, and a time limit to be set for African dependency.[47]

The CAA event revealed how America was linked to the exploitation of Africa and pointing out that "the American government was getting uranium from the Belgian Congo for atomic bombs and that American companies were prospecting for oil in Ethiopia and for minerals in Liberia."[48] Revealing Americans' role in African exploitation showed why the United States remained neutral on the issue of colonialism. The CAA rally did not end with just speeches; the group also put together a list of demands for President Truman, the State Department, and United Nations delegates. The demands included "To translate immediate action pledges of democratic rights and self-determination for all people"; "To welcome colonial peoples into the United Nations family"; "Full recognition of Ethiopia's territorial and reparation claims"; and "Investigation of race discrimination in South Africa by the UN."[49] The CAA rally was highlighted by the *New York Times, Chicago Defender, Baltimore Afro American,* and *New York Herald Tribune,* allowing its message to be received across the nation. As a speaker and attendee of this major event, Bethune demonstrated her growing public support of decolonization efforts. This radical call for freedom, supported by thousands, gave her an even greater understanding of the significance of her work with the United Nations. Over the next few years she would channel her energy into advocating for decolonization through her work with the UN, but the CAA left a lasting impact on her activism.

The Red Scare

Established in 1938, the House Un-American Activities Committee (HUAC) was one of the most pervasive departments of the government. During the late 1940s and throughout the 1950s HUAC investigated possible cases of communist activity, sending some to prison or into exile or deportation. Communists supported and participated in the CAA, which made the organization a target during the "Red Scare," a period in which communists and possible communists were targets of government action. Due to its affiliations, by 1947 "Attorney General Tom Clark placed the Council's name on the list of subversive organizations that threatened to overthrow the U.S. government."[50] The following year, in February 1948, Executive Director Max Yergan, fearing that the organization would suffer consequences for their communist associations, pushed for CAA to make a public statement saying it was "neither fascist, Communist, nor subversive."[51] Robeson, CAA's chairman, did not agree with the move, and soon the organization began to crumble as some members took sides with Robeson and others with Yergan. Bethune sided with Yergan's anticommunist viewpoints and continued to support the organization. Although it is unclear if she accepted the position, after an April 21, 1948, meeting Robeson found that Bethune had been selected to replace him as chairman by the Yergan faction, according to newspaper reports.[52] As the feud between the two began to come to a head, Bethune left the organization. In a letter to both Robeson and Yergan on June 14, 1948, she wrote: "Both of you know how earnestly I have tried to help our African people through the Council on African Affairs. Because of the confused situation there now, there is nothing else I can do. Please accept my resignation from the council with hope that you will work out some plan to carry on the work."[53] By September 1948 Yergan was officially expelled from CAA and began to supply information about the organization to the FBI.[54]

During 1952 Bethune's stance against colonialism and her affiliation with CAA in the previous decade became the source of accusations against her for alleged communist sympathies. In May 1952, she was scheduled to speak to a group of junior high school students; however, she was "accused of affiliation with 22 'subversive' organizations" and was refused entrance into the school.[55] Leaders from across America including Eleanor Roosevelt and Daisy Lampkin came to her defense. In the early years of the HUAC Bethune was also publicly called a communist by Representative Martin Dies, but she was quickly cleared of the accusation with the help of her lawyer, Charles Hamilton Houston. Although HUAC did not solely accuse African Americans, it did focus on leaders, particularly those with international ties. Paul Robeson, chairman of CAA, was accused of being a communist and was stripped of his rights to travel internationally. In his statement before HUAC, he gave the reasons he believed that he was accused of being a communist: "because I have struggled for years for the independence of the colonial peoples of Africa and . . . that when I am abroad I speak out against injustices against Negro people of this land. . . . I am being tried for fighting for the rights of my people."[56]

Political activist and journalist Claudia Jones was imprisoned and exiled for being a member of the Communist Party. As a writer for *The Worker*, the newspaper of the Communist Party (CPUSA), Jones wrote essays on women's issues in her column entitled "Half of the World." "An End to the Neglect of the Problems of Negro Women," one of her most compelling essays, uses Department of Labor data that indicate Black women's pay to be half of white women's, lack of Black women's representation in unions, and the exploitation explanations of Marxism to theorize "the super-exploitation of the Negro woman worker."[57] In 1955, Claudia Jones was imprisoned for violation of the McCarran Act, also known as an anticommunist law, and she served nine months in jail before she was deported to London. The charge of communism was detrimental to African American activists and their organizations. Many organizations dissolved or drastically reduced their activism to ensure that they would no longer have any affiliations with communists or communist activities. There is no indication that Bethune worked with the CAA again after the submission of her resignation letter.

San Francisco and the Global Stage

When Bethune joined the NAACP in 1945 as a consultant to the founding of the United Nations in San Francisco, she had led a charge for Black women to be involved in a global fight for democracy, and she armed herself with knowledge of the state of colonization in Africa through her work with CAA. Well prepared to take her place in conversations among global leaders, she found that it was not easy to gain acceptance as a Black woman. For years she had been involved with the NAACP, but the path to representing the organization in San Francisco would prove difficult, yet not unobtainable, for Bethune. Not only was she a member of the NAACP and recipient of the prized Spingarn Medal, but she served as vice president and a member of the Board of Directors for a decade. In 1943, Bethune served on a committee in support of the NAACP's anticolonialist efforts, which "present[ed] the cause of the Negro not only in America but [also in] the West Indies and Africa."[58]

In her work with the organization she became acquainted with Walter White, the organization's executive secretary from 1931 through 1955. White had also been concerned about the treatment of African Americans troops during World War II, and he traveled to Europe to investigate the soldiers' environment. Realizing that African American soldiers were fighting in the war for their own freedom from oppression and that there were African troops fighting against a common foe in the form of colonialism, White stated: "World War II has given to the Negro a sense of kinship with other colored—and also oppressed—peoples of the world. Where he has not thought through or informed himself on the racial angles of colonial policy and master-race theories, he senses that the struggle of the Negro in the United States is part and parcel of the struggle against imperialism and exploitation in India, China, Burma, Africa, the Philippines, Malaysia, the West Indies, and South America."[59] As the head of the NAACP, White fought for not only African Americans but people of color throughout the world, making him an important voice on global affairs.

Despite being the leader of her well-known women's organization, Bethune would find that her connection to the NAACP would prove to be more important to gaining attendance at the historic meeting in San Francisco that would lead to the formation of the United Nations. For months, in his role as director of special research for the NAACP, W. E. B. Du Bois had petitioned the State Department on behalf of the organization for either consultant or observer status, and his persistence paid off.[60] On April

10, 1945, Secretary of State Edward R. Stettinius sent invitations to forty-two national organizations—the NAACP being the only one of them composed predominantly of African Americans—to send representatives to act as consultants to the United Nations Charter.[61] Women's organizations including the National League of Women's Voters, the Women's Action Committee for Victory and Lasting Peace, the American Association of University Women, and the General Federation of Women's Clubs were all invited, but the NCNW did not receive an invitation. Knowing how vital it was to attend this international event, Bethune had her executive secretary, Jeanetta Welch Brown, contact the assistants to US Secretary of State William L. Clayton and Archibald MacLeish, insisting that the NCNW, with its membership of nearly six million African American women, should be represented. In an April 11, 1945, letter to MacLeish, she stated, "the council is entitled to representation."[62] Clayton not only denied them an invitation, but he also insisted that inviting the Council would force them to invite other women's organizations, such as the councils of Jewish and Catholic women.

Bethune continued to press for the opportunity to attend the San Francisco Conference. Despite the denial of her request on April 12, she expressed to Walter White that she, along with the NCNW, fully supported the NAACP delegation. Her telegram included these words: "We offer the use of our name and the influence of the 6.5 million Negro women of America pushing for conference consideration of these points affecting the colonial and dependent areas of the world."[63] Bethune was not deterred, but she was willing to participate in any way that she could to assert herself as a global leader. Yet again she realized that even when shut out of male-dominated spaces, she still had a powerful voice among women. Ahead of the conference, she called for NCNW to start preparing for the historic occasion by creating World Security Month to be celebrated throughout April. During the month women were urged to listen to the conference on the radio, to plan their own community programs to invite speakers to discuss world affairs, and to reach out to state and local officials to get them to endorse the month.[64]

From April 25 to June 26, 1945, delegates from fifty countries would hold sessions to create the foundations of the United Nations. The NAACP saw their invitation to be a part of the San Francisco Conference as associate consultants as their moment to challenge the issue of colonization on the world stage. In preparation for the meeting the organization surveyed more than 150 African American organizations to determine what should be addressed at the conference, and the top issues that surfaced were colonization and discrimination.⁶⁵ Their goal was to not only represent their interests but to be a voice for Black America. NAACP Executive Secretary Walter White served as the consultant for the delegation and Director of Special Research W. E. B. Du Bois was named as an associate consultant. In a turn of events, by the end of April Bethune became the third person on the delegation. Accepting the honor to serve with the NAACP at the conference, Bethune was the only African American woman to serve as an associate consultant for the founding charter of the United Nations, and she did so proudly.⁶⁶

Upon her arrival at the San Francisco Conference, she immediately began to emphasize the NAACP's main objective: to address the issues of colonialism and discrimination. She set the tone for her tenure at the conference in an address captured by *Chicago Defender* correspondents on May 5 where she stated:

> Through this conference the Negro becomes allied with all the darker races of the world, but more importantly he becomes integrated into the structure of the peace and freedom of all people everywhere. I am particularly interested the trend of thought of the darker people of the world who are no longer a numerical minority. One of the big questions of the conference will be how best to set up machinery for the inclusion of small and dependent peoples whose status is undetermined, yet whose voice is needed in clinching and durable peace.⁶⁷

White, Bethune, and Du Bois sent a letter to Edward Stettinius, the chairman of the American delegation, critiquing the proposals. Chapter 1, paragraph 3, of the declaration called for human rights and freedom from discrimination; however, the consultants pointed out that it left out "the mass of people living in colonies, against whom discrimination is customary and unjustifiable."⁶⁸ They also criticized the conference for denying representation to the countries that the United Nations had taken under colonial trusteeship. They argued that it was "unthinkable that the mandated colonies distributed after the First World War should be returned to the position of colonies owned by other countries."⁶⁹ In the joint statement the trio called for those under the colonial system to obtain autonomy through the revision of the declaration.

Bethune kept the NCNW abreast of the progress being made during the conference. She also put together an impressive group of NCNW members to serve as observers including Mamie Davis, Dr. Dorothy Ferebee, attorney Eunice Hunton Carter, and Sue Bailey Thurman. They joined Bethune in communicating and keeping members abreast of the important conversations that were taking place.[70] In a letter dated May 10, 1945, Bethune discussed her role as liaison between the masses and the delegates. She stated: "We are greatly concerned as to the fate of people of the world. Colonial problems are in the forefront, and human rights for all people everywhere must be insisted upon."[71] She also let readers know that Du Bois, White, and she were the only African Americans among the conference's 126 consultants from the United States. Her purpose at the conference, and that of the African American in general, was to use this global event to put forth ideas that would eliminate discrimination and colonization. To this end, she noted that "To the Negro people, the World Security Conference in San Francisco has but one meaning, that is how far democratic practices shall be stretched to embrace the rights of their brothers in the colonies as well as the American Negro's own security at home."[72] Bethune's letter showed her position not only as an African American leader but also as one with concern for all those living under the thumb of colonization.

The African American press was well aware of the consultants' plans to raise issues of colonization and discrimination on the world's stage. The May 19, 1945, *Chicago Defender* article titled "Hit U.S. Stand on Colonies" addresses the presence of White, Du Bois, and Bethune at the San Francisco Conference, and a wire sent on behalf of the trio that pointed out the declaration's inadequacies and called for the "eventual disappearance of the colonial system."[73] All eyes were on the trio in support of their stance against colonization. In a May 26, 1945, issue of the *Chicago Defender* titled "Hit U.S. Opposition to Colonial Independence," US officials were called out for their attempts to maintain colonialism.[74] Both the American and British delegations stood against the mention of colonial independence in the Bill of Rights. An enraged Du Bois pointed out how "undemocratic" the colonial system had been, while highlighting the fact that the United Nations declaration called for democracy.[75] Du Bois and Bethune continued to link promises of democracy to anticolonialism, swiftly using the terms to condemn the delegation.[76] In a wire to the US secretary of state, White asked the country to reconsider its position on colonialism. White noted that not supporting freedom for colonized people negated the image of World War II as a struggle for the freedom of all people, and wires from African Americans from across the nation were sent to the conference organizers and President Harry Truman.[77] The American Council on Race Relations protested to Truman through a wire stating that America's opposition played "directly into the hands of the enemy propagandists . . . that allies are interested only in white freedom."[78] In his recap of their representation, Walter White wrote in the *Chicago Defender,* "The consultants were a unit of insistence on the speediest possible abolition of colonialism and all its evils."[79] White spoke highly of the differences in the presentations and the powerful impact they made, writing that Du Bois presented facts on colonial exploitation while Bethune "made a stirring plea at one session for the disadvantaged people of the earth, particularly American Negroes."[80]

As the only African American female consultant, Bethune was one of many African Americans who took issue with colonization and placed their expectations for its end upon the fledgling, global organization that was supposed to represent democracy. Bethune did not take lightly her responsibility of receiving the demands of the masses and communicating them, but it was still problematic that so few women were a part of the historic occasion. Eslanda Robeson (wife of Paul Robeson) attended and participated in events and briefings, and during the conference she and Bethune reconnected over dinner.[81] As an unofficial observer, Robeson criticized the historic occasion for its underrepresentation of women.[82] Unfortunately for Bethune, she faced her own challenges, particularly sexism, while working with White and Du Bois. Although she had been an influential leader among women, it was the insistence of Eleanor Roosevelt that had been a key factor in her invitation to serve with the NAACP, not the graciousness of the men or the organization. Historian Brenda Gayle Plummer discusses the tension between the three and the men's overall disregard for Bethune's expertise and leadership. She notes that Du Bois and White "were less than enthusiastic about having her as a colleague" and that "The NAACP did not offer to pay her fare and did not even inform her that she was a consultant-observer until the last minute."[83] Du Bois biographer David Levering Lewis confirms the contentious relationships, noting that off the record Du Bois called Bethune "a nuisance, but a harmless one."[84] Despite the supposed feminist leanings of Du Bois, Bethune was never a beneficiary of his.

It would seem that the conference was where the issues began, but correspondence between Bethune and Du Bois dating over a decade before the meeting reveals that the three of them had not been the best of friends, although they were often in positions in which they had to work together. In a December 1929 letter to Bethune, Du Bois accuses Bethune of gossiping about being neglected by the NAACP during her visit to New York.[85] In her response the following month she played it down, stating, "I was having a little spat with Walter White, and I did not think it would be taken seriously."[86] She was in town for two months and had not seen either of the men as she had expected to. Du Bois's letter seems to indicate that he did not feel that he had to make these types of accommodations for Bethune. From these short exchanges it is clear that, though they tolerated Bethune, the men saw her as their subordinate and they treated her as such. She may have risen to great heights to work with presidents, but that meant very little in the eyes of Du Bois and White. They were well-educated, mixed-race men, and she was their complete opposite with her African features and dark complexion and seminary/missionary training. Despite what they may have thought of her, Bethune did not let that change how she saw herself, and she believed that it was her rightful place to work with Du Bois and White, and she did so proudly.

Continuing for Justice

Upon returning to her home in Daytona Beach, Florida, Bethune shared her experiences with the local African American community by hosting a discussion at Bethune-Cookman College, where she spoke to students and community members. Expressing her disappointment in the US delegation, she stated that one of its mistakes was "the failure of the U.S. to assume leadership in the matter of representing 750,000,000 colonial people who had no voice in the gathering."[87] At the time, much of Africa was ruled by European colonial forces, severely limiting the independence of the continent. Bethune told her audience that her position at the conference had been to represent both "colonial" people and African Americans whom she felt were in a similar condition because they were "not permitted to exercise their rights under the constitution of the U.S."[88] In this comparison Bethune recognized that although African Americans lived in a "free country," they were in no way more free than Africans living in the colonies. As a person who had studied the conditions and worked with local communities to better their positions, she was well aware of what issues African Americans faced. She urged the audience to prepare and become aware of these issues, stating: "Do your part. Study, become skilled, be able to stand on your feet."[89] She utilized her experience and her disappointment with the US delegation to rally African Americans to become more engaged in the global struggle for freedom.

Bethune also turned to African American leaders to see how they could build on the momentum of the San Francisco meeting. In a June 23, 1945, meeting in Washington, DC, she met with leaders including Mary Church Terrell, Adam Clayton Powell Jr., Charlotte Hawkins Brown, Dr. Rayford Logan, Charles Hamilton Houston, Dr. Channing Tobias, Walter White, and Max Yergan.[90] The National Conference of Negro Leaders addressed issues including the challenges faced by returning veterans, continued practices of segregation in the government, and the colonial question.[91] In her speech given during the meeting Bethune emphasized the need for a resolution to colonization: "UNCIO has to no less degree focused our attention on the position of more than 100 million colonial peoples throughout the world with whom we have a common bond and who are demanding a major role in the shaping of a new civilization. . . . The confidence of the masses cannot be retained if they must sit by and permit a handful of the vested interest group to shape the contour of civilization which they have done so much to destroy."[92]

Just as she compared African Americans and those who were colonized in her speech at Bethune-Cookman College, Bethune continued to remind leaders of the similarities in their struggles while also advocating for their autonomy. The colonial question was on the minds of many. Howard University president Mordecai Johnson said that he was disappointed that the United States "gave substantial comfort to the colonial powers," but they also understood that the UN could potentially be a part of the path to decolonization.[93] As a result, at the urging of the Council of African Affairs leader Max Yergan, they agreed to approve the charter's adoption. As the leader of CAA, an organization whose founding principle was to end colonization in Africa, his opinion carried a lot of weight. Bethune compiled a team of leaders she knew would take action.

On October 24, 1945, the United Nations Charter was ratified, and the United Nations came into existence without the complete abolition of colonialism. Although the Declaration on the Granting of Independence to Colonial Countries and Peoples would not be adopted by the United Nations until December 14, 1960, Bethune and NCNW continued to call for true democracy for colonized countries and an end to discrimination. NCNW's report on the United Nations offered suggestions on how the Council could create change as a member of the United Nations.[94] One of the suggestions included becoming educated on the charter and electing officials who would implement its provisions. NCNW's key suggestion was to "establish contact with the women of other minority groups and of dependent countries and unite with them in working on the ultimate goal of full citizenship for men and women everywhere."[95] Her participation in San Francisco had been an important step toward further internationalizing NCNW. In a public conference report she announced that Indian ambassador Vijaya Lakshmi Pandit had become a life member and that plans were also underway for Liberian women to become affiliated with NCNW.[96] As India was in the midst of its struggle for freedom from the British, Pandit traveled to the United States as a diplomat and was able to attend the San Francisco Conference, where she met Bethune. Pandit had been heavily involved in the independence movement, often serving time in jail for her political beliefs. Expressing how impressed she was with Pandit, Bethune stated, "I have found Mme. Pandit of India most interesting with a yearning in her heart for the delivery of her people."[97] As two women working in a male-dominated atmosphere and trying to insert freedom into a conversation of imperialism, Bethune and Pandit made a connection that not only brought them into a friendship but also built a bridge between the NCNW and the women of India.

Immediately following the conference, NCNW created programs to support the United Nations. In a September 25, 1945, letter to Chinese ambassador Dr. Wei Tao Ming, Bethune urged him to attend NCNW's "World Community Night" as a representative of China. This program was one of the earliest NCNW programs in its attempts to implement United Nations Charter principles.[98] Another important facet of supporting the United Nations was studying and becoming fully aware of its tenets. By ordering resources such as *The United Nations Primer* by Sigrid Arne, NCNW built a library containing information to educate its members.[99] In April 1946 NCNW applied to be a nongovernmental organization to gain its members access to meetings of the United Nations as consultants. In sharing its specific interests on the form, the organization stated, "The council is interested in raising social standards of not only the Negroes in America but darker races everywhere."[100] This short statement speaks volumes about the consistency of NCNW's mission. Even in its relationship with the United Nations, the main purpose for NCNW was the improvement of conditions of people all over the world but particularly the conditions for people of color. Although official consultation status was not given to NCNW in 1946, the organization continued to assert itself into United Nations affairs.

Although the United States did not agree to take a stance against colonialism, Bethune, White, and Du Bois spoke on behalf of those living under imperial forces, ensuring that their voices were heard. Africans living in colonies felt disappointment too, but many were proud to see African Americans representing on their behalf. Expressing his pride in the work of the consultants, Nigerian student and activist Nwafor Orizu wrote:

"The objective of the Negro has changed totally. He is grown to demand his right with irresistible determination; He is grown to say: 'although I am an American, I want to remain an American by right but I am proud that I descended from the noble Africans whom we shall no more stand by and see the European gangsters devour them.' That is the significance of the Negro in San Francisco."[101] Not only did Orizu express pride in African Americans, but in some ways, as an African affirming their actions, he validated the work of the consultants.

Over the next few years Orizu would seek Bethune's support for his mission to educate Nigerians. He was the founder and president of the American Council on African Education, an organization that provided scholarships for Africans to attend college in the United States. Hailing from Nnewi, a British protectorate of Nigeria, Nwafor was a graduate of Columbia University and Ohio State University who believed that "universal free education" would be a means by which Africans would make progress.[102] It was his goal to equip Africans with education and knowledge from American universities so that they could return home to make valuable contributions to their country. With a primary focus on Nigeria, some of the goals of the organization were to establish libraries and science labs for research, to secure scholarships to study in America, to promote goodwill and understanding between Africans and Americans, and to create a space to house African students in the United States.[103]

Orizu enlisted the help of an interracial group of leaders from institutions including Fordham University, Howard University, Western Reserve University, Morehouse College, Yale University, Wilberforce College, and Lincoln University.[104] Bethune-Cookman College accepted students as a part of its partnership with the American Council on African Education, and in 1948 Chukwuemeka Okeke and Austin A. Njakar were awarded scholarships to attend, bringing the total number of awardees to more than 150.[105] Bethune personally supported the work of the organization that year by serving as a speaker for their benefit drive, which was working to raise $25,000 to continue to provide scholarships to African students.[106] The support for decolonization of Africa in San Francisco was also a vital step in the right direction in strengthening relationships between continental Africans and African Americans. It is unclear if Bethune met Nwafor at the conference, but she became a supporter of his educational work, which included a comprehensive plan to rebuild Africa by equipping its young people with the tools to do so. In later years Bethune joined an advisory board led by Joseph Acquah in support of the building of a college on the Gold Coast, continuing her support of educational efforts for Africans.[107] Understanding how education had transformed her life and the lives of her students, Bethune saw it as one of the ways to create change, be it in Florida or Nigeria. For her, Nwafor's organization was a vital part of liberation, and their association emerged after the UN meeting.

Bethune takes her rightful place as an activist on the global stage, despite those who sought to keep her from doing so. She saw World War II as a vital step toward the world recognizing Black women as being participants in world affairs who deserved equality. As a supporter of CAA, she broadened her understanding of Pan-Africanism, working with younger activists who challenged her to become even more engaged in decolonization efforts. Even when faced with experiences of sexism as a part of the United Nations delegation, Bethune was not deterred because she understood the bigger picture, which was to advocate for those who were colonized. Understanding her role as a part of the African Diaspora, as a daughter of Africa who could now use her influence to bring about change, she was determined to be heard as a voice representing those who were not able to speak for themselves. As the president of NCNW she challenged members to take their international engagement to greater heights in the coming years.

5

National Council of Negro Women's Postwar Leadership Abroad

The events that took place during World War II and the war itself changed the landscape of activism as it opened the minds of many to the revolution and struggle of Africans abroad. As they fought in the war to sustain democracy, Africans in both the United States and on the continent envisioned democracy for themselves. They were not fighting aimlessly but with intentionality and forethought, with their own agenda. World War II sparked a fire in African Americans that laid the foundation of the modern civil rights movement and a fire in Africans that ultimately led to decolonization across the continent. Women had been a vital part of winning the war, and they worked to continue to have a voice in postwar planning and the rebuilding of the world. Recognizing the parallel struggles of people of African descent, Bethune and NCNW navigated the postwar years by creating initiatives to advance the cause of democracy. They did so by increasing their involvement with the United Nations, strengthening coalitions with women across the world to address issues that were plaguing their communities, and educating themselves on world affairs with the establishment of an international committee.

Bethune's increasing international experience became a driving force in her leadership of NCNW, and she was even more committed to seeing it grow as a respected voice on global affairs. She called for members to concern themselves not only with what was happening in America but also around the world, particularly the plight of those of African descent. NCNW members traveled to Trinidad to join women from Jamaica, Barbados, and British Guiana to expand their understanding of the issues faced by women in these respective areas, gaining firsthand insight through workshops and conversations. It was important for NCNW to show up for women in person when possible, to make personal connections and show their commitment to creating solidarity and their support. Building on Bethune's relationship with Madame Pandit, they welcomed Indian women to visit their headquarters while also publishing literature about India to build awareness of the challenges that country faced as a colonized nation. The journal informed readers by including voices of those from other countries, giving vital opportunities to hear directly from the people. As they expanded their presence on the international front, NCNW became a model for women like Sarah Simpson George, who organized the Liberian Women's Social and Political Movement after meeting with NCNW and returning to her country. The international influence of the organization expanded, particularly among women, and the seeds of activism that Bethune planted over the years were now germinating in a way that she had only dreamed about. In the last year of her presidency, she was afforded the chance of a lifetime when she was invited to Haiti by the country's president to receive the Haitian Medal of Honor and Merit. After years of asserting herself as an international leader, she was finally being respected as one by a country that epitomized ideals of Black Liberation that were near and dear to her heart. Haiti was a symbol of freedom for Bethune, and she did not take it lightly that the country and its people celebrated her work.

International Relations Committee

As NCNW's international exchanges and travels continued, Bethune felt that it would be in their best interest to create an official International Relations Committee to help guide the activities of the organization. Although the *Aframerican Woman's Journal* had much success under the leadership of Sue Bailey Thurman with its trip to Cuba and the addition of foreign correspondents, Bethune sought to expand the educational component of their activities by including academic experts. She solicited the assistance of scholars who specialized in international affairs, history, and culture, and in her invitation she stated that the committee's purpose would be to "create better understanding of the people who live in our neighboring countries and in other countries of the world."[1] The committee would serve as a vehicle for promoting awareness through its educational programs and by studying foreign affairs. Several of the invited speakers were professors at Howard University. Over the years Bethune often worked with Howard

University, speaking at programs for the school, ensuring that the university benefited from National Youth Administration funds when she was its head, and maintaining close relationships with its faculty. During the first few months of NCNW's existence the organization's principal business address was the office of Lucy D. Slowe, who served as the dean of women for the university.[2] Some of the most respected Black scholars came from Howard, including United Nations delegate Ralph Bunche, and issues of internationalism and imperialism were debated and discussed heavily among scholars at the university.[3]

On Monday, January 28, 1946, the committee held its first meeting at the NCNW headquarters, led by Vivian Carter Mason. She listed the main objectives of the group as building friendships with women abroad; visiting women, "especially [in] the West Indies, South America, Africa, Virgin Islands, Central America"; and bringing international affairs educational programs to NCNW.[4] Mason suggested creating "International Night" programs to study the conditions of those across the world and to get a sense of other countries' histories and languages. She also added that the program would bring unity with other countries. With eight committee members present, the group resolved to find representatives from various countries to be a part of the committee, to find existing international programs to attend, and to take a special interest in the conditions of women, particularly those fighting for suffrage.

Howard University was well represented among the committee members, with three of its faculty serving. Margaret Just Wormly (later known as Margaret Just Butcher), the chairman of the committee, was a professor at Howard University. In later years Dr. Wormly worked alongside Alain Locke to complete the book *The Negro in American Culture (1956–71)*.[5] World-renowned scholar, archivist, and librarian Dorothy Porter Wesley served as a member of the International Relations Committee. Her academic works included *A Selected List of Books by and about the Negro* (1936), *North American Negro Poets* (1945), and *Afro-Braziliana: A Working Bibliography* (1978). Her work as an archivist at Howard was instrumental in establishing what is now known as the Moorland-Spingarn Research Center.[6] Dr. Merze Tate, a world traveler, Fulbright scholar, and the first African American woman to graduate from Oxford University in England, provided much international insight as a committee member.[7] Her works include *The United States and Armaments* (1948), *The United States and the Hawaiian Kingdom; A Political History* (1965), and *Mineral Railways in Africa* (1989). Just as Bethune forged relationships between her school and the Daytona community, she challenged Howard University to do the same by welcoming its faculty to serve on the newly formed committee. The women's participation demonstrates the importance of historically Black colleges and universities as centers of education that go beyond their physical locations, by being active participants in their communities.

The committee hosted its first "International Night" on March 1, 1946, nearly a month after its formation, and the selected region for the discussion was the West Indies. The special invited speakers were Howard University professors Dr. Mercer Cook and Dr. Angel Suarez Rocabruna. Dr. Cook had recently returned from a two-year stay in Haiti, where he led an English-teaching project.[8] He was asked to speak on Haiti's economic, political, and social structure with a special focus on "the position of women in the country and the activities which they engage in on a political and economic level."[9] Originally from Cuba, Dr. Rocabruna was a visiting professor of Spanish at Howard. During his tenure he worked to build relationships by hosting meetings between African American scholars and activists and Afro-Cubans, particularly members of Club Cubano Inter-Americano.[10] Though the committee addressed international issues overall, there was a particular focus on people of African descent, and, with the first topic being the social and political conditions for Haitian women and Afro-Cubans, the organization got off to a great start. Bethune brought together an impressive group of women, each of them at the top of her field, to create programs that would help prepare NCNW to take part in postwar planning. The women were participating in intellectual conversations to educate themselves on how they could use their positions and resources to effect change on a deeper level.

Joining Forces with Women Abroad

When opportunities presented themselves for NCNW to engage in global conversations whether in the United States or abroad, they made every effort to do so. It was important for them to be at the table, particularly among other like-minded women. Following an invitation to Bethune from Coterie of Social Workers president Audrey Jeffers, NCNW sent four of its members as delegates to join women from Trinidad and Tobago; Barbados; Kingston, Jamaica; and British Guiana in the celebration of the Coterie's twenty-fifth year. Baltimoreans Mrs. Henry Welcome, Mrs. John Coasey, and Mrs. Bernard Hatcher set out for Trinidad as representatives of NCNW.[11] NCNW vice president Estelle M. Riddle also joined the women as an attendee.

Audrey Lane Jeffers founded the Coterie of Social Workers of Trinidad and Tobago in 1921 with the motto, "We lift as we climb, and we give the best, or nothing."[12] Over its twenty-five-year existence the Coterie established Children's Breakfast Centres to feed children in Trinidad and Tobago, the St. Mary's Home for Blind Girls and Women, and a nursery to provide daycare for working mothers.[13] The Coterie was "the first non-white organization to offer an outlet for middle-class black and colored women to help underprivileged working women and their children" and their work resonated with NCNW's ideals of improving the status of women.[14]

From April 29 to May 17, 1946, women gathered in Port-of-Spain, Trinidad, for lectures and discussions on topics including "Youth, Their Place in the Post-War World," "Health and Social Service," and "The Value of Higher Education."[15] As part of the convening, they gave back to the community by hosting a special Mother's Day for the local women. Serving breakfast to children, providing dinner for the poor, and visiting local institutions were also parts of the program that allowed the Coterie of Social Workers and its visitor delegates to continue the legacy of community service and involvement that had been the core of the organization's work for more than two decades. In a letter from Estelle M. Riddle to NCNW executive director Mame Mason Higgins, she wrote, "These women have done a wonderful job against great odds."[16] For NCNW, the trip was an invaluable opportunity to understand the issues faced by the women in the Caribbean and to stand in solidarity with the Coterie by serving the community. This firsthand experience of meeting local people, seeing their challenges and the conditions they faced, informed the organization in ways that their research and news reports could not.

Just as NCNW was welcomed to Trinidad by the women of the Coterie, they invited women who traveled to the nation's capital to visit with them during their stay in the United States. During their meetings they often mentored women, giving them the tools to return home to organize in their local communities. Under Bethune's leadership the organization became a powerful example for women across the globe, providing a model for many, including Sarah Simpson George. An educator from Liberia, George met Bethune and members of NCNW during her visit to the United States, leaving a lasting impact on her. In a letter to Bethune she wrote, "You are my 'Ideal Woman,' and I do so much admire you, all you represent and stand for."[17] She also requested copies of *Aframerican Woman's Journal* to share with the women of Liberia, and she asked Bethune for any suggestions or advice on how to strengthen the country. During her trip to the United

States Bethune had arranged a meeting with First Lady Eleanor Roosevelt for George, and she was also able to discuss her work of setting up kindergartens in Liberia, most likely sharing her experience as the founder of a school. Roosevelt noted the visit in her newspaper column "My Day."[18] George came to America to gain insight on the kindergarten system and to gain support for her education efforts, and Bethune was willing to extend her political connections by introducing her to one of the most powerful women she knew. Bethune also encouraged George to become a member of NCNW in an effort to build "a solid foundation for our international program."[19]

In October 1946, just a few years after her trip, George founded the Liberian Women's Social and Political Movement.[20] Continuing to foster relationships with Bethune and NCNW, the organization's president, Mary McCritty Fiske, attended the NCNW convention as an official delegate just one month after its founding.[21] Fiske was the recording secretary, George was the founder and president, and Jeanette L. Cooper was the national vice president. After attending the conference, Fiske wrote to NCNW executive director Mame Mason Higgins: "To have been in company and association with ladies as you all was an education in itself. I am sure you and Bethune can be immense help to me."[22] George founded the organization as a means of mobilizing women to call for suffrage and for positions in the Liberian government and politics, and much like NCNW, the organization was heavily focused on women's and children's rights. During the first few years of its existence, they hosted community rally/children's fund drives to raise funds to feed starving children; provided much-needed political support to Vice President Benjamin Green Freeman in 1950 for the 1951 election; and worked with President Tubman to acquire positions for women in the executive branch.[23]

In the years that followed Bethune began to emerge as an influential figure to Africans, and she often received letters from the continent seeking assistance and encouragement. On December 30, 1946, Ekekwe Obiora from Aba, Nigeria, wrote to Bethune expressing admiration toward Bethune for having the courage to start Bethune-Cookman with $1.50 and faith. He stated, "This maxim has fired my mind and for long I have desired to help my race."[24] He also asked for assistance to study at an American university. On July 4, 1947, Joe Columbus Wobil from Takoradi, Gold Coast, wrote Bethune thanking her for encouraging him to attend Madam C. J. Walker's School of Beauty Culture: "I shall not forget the moral support you have given me. To me it is history in the making" in appreciation to Bethune.[25]

On December 12, 1947, Felix U. Zeh from southern Nigeria wrote to Bethune seeking financial assistance, calling her a "fellow descendant from Africa."[26] Numerous letters arrived for Bethune praising and admiring her and sometimes asking for help to seek an education, and she took the concerns of the people into consideration as she went about her work, particularly as she implemented programs and initiatives.

Relations with Indians

Historian Joseph E. Harris argues that it is imperative to include India in African Diaspora studies, noting evidence of the presence of free Africans in Asia before the Atlantic slave trade and the numerous Africans who were enslaved by Arabs in places including India.[27] Recognizing India as a part of the African Diaspora, promoting solidarity with its people, is a tenet of Pan-Africanism. The oppression that Indians felt as a nation colonized by Europeans resonated with African Americans, whose status in a segregated country relegated them to second-class citizenship in a country dominated by white supremacy. Bethune's relationship with the people of India began during her tenure with ICWDR; the organization included members from the country, and involvement in the organization presented an opportunity for her to forge relationships with "peoples of color the world over."[28]

As they continued to learn more about the challenges facing women across the globe, NCNW embraced the women of India, building upon Bethune's relationship with Vijaya Pandit. She was not alone in the belief that there were shared struggles between African Americans and Indians. Marcus Garvey often spoke about India in *Negro World,* once stating "Indians and Africans have the same fight."[29] He had seen firsthand how Jamaicans were impacted by British colonization just as Indians were in their country. Visiting India and meeting Mahatma Gandhi had a profound impact on the work of theologian Howard Thurman, leading him to become more focused on social justice and the philosophy of nonviolence. Having witnessed the mistreatment of people of color a world away and their struggle to earn independence, Thurman saw parallels between the Black and Indian experience.[30] Just as other African American leaders sought to link the struggles of Indians and African descendants, Bethune did so also.

Madame Vijaya Pandit became a life member of NCNW shortly after the San Francisco Conference. With one of India's most respected diplomats and women's rights activists as a part of NCNW, Bethune hoped that other women from her country would also be interested. In a memo on NCNW activities written by Bethune to the National Council of Women, she discussed Pandit's role as a workshop facilitator contributing to the international activities of NCNW.[31] In *Telefact,* the newsletter for the NCNW, the organization discussed the impacts of colonization: "India, long a victim of British domination, with all that implies, is today in a state of turmoil. There is a division in the ranks of the masses, which division plays, as always into the hands of the exploiter."[32] Nearly seven months later, the people of India won their independence from the British; however, the "British domination" that NCNW highlighted had been very real for almost nine decades, dating back to the 1850s. Students from India, Svati Puwaiah and Lakshmi Rao, visited Bethune and NCNW members in the organization's headquarters in Washington, DC. During their conversations the women discussed the status of the women of India and revealed their progress, noting that the University of Madras now had women in all departments, including those that had been traditionally exclusive to men, such as engineering. About the conversation and the exchange Bethune wrote, "We felt the spirit of unity with all of these women."[33]

During his first visit to the United States, Bethune met Madame Pandit's brother, Jawaharlal Nehru, the first prime minister of Independent India. Both he and his sister had been activists during the Indian independence movement. Having witnessed the impact of British imperialism on his home country, when he became prime minister in 1947 to the newly freed India he vowed to remain independent by avoiding "entangling alliances."[34] He was well read on American history, and in his book *Glimpses of World History* he criticized America's treatment of African Americans and American Indians and its control of Central and South American governments through domineering banking practices.[35] In 1949 Nehru visited the United States as a guest of the State Department, but he maintained his stance of nonalignment, pledging no particular allegiance to America. It was believed that the State Department had purposely left meetings with Black leaders off of Nehru's three-week itinerary although he had expressed prior interest to meet with them.[36] On his own accord he set up a meeting in New York with top Black leaders with the assistance of Walter White and Ralph Bunche. Bethune's presence was requested, and she attended along with Mordecai Johnson, George Weaver, Claude E. Barnett, and Roy Wilkins.[37] In anticipation of the meeting Nehru came prepared with questions about the status of progress being made by African Americans, their satisfaction with the United States, their interest in Africa, and their employment status.[38] He was also interested in knowing what legal resources were available to African Americans to utilize in their struggle for equality. Bethune was asked to attend specifically to discuss the progress that African Americans had made in education, a moment that allowed her to enlighten the world leader on the hard work that they undertook while managing the limitations of Jim Crow segregation. She accepted the invitation, understanding that she would be a part of an important conversation with an emerging leader who was seeking to understand the status of African Americans from the people themselves.

Although Bethune did not travel to India, her influence touched the lives of the people. In 1946, the year after the UN meeting, a young man from Sialkot City, India, named Rana S. Singh began to reach out to Bethune, admiring her for her leadership and her role as an educator. In his letter he called Bethune "Respected Grandma," as many of her students and those closest to her affectionately called her. From as far away as India, Singh was knowledgeable of Bethune's impoverished background, "African ROYAL blood," and her courageous efforts to found Bethune-Cookman College.[39] He also expressed that his sister was interested in Bethune's work and was very much impressed by Bethune's friendships with Pandit and Nehru. Singh's letters are among many that reveal her growing influence internationally. Bethune did not take the letters lightly; she wrote back and provided information about African American news sources in response to his requests, and she also gave contacts for his sister to correspond with. She was an advocate for cultural exchange and building relationships among people facing similar issues of discrimination and maltreatment. To Singh, Bethune wrote, "Though you are far away in India and I am here in Florida, our interests draw us together and together we understand that the world is better when people understand each other," further demonstrating her persistence in building cultural understanding and unity.[40]

Madame Pandit visited Bethune at her home in Florida in 1951, where she invited hundreds of students and community members to hear her speak about "her personal fight for the release of her people and her determination to release mankind the world over."[41] Having followed the nonviolent philosophy of Mahatma Gandhi, Pandit had been a leader, speaker, and a political prisoner during her involvement with Indian freedom movements. She also spread Gandhi's message of equality among Indians, and after attending a conference under his tutelage, she spread his message of abolishing untouchability.[42] In her address at Bethune-Cookman College she infused her past experiences as a freedom fighter to give the community a snapshot of what it would take to gain true liberation. She also encouraged her audience to "remain steadfast in the fight for freedom, for brotherhood—for security," which made a strong statement against the bondage of colonialism, imperialism, and Jim Crow.[43] Bethune introduced both her students and the women of NCNW to the commonalities of the struggles of Indians and African Americans not only in the printed pages of her newspaper columns, writings, and memos but by inviting Pandit to speak in person. In this time of transition after World War II when African people around the world were still processing the impact of the war, she seized the opportunity to continue the momentum that inspired the call for "victory abroad, victory at home."

Bethune began to be more vocal about America's relationship with India, addressing her concerns in the *Chicago Defender*. In 1950, India began to experience a major food shortage, and by November, India's minister of agriculture called on the United States for assistance, stating that "foods from the previous summer combined with a subsequent drought had already destroyed an estimated 2.6 million tons of grain."[44] At the time, India was a part of the Non-Aligned Movement during the Cold War, it was not aligned with the Eastern Bloc (Communist countries) or the Western Bloc (democratic countries, including the United States). Because the United States wanted a vow to align from India, and the country did not make a promise to do so, America did not quickly respond to their pleas for assistance. In a public address Nehru vowed that India would not be bound to any country in exchange for food, stating, "we have made it clear that such help must not have any political strings attached to it."[45]

Many Americans including Walter White, Eleanor Roosevelt, and YMCA leaders began to criticize the United States for its slow response, and Bethune was among them.[46] In her April 28, 1951, column she wrote: "Our law-makers have haggled too long with hunger and distress. They have held out for hard bargaining in terms of cash and of basic war materials from India, in return for the grain she needs, while[,] as one bishop wrote back from South India, little children are starving by the roadsides."[47] Bethune was appalled by the government's decision to withhold humanitarian efforts to assist a newly liberated country when the United States had the power to do so. Even as a country that was no longer colonized, India still had not earned the respect of the United States. Using her column to address the government indirectly, she focused on the devastating effects of what would happen if the United States did not intervene. On June 15, 1951, President

Truman signed the India Emergency Food Aid Act, appropriating a loan of $190 million for the purchase of grains.[48] Although he accepted the much-needed assistance, Nehru was not moved to change his position of neutrality as the polarizing Cold War continued.

Haiti

After years of welcoming Haitian leaders to the United States and learning about the country through the work of the International Relations Committee in 1949, Bethune received an invitation from its government to visit. The chance to visit the first Black republic was an exciting opportunity for her, and she did not take it lightly. Before leaving for the trip, Bethune began to make plans to make the most out of each day. She spoke in the *Chicago Defender* about her intentions to have conversations with young leaders and women in the hope of broadening her relationships, and she shared her excitement about seeing "men of the darkest hue" in high positions.[49] Visiting a place where segregation was not a hindrance to Black achievement gave Bethune hope, and she referred to Haiti as "the high country of Toussaint L'Ouverture and his brave blacks."[50] In many ways, the pride that she showed in her attitude toward Haiti embodied the reverence that African Americans felt toward the historic place that had once been a beacon of hope to those who were enslaved.

One of the most influential and recognized slave revolts was the Haitian Revolution of 1791 to 1804. After the successful battle for freedom, the country became a symbol of success for enslaved and oppressed African people throughout the Diaspora. As the French Revolution was taking place in the closing years of the eighteenth century, across the seas in the French colony of Saint-Domingue, which at the time was the largest sugar-producing colony, rebellion was set to take place. Enslaved Africans, including Kongolese, Fon, and Yoruba peoples, utilized spirituality in their destruction of slavery, as evidenced in Vodun rituals performed before the insurrection. When Haiti won its independence in 1804, it became the new world's first Black state, becoming a model for enslaved peoples across the hemisphere who now looked to achieve what Haiti's enslaved had—freedom. C. L. R. James's classic text *Black Jacobins* examines the rise of enslaved African Toussaint Louverture and his role as a revolutionary leader of Haiti and the conditions that led Africans to seek and ultimately obtain freedom.[51] The narrative of people who had endured slavery coming together and rising to defeat the powerful nation of France became a source of inspiration for Africans for years to come. Just a few years later, in 1812, the leader of the Aponte Rebellion in Cuba was found with drawings and books that demonstrated Haiti's overthrow of the French, and in South Carolina in 1822 Denmark Vesey modeled plans for rebellion after the Haitian Revolution.[52] Sharing the sentiments of what Haiti meant to African people, Bethune called it "a spiritual haven to the oppressed of African descent" and a "symbol of freedom to those beyond her shores."[53] She saw her visit as a pilgrimage to a sacred place, and the solidarity that emerged out of the Haitian Revolution was the foundation on which she would build upon.

Three years into the presidency of Dumarsais Estimé, he created the Haitian International Exposition to celebrate the two-hundred-year anniversary of the founding of Port-au-Prince.[54] This would be an event to showcase the culture of Haiti to the world while also exemplifying that Haiti was a great country to be recognized by all. Haitian artists and performers would showcase their talents to a worldwide audience during the exposition. In recognition of the achievements of people of African descent, Bethune would be honored with the Medal of Honor and Merit as a part of the exposition. For years to come she would continue to reflect on this moment of recognition and the ten days she spent in Haiti. On June 9, 1949, Bethune received an official invitation from Joseph D. Charles, the ambassador of Haiti. Written in French, Mr. Joseph stated: "It gives me great pleasure to convey to you officially the invitation of my government has come to visit Haiti. I will be happy to welcome and receive one of its congeners whose value and personal merits are great."[55] Bethune accepted the invitation, and on Tuesday, July 12, 1949, she left Florida for a ten-day trip to Haiti. Stopping over in Montego Bay for a layover, during which she connected with local Jamaicans, inquiring about how many people of African descent lived on the island and what the main employment industries were.[56] She reached Port-au-Prince in the afternoon and began her journey in Haiti along with fellow NCNW colleagues Constance E. H. Daniel and Fannye Ayre Ponder.[57]

Much of the time Bethune spent in Haiti was dedicated to meeting local people and exchanging ideas while listening to their perspectives and learning more about the history and culture. She kept an extensive diary of the trip detailing the conversations that she had each day, along with entries on the places that she visited and the people that she met. On the second day of the trip, July 13, 1949, Bethune spent the day with the nation's First Lady, Madame Estimé. The two talked for hours about unity and the issues faced by the people of Haiti. Bethune expressed her purpose for coming, stating that she wanted "to try to bring about a better understanding and inspire the women of Haiti to work with her in trying to bring about peace and unity."[58] She discussed the founding of the National Council of Negro Women and expressed interest in starting a chapter of the organization in Haiti. NCNW had been quite successful in creating a united voice for women of color, and Bethune wanted the women of Haiti to be a part of the movement. It was her goal to make the organization one that would reach women in all parts of the world, and establishing NCNW in other countries was a part of her plans. By the end of the conversation Madame Estimé was honored to be considered to lead a Haitian council, but she would first start with becoming a lifetime member. For the NCNW and Bethune, this was another major step in expanding the influence of the organization and in uniting women across the globe, all facing similar issues as women of color.

The day would not end with the long discussion with Madame Estimé; Bethune was also hosted by William E. DeCourcy, American ambassador to Haiti. Having been appointed as US ambassador in 1948, DeCourcy had seen much of the world during his three-decade career in military and foreign service, which led to an interesting talk between the pair.[59] The two discussed racism, the issues faced by people of color in the public school systems of America, and Bethune's fellow UN colleague Ralph Bunche and his recent decision.[60] She told DeCourcy that she was impressed that Bunche had done "a fine thing to demonstrate the whole spirit of democracy" in his refusal to accept the position of assistant secretary of state.[61] President Harry Truman offered Bunche the position, but he declined the offer in protest of Washington, DC's segregated housing policies. Ending their discussion around noon, Bethune was continuously seeking to learn and expand her knowledge of the world through conversations with global leaders and those who were experts on foreign affairs. DeCourcy's experiences as a Black man living abroad varied greatly from Bethune's, but the two shared similar issues facing racism and discrimination and an apparent desire to build a connection with Haiti.

On Thursday, July 14, 1949, Bethune's third day in Haiti was spent assessing the needs of the country to better understand how she might be able to assist in her many roles in the United States. During her time with Monsieur Timoleon Brutus, the country's minister of foreign affairs, she was able to both interview him and learn more about Haiti's history. She was deeply concerned about the welfare of the masses, and in turn he shared his desires to improve education in Haiti and that he was looking forward to working with Bethune to bring some of the goals he set for the country to fruition.⁶² Her expertise as an educator who built a college from humble beginnings of $1.50, faith in God, and five little girls was inspiring, and the wisdom and knowledge that she shared was invaluable. As always Bethune was a fierce advocate for women's rights, leading her to question the minister about the status of women's suffrage. As someone who remembered a time when women in the United States could not vote, Bethune understood the transformative power of the ballot, and she wanted to ensure that the women of Haiti had the same rights. However, they had not gained suffrage by 1949. Unsatisfied with the minister's answer, she pressed for more information about when they would gain those rights, asking, "How far removed are they?"[63] On her return to the United States she advocated for women's suffrage in Haiti, utilizing her column in the *Chicago Defender* to do so.[64]

The third day of the trip was one of the highlights of Bethune's voyage to Haiti as she sat down for a meeting with President Dumarsais Estimé. His term as president lasted from 1946 to 1950, and he was the first Black president to serve after the 1934 ending of the US occupation. Bethune was overjoyed to be in the presence of the young leader of Haiti, stating: "As I look on you I have the realization of the prayers and yearning of the Black republic of the world. I feel like I am on my own soil."[65] For a woman who was born just a decade after the ending of slavery, having known the horrors of slavery from her parents and siblings, to witness a Black man in the powerful position of president was an emotional moment for Bethune. Haiti was a symbol of what Black people could accomplish if given the chance. Expressing her desire to help improve conditions in Haiti, Bethune pledged to do all that she could to strengthen the country. During the conversation with President Estimé, Bethune, who had always had a relationship with Haitians and its people from afar, gave her word to its leader that she was now one with its people. Given her influence in the States, Bethune was a very important ally for Haiti.

Connecting with the Masses

Bethune's love for people and desire to understand the shared plight of people of African descent throughout the Diaspora was expressed throughout her journey in Haiti. Although much of her time was spent meeting and connecting with political leaders, she also made sure that connecting with the masses in Port-au-Prince was a major part of her trip. Bethune traveled to Ecole République d'Argentine, a local elementary school where she met nearly 475 students and twenty teachers.[66] As an educator, she was always concerned about the future of young people, and this was no different on the trip to Haiti. Many years before her work with the National Youth Administration, during her tenure as president of the Florida Federation of Colored Women (1917–24) she helped establish the Delinquent Home for Colored Girls in Ocala, Florida. She saw housing and having a place to call home as being just as important as education in the classroom for youth; both were needed to be successful. On the fifth day of her visit, she met the children of the Sunshine Orphanage, and her heart ached for them just as it had for the girls for whom she set up homes in Florida. She was overwhelmed by the children's malnourished bodies and the poorly kept space, yet encouraged by their desire to overcome. Making a donation to the orphanage before she left, she was humbled by the visit.[67] A few days later Madame Estimé showed Bethune the orphanage she was building, which Bethune would later financially commit to assisting.

In the short visit Bethune did her best to build as many meaningful relationships as possible, often sharing her knowledge and wisdom with the women she encountered. She met with teachers at the School Republique of Venezuela on July 20, 1949, to share the story of how she built her school.[68] What she accomplished was not an easy feat, so surely she could relate to the hard work that the teachers were putting forth to educate students with few resources. The success of turning the small all-girls school into a college made Bethune's story one that contained many lessons and strategies for the teachers she met. During the visit she dedicated herself to using her resources to help make the educational system in Haiti an even better one, stating that she would "do all she can to help Haiti when and while every opportunity presents itself."[69] Bethune also met with policy makers including the minister of education, Andre Vieux, to discuss the expansion of educational programs in rural areas, which was her specialty, considering those early years in the newly incorporated town of Daytona.[70]

Working for the betterment of women and children was at the core of Bethune's activism throughout her life, and while in Haiti she consistently sought to learn more about the needs of both. She understood the importance of meeting face-to-face to discuss issues to gain a greater understanding of what was needed by the people, versus making assumptions. Following her talk with teachers, later that afternoon she attended a meeting with the Ligue Feminine d'Action Sociale, a women's organization concerned with women's rights and equality. Formed in 1934, it was Haiti's first feminist organization, initially starting in response to women's opposition to the US occupation but later taking on issues including "women's full political rights, rights and autonomy within marriage, an equal minimum wage, a three week paid maternity leave and protection for children."[71] Although its members were mostly educated women from elite backgrounds, their work did impact women who were not of the same socioeconomic status. A 2002 oral interview of Paulette Oriole, a lifelong member of the organization, conducted by Chantalle F. Verna, revealed the significance of the women's work. Oriole's mother was a member of the league during its early years, and she remembered going to meetings as a child before becoming a member herself in 1950 and president in 1987 (serving until 2011). In a discussion of the community work of the league, she stated:

> Those women, the founders, they wanted to help where help was mostly needed. They started to go to the public hospitals to see how the women were treated, not only for medical treatment but also to see if [the female patients] were treated like human beings. They started visiting the prisons, and the asylums. I remember as a child going with my mother with big straw baskets with bread, with food, for Christmas, for New Year, for Easter. We would bring them food... toiletries. They love to have good smelling soaps and toothpaste and some socks or cute dresses and so on. [The Ligue members] did a wonderful job.[72]

From her years of membership in various women's organizations, Bethune was familiar with the community service work aspect of the organization and was involved in similar projects, particularly during her NACW tenure. The work of the league was reminiscent of the earlier years of NACW, which focused largely on improving conditions within the local community for women and children. And just as the women of NACW had been mostly well-to-do educated women, with the motto "Lifting as We Climb" the Ligue Feminine d'Action Sociale was also composed of women of the upper socioeconomic echelon who utilized their positions to advocate for women. In Oriole's interview she highlights some of the achievements of the league in the 1940s, which included gaining a woman's rights to spend her own salary, the opening of schools for women, and modifications of laws pertaining to nationality for women who married foreigners.[73] Bethune developed a very close relationship with the members of Ligue Feminine d'Action Sociale, particularly First Lady Estimé. The pair "were good friends, corresponded frequently, and encouraged collaboration between their respective organizations."[74] Bethune welcomed the women of the league to become affiliates of NCNW and pledged that her organization would back their efforts to gain suffrage. Building bridges with women who were leading and shaping their communities was a vital and consistent part of Bethune's trips. She saw women as conduits through which her activism was the most effective, and much of her time was spent connecting with them.

The 1949 Haitian Exposition presented an opportunity to highlight the country's art and culture during a celebration of the bicentennial of the founding of Port-au-Prince.[75] For Bethune, the exposition would bring one of the most important honors of her lifetime when she received the Haitian Medal of Honor and Merit on Thursday, July 21, 1949. The night included a ceremony honoring Bethune for her many achievements, including being the first woman to receive the award. In a speech honoring Bethune on the night of the award, one of her presenters stated that "her works for mankind had changed the face of the world."[76] Bethune had led a life in which she fought tirelessly for equality and inclusion, and now her efforts were being honored by a country she respected greatly. For her, being recognized by a historic country that was liberated by the hands of Black people and was now governed by Black people was an especially significant moment. Reflecting on all that had taken place, she stated, "I realize that I am treading for the first time on the soil of a great country controlled by Black people—I have never been so thrilled!"[77]

Renewed Dedication to Haiti

The visit to Haiti ignited a spark in Bethune that was very different from prior travels; she returned ready to act immediately to effect change in Haiti. Bethune's model of creating unity between the people of Haiti and African Americans utilized "small p" Pan-Africanist methods, which involved basic people-to-people contact. In traveling and meeting both the masses and the political leaders of Haiti she was able to contribute to the larger scope of "capital P" Pan-Africanism, which involved political movements.[78] In many of the photos after the trip you see her beaming with pride as she wore the Haitian Medal of Honor and Merit as a necklace. She begins to focus more on the plight of Haitians, particularly women, in her speeches and in her writings in the *Chicago Defender* as she advocates for suffrage and calls attention to the powerful history of the country.

Before her trip, Bethune had developed a relationship with Haiti mostly through its ambassador, Joseph D. Charles, but having gone to the country for herself, she expanded upon the relationship. Nearly two years prior to her visit, Ruth Clement Bond had written to Bethune requesting her assistance in building orphanages in Haiti, but it was not until after seeing a firsthand account of the devastation in orphanages in Haiti that she actually became active in the program.[79] Calling on all members of NCNW to join her in assisting Madame Estimé in building the orphanages, she began a campaign to raise funds. In a letter to Constance Daniel, her assistant, she requested that she write a letter:

> Send out a statement as to the great needs of the orphans of Haiti and our desire as American women, to help Madame Estimé in the gigantic task she has undertaken. For that sacrificial service I am asking all men and women of ALL races, and creeds—not in any organized form, but any individual that might like to help to complete this shelter for the orphans in Haiti.[80]

In her pleas Bethune called on anyone who was willing to help her meet the goal of assisting Haiti. She made plans to send volunteers to Haiti to assist and to present the collected funds. At Bethune-Cookman's 1949 Southeastern Conference, which was themed "Working towards World Peace and Prosperity," Bethune addressed women from twelve states and 150 Cubans on international affairs including raising funds for the Refuge Home for Orphan Children in Haiti.[81] She made personal pleas to NCNW women to join her in working to raise twenty-five thousand dollars to construct the orphanage, stating, "I want the women of America everywhere to open their purses and help this worthy cause."[82] She was committed to assisting Madame Estimé in her efforts, and she wanted other women to see this as a worthy cause too.

Bethune advocated for Haitian women's right to vote, particularly through her *Chicago Defender* writings, allowing her to reach a wide audience. During her meeting with Ligue Feminine d'Action Sociale, and its leader, Madame Augustine Garoute, she gained insight about the challenges they were facing in obtaining suffrage. In a June 1950 article of the *Chicago Defender* about suffrage in Haiti, she stated, "Women astute enough to drive a hard bargain in the market place, are astute enough to drive another at the polls!"[83] Still struggling with factors that often limited their ability to vote, African Americans understood what it was like to be denied suffrage. At the time the newspaper was a powerful means of communication, and as a columnist in the *Chicago Defender* she wrote articles that directly spoke to African Americans, putting them in connection with Haiti. While African Americans were fighting for equality and desegregation, they were able to draw strength from the richness of Haiti's history while also realizing that the oppression they faced was similar and relationships could be built through the struggle.

Upon her return Bethune conducted an analysis of the country and offered solutions to President Dumarsais Estimé outlining her assessment of the four main needs of Haiti: employment, health, housing, and education.[84] In an effort to increase employment and create a more stable economy, she advised the president to consider producing bananas to export to the United States while also encouraging more focus on agricultural development. She recommended selling handcrafted furniture as an export item, and having enjoyed the food on her visit immensely, she promoted the creation of a cookbook with authentic Haitian recipes as an export product. To increase the interactions and exchange between African Americans and Haitians, she suggested sending African American newspapers to Haiti and vice versa to "bridge the information gap between them."[85] She concluded her analysis with a pledge of direct assistance and a vow to continue to support the country.

Bethune offered advice to President Estimé out of the wealth of knowledge she had gained through her own experiences. She was very resourceful in the building of her school and often utilized agriculture and farming as a fundraiser, growing sugarcane and making sweet potato pies to sell to the local Daytona community. As the director of Negro Affairs in the NYA, Bethune also ensured that African Americans benefited from programs that provided training opportunities to rural farmers. The NYA vocational training offered "centers focused primarily on training young men in modern farming techniques and offered young women instruction in dairying, raising poultry and food preservation."[86] She advised Estimé to explore similar methods for economic development in Haiti. Having understood America's desire for coffee and Haiti's initial development of the crop, she gave Estimé very practical advice, stating, "It seems to me very wise that more stress is now being placed on the increased cultivation of this crop."[87]

Bethune urged President Estimé to support women's suffrage, using Frederick Douglass as an example of a great historic figure who had done so during the nineteenth century. On the subject of democracy, she wrote that Douglass had "called also for the broader application of the term, to include all women."[88] The great abolitionist was one of the few men to attend the 1853 Seneca Falls Convention, which is known as the birthplace of women's suffrage in America, and up until the end of his life he was a fierce advocate for women's right to vote. Having served in Haiti as the minister resident and consul general, he spent two years (off and on) in the country as a representative of the US government. Douglass considered his post to Haiti and the invitation to represent Haiti at the 1893 World's Columbian Exposition to be the "crowning honors" of his career.[89] Bethune uses the familiarity of this great man who had served in Haiti and represented it while also advocating for women as a model for Haitian men to follow. Surely, if Douglass used his influence to join the cause for women's suffrage, President Estimé could do so also. The women of Haiti, led by the Ligue Feminine d'Action Sociale, organized and advocated for their rights for decades, while also bringing attention to the conditions faced by women. On November 4, 1950, their efforts paid off greatly, when they won the right to vote in all local and national elections.[90]

During the years of World War II Bethune and NCNW were fierce advocates for the inclusion of Black women in an event that impacted the world, and after its ending they continued to demand that their voices were heard. The war had opened new possibilities, and they were not willing to reverse the progress that had been made toward being recognized as global leaders. They were now being called on by women around the world for their counsel and tutelage, and the NCNW headquarters became a sought-after destination for foreign leaders. The creation of a space for women to establish their autonomy is exemplified through Bethune's work, whether it was through the mentoring of Sarah Simpson of Liberia, advocating for suffrage of Haitian women, or by giving voice to the women of India to speak freely about their experiences with the women of NCNW. With leading internationally minded women by her side, Bethune expanded the scope of the organization, opening their doors to women from throughout the African Diaspora while traveling abroad to stand in solidarity with other women who were seeking change in their countries. Bethune and NCNW addressed broader issues impacting people throughout the world, but they did so primarily through their connections with women, allowing their voices to be heard loud and clear, creating a platform that they may not have had otherwise. As a woman who experienced being the only woman in the room as a member of the Black Cabinet and as one of the San Francisco delegation, she understood the importance of women-led spaces. Bethune's success as a leader could not have been possible without women, and when developing an international agenda, she considered women to be her closest allies. Even as she faced a transition into retirement, the goal of continuing to build solidarity and create change internationally was at the forefront of her mind.

6

Bethune Advances Her Global Agenda beyond Retirement

Fall 1949 marked a turning point in the life of Mary McLeod Bethune. After fourteen years as the leader of the National Council of Negro Women she retired with international acclaim and she was revered by many. In honor of her retirement, President Harry S. Truman attended the NCNW meeting and commended Bethune on her work with the National Youth Administration and for how she challenged the program to provide better housing, more employment opportunities, and fair employment practices.[1] In the hope that she would continue to be involved with his administration and NCNW, he expressed that he was sure that she would not "retire from public life."[2] The president also urged Bethune to continue to work with him on civil rights issues: "We are going to continue to advance in our program of bringing equal rights and equal opportunities to all citizens. In that cause there is no retreat and no retirement and I know Mrs. Bethune is going to stand by me as she had from the beginning."[3] The president was right. Bethune was not seeking to retreat or retire from activism; instead, she was committing herself to her personal mission to be an advocate and a voice for women throughout the African Diaspora beyond the bounds of her organization. Retirement from NCNW gave her the freedom to continue her work of organizing and meeting women abroad no longer at the helm of NCNW but standing solidly on her own. After graduating from Moody Bible College she dedicated her life to education and women's work, toiling and building organizations with the idea to open others' minds to her global agenda, and she had been largely successful in doing so. Shifting her primary focus from leading a US-based organization, Bethune imparted the expertise and knowledge that she acquired throughout her lifetime to activists around the world.

Her official retirement was announced at the organization's annual meeting, held at the United States Department of Labor Auditorium. The lavish event featured activists, leaders, and ambassadors from around the globe representing thirty-two countries including Liberia, Israel, France, Ethiopia, Haiti, and Spain.[4] Madame Vijaya Lakshmi Pandit brought greetings along with United Nations mediator Ralph Bunche. As a part of the program, NCNW gave awards to various individuals including Mary Church Terrell, Walter White, Dr. Channing Tobias, and Dr. Carter G. Woodson for their work as change agents. The event brought together people from around the world to celebrate the founder of an organization that strived for better conditions for people across the globe.

For the seventy-four-year-old leader who had spent much of her life building institutions, this was the ending of an era and the beginning of a new chapter. She had risen from starting a school in Florida with $1.50 and being relatively unknown to becoming a global leader who was sought out by people around the world for her counsel and knowledge. The records of National Council of Negro Women indicate that during Bethune's presidency several women's organizations wrote her to seek guidance on how to implement the ideals of NCNW in their countries. In a June 1945 letter the Ladies Welfare Group (Junta Femenine de Beneficencia) of Panama reached out to Bethune for suggestions on how to strengthen their organization, having been established "for the purpose of engaging in charitable and general welfare work."[5] In turn Bethune provided NCNW's ten-point program and encouraged the women to write to her at any time, acting as a mentor abroad. As Bethune's international work continued with NCNW, she also became a role model to women throughout the African Diaspora.

On November 15, 1948, the *Costa Rica Star* (*Estrella de Costa Rica*) monthly magazine wrote to Bethune in the hope of featuring her in an upcoming issue. The magazine's mission to "awaken a once dormant racial pride by bringing to the front, wherever possible, eminent men and women of the race: of whom we are justly proud" led them to contact Bethune for biographical information and photos of herself to help instill racial pride.[6] She supported the idea and sent the requested materials and agreed to promote the magazine. Bethune was looked upon by the people of Costa Rica as someone who was a great representation of Black pride, and they wanted to learn more about her. The African Academy of Arts and Research president, Kingsley Ozuomba Mbadiwe, presented Bethune with a hand-carved table on behalf of the Ashanti people of the African Gold Coast. The gift of appreciation was given by the Ashanti "as their token of esteem for the encouragement which she has given to Africans in this country."[7] Bethune was beloved by Africans throughout the Diaspora, many of whom lived in places to which she had not traveled, but her name and the great work she did was well known. Leading NCNW had given her a platform that made her a powerful voice among the people of the world.

In the coming years she would travel to Liberia as a United States ambassador, finally fulfilling her dream of going to Africa while being honored by the country. Bethune continuously encouraged solidarity among African Americans and Afro-Cubans and used her voice as a columnist in the *Chicago Defender* to speak against the United States' domineering relationship with Cuba. No longer representing an organization, she could now speak freely on behalf of herself as an international activist, condemning South African apartheid and celebrating Kwame Nkrumah's path toward the liberation of Ghana. In her travels to Canada she recognized the significance of emancipation throughout the Diaspora while learning important lessons on the history of the country's African descendants.

Building Bridges between Cubans and Americans

Receiving the honor of being inducted into the Cuban Society of Letters had been an important milestone for Bethune as it gave her further credibility in the Afro-Cuban community. On her mission to continue to foster those relationships within the United States she collaborated with the Cuban American Goodwill Association, serving as a speaker for the organization's inaugural banquet in November 1950. Founded by Pedro Portuondo and Calá Henry Grillo, the organization "promoted cultural exchanges between Afro-Cubans and African Americans" and assisted in tour opportunities for travelers.[8] During its inaugural banquet Bethune encouraged the organization to continue its work of linking African descendants, stating, "We must know each other, love one another, build each other up and encourage one another."[9] Cuba native and attendee Nora R. Tucker mirrored Bethune's words as she called for better relations between the "darker people" of Cuba and the United States.[10] The cultural exchanges and mutual understanding that the organization promoted were important aspects of building solidarity, and Bethune was among their supporters and was willing to lend her voice to the association in their efforts to do so.

Bethune's relationship with the organization's founder, Henry Grillo, had begun during his youth. A work by Evelio Grillo (Henry's brother), *Black Cuban, Black American: A Memoir*, notes that Henry had "become very close to Mary McCloud Bethune while at Bethune-Cookman."[11] In 1930 Henry was in Bethune-Cookman's junior high school class, serving as a business manager for his class, music editor for the school's *Wildcat* yearbook staff, and a member of the Tampa Club.[12] Over the years he stayed in contact with Bethune and volunteered in the National Youth Administration during her tenure as the director of Negro Affairs.[13] In a 1954 photo of Grillo as an adult, along with Bethune and her great-grandson Donald Bethune pictured at her home on the back of the photo, Grillo wrote: "To Mother Dear: Just reminding you that the Grillos will continue your good work for many years to come. Your boys, Rafael and Henry, May 20, 1954."[14] Bethune considered her students to be family, and she demonstrated this same love for Grillo. She supported his business ideas by using her voice to promote the work of the Cuban-American Goodwill Association and connected with the people of Cuba with his help.

In November 1950 Grillo wrote Bethune as the Washington representative of the Cuban-American Goodwill Association to submit to her a letter from Celia Planos, a Cuban woman who visited the NCNW Council House. It is unknown whether she may have traveled from Cuba with the Cuban-American Goodwill Association. It is clear, however, that she was highly impressed by her trip, and Grillo took the time to translate her letter into English in a letter to Bethune. Planos wrote to Bethune in the hope of becoming a member of NCNW, which she felt was "carrying out one of the most beautiful works that the world needs for peace, for international unity and culture, and for the general progress."[15] In his letter, Grillo assured Bethune that just as Planos was interested, there were probably enough Cuban women interested in NCNW to start a council there and that he would work to find out during his next visit. Writing from Santiago de Cuba, Planos anticipated becoming a member and assured Bethune that "the National Council of Negro Women will radiate in Cuban soil" through her work as a member.[16]

Planos was impressed by Bethune and the organization, and she was moved by her encounter with the women she met on her visit to the NCNW headquarters. Takkara Brunson discusses the significance of the letter, noting: "Planos's 1950 letter to Bethune indicates the likelihood that many Black Cuban women adopted African American women's activist strategies to pursue their specific goals. The belief that Black women living in the United States confronted similar issues of racial and gender discrimination facilitated this understanding as well as their commitment to international democratic discourses that circulated during the period."[17] NCNW's trip to Cuba a decade prior and Bethune's continued engagement with Afro-Cubans deeply influenced the women. NCNW and the work of its founder were seen as a model that could be useful, and women like Planos sought to learn more about how to implement their strategies in her country for gender equality.

Liberian Invitation

In January 1952 at the age of seventy-six, Bethune was finally able to make her dream of visiting Africa a reality when she was selected to be a delegate on behalf of President Harry S. Truman to the inauguration of Liberian president William V. S. Tubman. For a woman who once had been robbed of the opportunity to go to Africa to now be going as a dignitary must have been a moment of pride and validation. Truly, her life had changed so much over fifty-plus years. Bethune was one of four members of the delegation, which also included Edward Dudley, who served as the American ambassador to Liberia; publisher of the *Afro-American* newspaper Carl J. Murphy; and Major General James S. Stowell of the US Air Force.[18]

Before leaving, Bethune excitedly anticipated her trip, writing about it in her *Chicago Defender* column in an article titled "Trip to Africa Stirs Memory of the Founding of Liberia in 1822."[19] While reminiscing on her dream to be a missionary in Africa during her "Moody Bible School days," she paid homage to Lott Cary, an African American Baptist missionary who led colonization efforts in Liberia. Born into slavery in Virginia around 1780, Cary purchased his freedom and established himself as the pastor of the African Baptist Church in Richmond, Virginia.[20] Even with the success that he achieved as a free man who was a leader to hundreds, a homeowner, a father, and husband, he lived in a state that issued an 1806 law that targeted free Blacks, stating that those "who remained in the Commonwealth more than a year, would forfeit the right to freedom."[21] The law expressed the sentiment of many enslavers, who saw free Blacks as a threat. Essentially, and they were not seen as equals who deserved the same freedoms as white people. As a solution, many proslavery supporters advocated for sending Black people back to Africa. Founded by wealthy whites in 1816, the American Colonization Society (ACS) purchased land to establish the colony that would become known as Liberia. Scholars Toyin Falola and Raphael Chijioke Njoku discuss its problematic nature, stating that "the ACS wanted to make the practice of slavery less hazardous for the slave owners by reducing the potential danger already posed by idle and impoverished free Blacks in the light of discussions of general emancipation."[22] Rather than fulfill the promise of freedom to free Blacks, they were instead sent to Liberia, which presented its own set of challenges as they attempted to reconcile their American past with their present.

Cary and many others who left America for Africa may have left under the guise of missionaries, but their true intention was to escape the oppression they had faced in America. They were willing to leave everything behind to take a chance on the place that their ancestors had once called home. When asked why he was leaving, Lott stated: "And, in this country, however meritorious my conduct, and respectable my character, I cannot receive the credit due to either. I wish to go to a country where I shall be estimated by my merits, not by my complexion; and I feel bound to labor for my suffering race."[23] In her historical analysis, Bethune acknowledged the strength of Cary and the African Americans who returned to Africa "to build a new freedom."[24] At the time Bethune wrote the article, a large proportion of Africa was under European colonization. In the article she recognizes Liberia as a place of freedom not easily won or sustained. Calling out "powerful nations" who once threatened the sovereignty of Liberia was a subtle reference to the effects of European colonization. Overall, Bethune uses her article to discuss the past and current state of Liberia with her audience in preparation for the insights that she would share after the trip.

On January 6, 1952, Bethune arrived in Monrovia, Liberia. In her diary she wrote, "I was thrilled to set foot in this soil of Africa which I have so long dreamed of visiting—of returning to my homeland."[25] For Bethune, the trip was more than an opportunity to represent America; it was a chance to connect with the place she had been longing to go since she was twenty years old. She was finally able to see the continent from which her ancestors descended and the place from which her world began. It was a full-circle moment for her. As a delegate of the United States, Bethune was an honored guest of the Liberian government, which allowed her to meet President William V. S. Tubman and his wife, Antoinette Tubman, shortly after arrival, along with Vice President William R. Tolbert and his wife. The Tubman administration was particularly welcoming to America and its citizens, as it saw the country as being essential to their modernization efforts.[26] Bethune was among several African Americans attending the inauguration activities, including founder of the Associated Negro Press, Claude Barnett; opera singer Lillian Evanti; and Mrs. Charles S. Young (the widow of Colonel Charles S. Young).[27]

Over the course of her stay, not only did she attend the lavish celebrations for the second inauguration of President Tubman, but she visited Booker T. Washington Institute, an agricultural and industrial school named after Washington. Mr. Walter C. Wynn, a minister originally from Florida, was the principal of the school and, according to Bethune, "a former student of Bethune-Cookman."[28] Having embraced Washington's ideals of vocational education heavily during the early years of her school, Bethune must have been proud to see her former Bethune-Cookman College student bringing his knowledge to Liberia. As the first African American principal of the school, Wynn introduced woodcarving to the curriculum, which already included carpentry, brickmaking, and general construction skills.[29] She spent time with local teachers at the institute and had lunch with them. While visiting a church in Monrovia Bethune was received by the pastor and the congregation. She went to Liberia on an assignment to attend the inauguration, but she spent much of her time listening to the needs of the local people while learning more about their culture.

The trip would not be complete without gathering with the women of Liberia, especially her dear mentee Sarah Simpson George. Recollecting their meeting years before in the United States, Bethune wrote about how the pair "had met in Washington" and "made many plans for the women of Liberia."[30] While visiting with George in Liberia, she was able to see the fruit of their conversations and plans, which had evolved into the Liberian Women's Social and Political Movement. The women of that organization presented gifts to Bethune during a brunch held in her honor, with nearly 175 women in attendance.[31] Just five years prior to the visit, the organization became an affiliate of NCNW, and Bethune was finally able to see their work for herself. Although she was no longer the president, she still promoted the ideals of NCNW, and during her trip Bethune met with local women and formed the National Council of Women of Liberia. The group chose Maude A. Morris to be the temporary chairwoman. According to Bethune's writings, the organization was formed under the auspices of NCNW and structured to also be affiliated with the National Council of Women.[32] She further stated that the organization was "another link forged in the chain of strength of women united to advance the cause of understanding and practicing brotherhood, around the world!"[33] Born in New Orleans, Louisiana, Morris had lived in Liberia since 1903, when she had come to the country as the result of a her father's position as the United States minister to Liberia.[34] She was a graduate of Yale University and was honored by President Tubman during the 1947 centennial anniversary of Liberia for her "services rendered in the nation's development."[35]

A year after the founding of the Council, Bethune received word from Rae Dudley, the wife of United States ambassador to Liberia Edward R. Dudley, that the organization had not held any meetings or progressed since Bethune departed for the United States. Although there was still interest in the Council, Dudley suggested that the organization merge with the Women's Social and Political League since it was a more established organization.[36] Bethune still attempted to rally the Council through Dudley; she encouraged her to set up the organization again and sent her the constitution of NCNW and many other materials. However, there is no record that the Council became an active organization. Before leaving Liberia, she met with a group of women building a home for the elderly and the blind who named one of their buildings in honor of Bethune.[37] Bethune's work may not have generated the expected return or actions she had hoped for; however, she forged a connection with the women, which was an important part of her plan.

While there to celebrate the inauguration of President Tubman, Bethune was honored with the Order of the Star of Africa Commander Cross (known as the Star of Africa). Since its 1920 inception, the star has been a symbol to honor those whose service was important to the building of Africa or Liberia, and it was the country's highest award. Prior recipients of the award included Brig. Gen. Benjamin O. Davis Sr. (the first African American general in the US Armed Forces), Liberian journalist Henry B. Cole, and Bishop W. Sampson Brooks of Baltimore.[38] A decorated military official, General Davis traveled to Liberia in 1947 to represent the United States as a part of the country's centennial ceremony. Henry B. Cole was a correspondent for *Life* magazine, *Time* magazine and the *London West African Review,* providing pertinent news information from Liberia to the world.[39] A minister of the AME Church, Bishop Brooks established Monrovia College in 1922 through extensive fundraising efforts.[40] Bethune, along with Carl Murphy and Claude Barnett, received the Star of Africa in a private ceremony with the president and vice president. They were conferred with medals and diplomas marking their official presentation of the coveted award.[41]

The outpouring of love and respect shown to Bethune by the people of Liberia was overwhelming. In her diary she wrote: "My heart truly seemed to overflow as I could scarcely find the words with which to thank him for this great honor. Truly God is with me."⁴² The trip had been a pilgrimage to the continent where her bloodline originated, the place that she had proudly recognized as her homeland. Receiving Liberia's highest award for a lifetime of service was a testament to the wide reach of Bethune's work. Even though she was kept from Africa in her early years, her commitment to equality for African people throughout the world was always at the forefront of her activism. To be welcomed and honored in Liberia was vindication for the rejection that she'd faced when attempting to come to Africa as a missionary. Bethune had become a symbol of progress and a person whom the people were proud to have in the republic.

The Land of Opportunity

After her return from Liberia Bethune became quite ill due to fatigue, but she did not let it stop her from sharing her experiences in Liberia.⁴³ From her hospital bed she described Liberia as "Land of Opportunity" in the February 2, 1952, issue of the *Chicago Defender*.⁴⁴ In her thoughts regarding her visit, Bethune was impressed with the dedication local people had shown to President Tubman, the professionalism of the Liberian government, and Tubman's vision for moving the country forward. Having met with local chiefs and visited schools and churches, Bethune was inspired by Liberia's economic, spiritual, and educational development. She saw Liberia as a model for Africa, writing, "I realized, fully, that in Tubman of Liberia and those around him, I was seeing the potentialities of all Africans."⁴⁵ She also encouraged others to join hands with Liberians to expand educational, economic, religious, and health programs.⁴⁶ On December 22, 1950, during the midst of the bitter Cold War, Liberia and the United States signed the "General Agreement for Technical Assistance and Cooperation," which created an exchange of technical skills between the two countries. Through the program several Liberians "received technical or professional training abroad at the expense of the joint U.S.-Liberian program."⁴⁷ During the US push for more allies against the Soviet Union, Liberia received benefits of the "General Agreement for Technical Assistance and Cooperation" in exchange for their loyalty. Bethune's position as a delegate required that she report the conditions in Liberia to President Truman, which was one of the stipulations of the assistance program.

 Recognizing herself as a citizen of America but a descendant of Africa, she spoke of the two places as "the land of my ancestors and the land where I was born!"⁴⁸ She encouraged greater cooperation between Liberia and

America because of the connection she felt as one of its descendants. Although political gain heavily influenced America's relationship with Liberia, Bethune was interested in ways that America could lead humanitarian efforts on the ground, but she was careful in her approach. She asked the US Department of State to create a position to help develop the continent and Liberia, stating, "We are calling on the U.S. Department of State to set up a Secretary of Africa, alone, so that a republic like Liberia and the interests of all Africans may be given adequate attention; that the means may be found to develop the rich resources of this great continent, which its people and for the advancement of mankind, without doing violence to the dignity and human respect of any man, or tribe or nation."[49] Understanding the dangers of imperialism, she wanted America to assist without infringing on the autonomy of Liberians.

In her *Chicago Defender* column Bethune spoke highly of the African Americans expatriates whom she met during her trip, and she called for Americans to "Look across the oceans to Africa. See there the possibilities," urging them to take their knowledge and skills to Liberia to seek out new opportunities and to be of service.[50] Although Bethune does not explicitly call for African Americans to go back to Africa, her sentiments about Liberia being a place of opportunity coincide with parts of the "Back to Africa" movements mirroring ideals of Pan-Africanists who urged Black people to return to their African homeland to free themselves of the oppression faced throughout the African Diaspora.[51] Alongside the encouragement for going to Africa, she highlights the success of Walter Wynn and his leadership of the local school; Dr. Max Bond in his role as president of the University of Liberia; and Colonel John West and his contributions to creating a Liberian radio station, giving readers a sense of what African Americans could bring to the country as well as what they stood to benefit. Living in a society free of Jim Crow was appealing, and she did not hesitate to urge others to see what Liberia offered for themselves.

Just a few years before her visit Bethune encouraged one of her Bethune-Cookman College faculty members to accept a position as an agricultural production specialist in Liberia. Lamar Fort served as Bethune-Cookman's director of agriculture for several years prior to arriving in Liberia in December 1946. Feeling indebted to Bethune for his new role as a part of the United States Economic Mission, he wrote: "I shall endeavor to do my best and not to let you down. After all, had you not had me at your college I never would have had this job. I feel exceedingly grateful to you for whatever I shall be able to accomplish."[52] During his tenure Fort "trained several hundred Liberians in the use of improved farm practices" and helped expand the trade of cocoa between the United States and Liberia.[53] While in Liberia Fort often wrote to Bethune, updating her on his work and inquiring about the status of students and faculty at Bethune-Cookman. Witnessing the success of her former faculty member and the impact of his role in bringing innovative farming methods to Liberia and the other African Americans whom she met on her trip impressed Bethune with the possibilities that awaited those who left America. She saw how they were able to create change and help improve a new country with the skills and knowledge they had acquired. For her this type of undertaking was an important step toward building a bridge between Africans and African Americans.

Writing

After her trip to Liberia Bethune became increasingly vocal about the plight of Africans throughout the continent and the Diaspora overall, particularly in her writings. As a columnist for the *Chicago Defender,* she expressed discontent with the conditions Africans faced, and she continuously highlighted similarities between the struggle of people throughout the Diaspora, oftentimes comparing experiences of racism under colonialism to Jim Crow. In the July 19, 1952, article "U.S. Democracy and Mrs. Bethune Have Reached Another Milestone" she praises the United States for how far it has come and also criticizes it for excluding African Americans from the promise of democracy: "We want everything and say so without hesitation or apology. We want exactly what everyone else wants—freedom to make a living, buy shoes, go to the theater, educate our children, acquire homes, be fed, receive medical services or otherwise exercise freedom and pursue happiness without reference to race, color or religion."[54] While honoring the 176th anniversary of the founding of the United States, Bethune was challenging America to live up to all that it promised in the words that its founding fathers had written. Not only did she challenge the country, but she specifically challenged African Americans to advocate for their own equality, while pointing to the activism of South Africans as an example to follow: "But it is wholly heartening to see the vigor and intelligence with which non-whites of South Africa are using the civil disobedience techniques advocated and initiated by the revered Mahatma Gandhi, who first fully sensed the tragedy and danger of race repression on South African soil. . . . [A]nd in a world of change the South African government cannot hold back the tide of democratic fulfillment"[55] Although she doesn't specifically discuss organizations or leaders, Bethune's article points to the Defiance of Unjust Laws Campaign started June 26, 1952, and led by the African National Congress. In an attempt to combat apartheid Africans and Indians throughout South Africa led protests and demonstrations against the government.[56] She urges African Americans to take a stand against discrimination, just as South Africans had begun to do, following their lead by no longer taking no for an answer when it comes to equality.

In her July 26, 1952, article "Words of South African Racists Compared with Hitler's 'Mein Kampf,'" she expressed dismay for the phrase "unnecessary discrimination" utilized by a United States presidential candidate. Bethune compared racial discrimination in the United States to apartheid and pointed out that in both instances it was "necessary" in the minds of those who chose to discriminate.[57] In comparing segregation laws in the United States to apartheid she drew a connection between the status of people of African descent, demonstrating that regardless of the location they suffered from racial discrimination. Bethune also praised the resistance methods of South Africans, stating, "Last week, in my birthday column, I expressed my satisfaction in the resistance of the colored peoples of the world to the pressures of racial discrimination."[58] Impressed by South Africans' usage of peaceful civil disobedience techniques, Bethune praised the people for their vigor.

In Bethune's January 24, 1953, article "Cuba to Celebrate 100th Birthday of Martyred Apostle of Liberty," she honored Cuba and exposed her readers to the country's rich history.[59] In 1953 José Martí, one of Cuba's independence movement leaders and founder of Partido Revolucionario Cubano, would have turned one hundred years old. As a Cuban exile, he was deported for his belief in Cuban autonomy. Martí organized other exiles and worked with Maximo Gomez and Antonio Maceo while living in the United States.[60] Nearly a month after returning to Cuba during the Second War for Independence (1895–98), he was killed on May 19, 1895. Bethune's article summarizes the history of Spanish colonization of Cuba, its struggle for independence, and identifies the assassination of Martí as a symbol of the sacrifices made for freedom.

In criticism of the United States, Bethune highlights the country's attempt to purchase Cuba in 1845 and the issuance of the "Ostend Manifesto" in 1854 "in order to protect the interests of slavery."[61] The Ostend Manifesto sought to purchase Cuba possibly by force, to secure the expansion of slavery; however, it was never fully manifested. Bethune also pointed out that it was the United States that chose to veto "Simon Bolivar's proposal to free

Cuba at the Congress of Panama in 1826," and for these actions Bethune calls the United States both "friend and foe" of Cuba.⁶² Also mentioned in the article is the Platt Amendment, which gave the United States extensive intervention and involvement in Cuba's domestic affairs, further evidence of its attempts to hinder its liberation. Bethune was hopeful that America would be able to move forward and was able to "see beyond Cuba's mines and Cuba's sugar—to Cuba's people."⁶³ While honoring the freedom fighter Martí, she used the occasion to bring attention to the United States' imperialist nature and attempts to promote slavery beyond its own borders. At a time when America was fully involved in the "containment" of communism with the advent of the Cold War, Bethune's article speaks volumes about the country's historic role of extending its power over other nations. Bethune also called for peace as she encouraged readers to embrace "brotherhood" with Cuba, possibly symbolically calling for peace in regard to the tensions of the Cold War. Ultimately in her writings she showed a deep level of respect for the legacy of Cuba and its ability to rise above slavery and colonization to become an independent nation.

Her writings in the *Chicago Defender* were an important way for Bethune to share information on conditions throughout the Diaspora, and in 1953 she highlighted the future president of Ghana, Kwame Nkrumah. Less than a decade before Ghana's independence, Nkrumah founded the Convention People's Party with the first of its six-point program ideals being "To fight relentlessly to achieve and maintain independence for the people of Ghana (Gold Coast) and their chiefs."⁶⁴ Nkrumah organized civil disobedience and protests to get the attention of British colonial authorities in an attempt to liberate Ghana. Neighboring countries such as Nigeria and Cameroon also created their own liberation movements. People from around the world were watching Africa as its people struck back against colonialism, and Bethune's readers were kept abreast through her articles.

In the April 4, 1953, *Chicago Defender* article "Writer Looks at Africa through Its Great Leader, Kwame Nkrumah,"⁶⁵ Bethune shared her thoughts on the newly elected prime minister of the Gold Coast. Having read the February issue of *Time* magazine, which featured Nkrumah, Bethune was impressed by the "young, hopeful leader" whom she saw as evidence of change that was coming to Africa.⁶⁶ She saw the liberation of the Gold Coast from colonization as an "awakening" that she linked to the work of missionaries like James Aggrey, stating: "Africa is awakening. How long have missionaries prayed and carried torches of faith. How many like Aggrey have given of their very life's blood to the dream that some day even the bushmen would realize that God attaches dignity and worth to the human being."[67] Bethune saw religion as a tool of empowerment, just as she did in her younger years when she desired to go to Africa as a missionary. Although he came to the United States to further his work as a missionary, Aggrey became an avid proponent of education and was deemed "Father of African Education" by many. Aggrey emphasized education as a vital part of Black advancement. He dedicated much of his life to his alma mater, Livingstone College, where he served many years as a faculty member, later leaving to become vice president of Achimota School, where Nkrumah would attend.[68] Just as Aggrey used his education at a historically Black college to lead Africans, Nkrumah followed in his footsteps, attending Lincoln University. In Bethune's opinion Aggrey's religious underpinnings had been an invaluable part of his ability to influence Nkrumah to be the great leader that he had become.

In the article Bethune also recounted her former desire to go to Africa as a missionary and noted that, although she was unable to do so, many of the African students at Bethune-Cookman College were able to return to serve their people: "I have dreamed of Africa. It has been Africa all along even though I have not been able to serve her with my heart, my head and my hands."[69] She does not see herself as less connected to Africa because she was not there; instead, she sees her school as the place where she is still able to connect with the continent through the training of young people. She names Bethune-Cookman College graduate Babs Fafunwa as one of her students who came from Africa to receive an education and was able to take on a position with the United Nations. Although she was no longer president, she also arranged for Reuel John Mugo Gatheru from Kenya to receive a scholarship to study at Bethune-Cookman. When speaking of his relationship with her, he stated, "She was a dynamic lady who also loved the African students very much."[70] Bethune's college was a place in which she was able to train leaders who worked for the betterment of Africa by either returning with newfound knowledge and a desire to serve or by bringing attention to conditions through their work in the United States.

Another aspect of her writings was the encouragement of African Americans to travel abroad. She provided lengthy descriptions of her trips, giving a sense of what to expect in various places while hoping to inspire. Bethune also highlighted others who traveled, including her close friend Marjorie Joyner. Having worked her way up from being a national supervisor for Madame C. J. Walker, Joyner founded the United Beauty School Owners and Teachers Association in 1945. In an article titled "Writer Pays Tribute to Negro Beauticians as Ambassadors," Bethune recognized Joyner and the organization for their recent trips to Haiti, Canada, and Europe, noting that their presence abroad "give[s] the world a gratifying picture of the Negro race."[71] Bethune had been very influential in Joyner's trips, and she provided important contacts for the women involved, enhancing their experience greatly. In their travels they not only learned about beauty methods but also met with officials to discuss "gender and economic inequalities" in Haiti, and they provided scholarships for Haitian girls to attend beauty school in America.[72] Bethune saw the women as ambassadors for the race, and they accepted the role, going above and beyond to have positive impacts on the places that they visited.

Bethune's *Chicago Defender* writings encouraged African Americans to stand in unity with Africans throughout the Diaspora by seeing the similarities in their struggles for liberation. She enlightened readers about current events that were impacting African people around the world, and she gave her firsthand accounts of traveling to various places to encourage African Americans to follow in her footsteps. After she visited Liberia her writings began to change focus, shifting to a more radical approach, where she is vocal with her critique of those in power who abuse that power, mistreating Africans, wherever they are. She sees herself as being connected to those who are seeking equality, and she uses the power of the pen to make others aware in the hope that they will take on the cause of freedom.

Bethune in the Bahamas

Just a year after traveling to Liberia, Bethune accepted an invitation in 1953 to speak to the women of the Carver Garden Club in Nassau, Bahamas. Before her trip to the Bahamas, Bethune's school welcomed students from the country, and by 1948, the school had enrolled students from "Africa, Nassau, and Honduras," according to the *Daytona Beach Morning Journal*.[73] Named after the world-renowned chemist and Tuskegee Institute professor George Washington Carver, the Carver Garden Club was founded in 1946 by a group of Black women who "saw the need to come together socially to build stronger roots to advance themselves—and to raise a standard for young women to follow."[74] Historically Black women's garden clubs have been active in the community in ways that went beyond horticulture. The text *Our Separate Ways: Women and the Black Freedom Movement in Durham, NC* discusses how Black women's garden clubs contributed invaluable funding to cover legal fees for civil rights activists who participated in school desegregation efforts and how they often invited student activists to their meetings to share their experiences.[75] Although learning plant and flower cultivation methods was a part of Carver Garden Club, the women were engaged in serving their local communities, and they invited Bethune to speak with them about how to further their involvement.

At the time there was heightened activism among Bahamian women as they were in the midst of a battle for the right to vote. By the time of Bethune's arrival, women in the neighboring countries of Jamaica (1944), Trinidad (1946), and Barbados (1950) were able to vote, but the women of the Bahamas were still without suffrage.[76] Throughout the 1950s the leading women of the suffrage movement included Eugenia Lockhart, Mary Ingraham, Georgiana Symonette, Mabel Walker, and Doris Johnson.[77] Ingraham petitioned Stafford Sands, a representative in the House of Assembly, for the right to vote in 1951, but her petition was rejected.[78] In October of the following year the Daughters of the Improved Benevolent and Protective Order of Elks of the World drafted a petition with the support of more than four hundred local women to be presented to the members of the House of Assembly in the hope of gaining suffrage for all women of the Bahamas, yet they were still denied.[79]

Bahamian women looked to Bethune for a word of wisdom from someone they knew had been a fierce leader among women around the world. Bethune attended conferences while on the island, meeting people from various walks of life and learning more about the country. She spoke to the women of the Carver Garden Club, encouraging them to commit to serving the community and continuing to work to "break down the barriers which have been erected by those who believe that we lack adequate preparation."[80] Identifying one of those barriers as denial of women's suffrage, she believed that strengthening the service aspect of their work would lead to gaining full equality for all, stating, "Such will make it possible for gates to be opened through which many may pass instead of one individual."[81] Having led the National Association of Colored Women with its mission "lifting as we climb," she encouraged the Carver Garden Club to adopt a similar mindset. She told them that it was not optional but rather their responsibility to help the underprivileged, realizing that many of them had access to resources that others did not and that unity among different classes of women was needed to change the plight of all women.

During the trip Bethune spent time meeting with Nassau's governor, Robert Arthur Ross Neville, and his wife, Lady Neville, and she also traveled to the Industrial Home for Boys to gain insight about their educational program. She visited the gravesite of Thaddeus Toote to pay homage to one of the country's first Black lawyers. Bethune consistently sought to connect with local people during her trips to learn more about what was needed in their communities while sharing her knowledge and wisdom as a seasoned leader. She sat down and talked, shared meals, and presented her ideals, seeking to have meaningful exchanges that would lead to more cooperation and unity. In an article in the *Chicago Defender* Bethune encouraged readers to build friendships with the people of the Bahamas and to "stretch our hands across the waters."[82] Bethune's travels to the Bahamas at the ripe age of seventy-seven to share her wisdom and strategies regarding how to improve the conditions of its people represents her continued work as a change agent. Even beyond her lifetime her visit would continue to inspire the women. Just a few years after her passing Bahamian suffragette Doris Johnson founded the National Council of Women, and she pointed to Bethune's speech during her trip as being what led her to create the organization, stating that it was "born out of a lecture given by Mary McLeod Bethune."[83] Similar to the National Council of Negro Women, the organization was "an umbrella organization for women's groups in the Bahamas," presenting a united front in the struggle for the right to vote.[84]

Emancipation Celebration in Canada

In 1954 Bethune accepted an invitation to come to Windsor, Canada, to be a part of its Emancipation Day celebration. Having been emancipated on August 1, 1834, Canadians of African descent hosted huge events for the occasion. For Bethune it was important that any remembrance of the ending of slavery was a moment to reflect while also addressing how to make the future better for people of African descent. As the daughter of formerly enslaved parents and the sister of formerly enslaved siblings, she had a deep understanding of what emancipation represented. She knew all too well how slavery impacted her family, separating them and limiting their chances in life. In an interview with Dr. Charles Spurgeon Johnson, Bethune spoke about how her parents sought to reunite their family after emancipation. She also remembered stories that were shared with her about the day that emancipation came:

> My oldest brother Samuel, and my oldest sister, Satira—odd names, eh!—heard tell when freedom came. They did not know they were actually free until called together a few days after, and they eventually found their way back to where my father was and father brought

mother home on the McLeod plantation and they all assembled for a family reunion. They brought the grandchildren that mother and father had not seen.[85]

Freedom presented the opportunity to unify and reunite the McLeod family. Bethune was the first child born free in her family, and her life was the manifestation of the promise of freedom. Having been impacted directly, she was a proponent of commemorating Emancipation Day, and as president of Bethune-Cookman College she ensured that her students understood its significance. For years Bethune led a huge January 1 emancipation celebration program, in honor of the passage of the Emancipation Proclamation. Open to the public and in collaboration with local Daytona Beach citizens, including public school teachers, churches, and organizations, the annual celebration included a parade featuring Bethune-Cookman's band.[86] The 1929 emancipation program included a "Spirit of Freedom" pageant and was held on the campus of Bethune-Cookman College.[87] She also used her column in the *Chicago Defender* to not only commemorate the passage of the Emancipation Proclamation but to address issues impacting the Black community and the need for more progress. She believed wholeheartedly that true liberation was possible but that more work needed to be done, speaking in a January article on the topic of "We Look Forward to Democracy and Brotherhood."[88]

Having visited Canada in 1946 as a guest of the Canadian Association for the Advancement of Colored People (CAACP),[89] Bethune had once before inspired the people of Canada as a speaker. Similar to the NAACP, the CAACP was founded by James Jenkins with the mission "to bring attention to the inequality faced by Blacks in areas such as employment, education and housing."[90] There were few details on the first trip, but her return in 1954 was well documented due to the popularity of the Windsor Emancipation Day activities, which were attended not only by Canadians but also by those from across the American border.[91] The text *Emancipation Day: Celebrating Freedom in Canada* notes that the Black press covered the event extensively while also using it as a time to "discuss challenges faced by its community and to bolster support and strength to tackle these issues."[92] The festivities included the church, feast, parades, and speeches. Bethune spent several days in Canada as the guest of the British American Association of Colored Brothers, an organization that had planned the emancipation events in Windsor for several years.[93] The celebration included a youth talent search along with an evening concert, but the main event, the Twenty-Second

Annual Emancipation Parade, was attended by upward of twenty thousand attendees.[94] Alongside the legendary musician W. C. Handy, Bethune was an "Emancipation Guest," taking part in the parade while she also gave an address that received "resounding applause."[95] Bethune spoke of Windsor's significance as a place of refuge for enslaved people while she encouraged the crowd to continue to challenge segregation and discrimination.[96] Having been denied entry into the Prince Edward Hotel during her trip, she knew all too well what Afro-Canadians were facing.[97] Remembering the incident and Bethune's trip, in an interview local activist Elise Harding-Davis recalled:

> I well remember Ms. McLeod Bethune's visit to Windsor, ON, in 1954. She and Eleanor Roosevelt came at the request of the Emancipation Committee—Walter Perry and a group of women called the Hour-a-Day Study Club (my maternal grandmother, Rachel Madison Harding, was a founding member of this group). One mishap that occurred during their visit comes to mind. Reservations were made by Mrs. Roosevelt at Windsor's then premier Prince Edward Hotel.
>
> When the Roosevelt entourage arrived, Ms. Bethune amongst them, the hotel refused to give Ms. Bethune a room. Mrs. Roosevelt cancelled the reservation, the entire upper floor of the Prince Edward, and moved her reservations to Detroit, Michigan, just across the river. It was quite a scandal![98]

Even as she was celebrating the anniversary of emancipation and the progress that had been made, the incident was a reminder that people of African descent still had a long journey toward achieving equality. With the segregated conditions that Black people were facing, events like these were important occasions in which they rededicated themselves to the fight for freedom in the present by remembering the strength of those who had overcome enslavement. Bethune had risen to great heights, and although she was known around the world, racism was still inescapable.

Bethune was honored to have been a part of the emancipation celebration, and she recapped her participation in the *Chicago Defender*. She was impressed not only by the celebration, which she deemed "World's Greatest Freedom Show," but also by the history of Afro-Canadians that had been preserved through historic sites.[99] Her tour of Underground Railroad monuments and historic places included a visit to Sandwich First Baptist church, a stop that aided those who were seeking freedom and was built by freemen and formerly enslaved. She connected with Reverends Brown and Dungy, local ministers of historic Black churches, while also learning more about the history of Afro-Canadians from a local study club that focused on Negro life and cultural appreciation.[100] Women played a significant role in curating Bethune's trip, assuring that she was able to gain a full understanding of past and present experiences of Afro-Canadians. The local study club that Bethune referred to was the Hour-a-Day Study Club. Formed in Windsor in 1934, the organization was a group of Afro-Canadian women who dedicated themselves to studying an hour a day to expand their intellect.[101] Bethune was extended an honorary membership into the organization. According to Ms. Harding-Davis, the club had been a part of the delegation that invited Bethune, making her one of the first Black women to speak at the Emancipation Day celebration.[102]

The International Women's Committee of the British American Association of Colored Brothers hosted a luncheon to honor Bethune as one of the final emancipation events of the four-day celebration. Led by community women, upward of six hundred women were expected to attend the event, coming from both Windsor and Detroit.[103] In her speech she discussed the humble beginnings of her school and how she was able to expand it with hard work and the help of the community. As she shared her wisdom with other women organizers, she advised the women to use their talents to serve and to be "dedicated individuals who are not afraid to stand for what they believe in."[104] As she was honored by the women of Canada, she hoped to inspire them with lessons learned through her work as an activist and educator. For Bethune, this trip was another opportunity to be in solidarity with people of African descent and to remember their shared history, which connected them in the present. Attending a gathering with thousands of people, where the single most important topic was freedom, gave Bethune another platform to continue to unify people of African descent.

* * *

Following her retirement from NCNW, Bethune sought to move beyond formal organizations as a means of creating solidarity with Africans throughout the Diaspora, focusing more on traveling and meeting people where they were. Although she had traveled abroad prior to this time, retirement from NCNW allowed her to focus more on listening to and learning from the people from whom she met. Visiting historic sites, speaking with local leaders, immersing herself in the local culture while sharing her philosophy on how to create change allowed her to have more meaningful connections. She created an agenda that consisted of meeting the masses and understanding their challenges and successes while also having conversations with leaders to be a voice for those whom she met. On each trip she consistently visited churches and schools, places where she would meet people from all walks of life. On most of her travels she was invited by governments and organizations who were decision makers or those who had access to resources, and her goal was to challenge them to lift those who might not be in similar positions, particularly women. Just as she urged the women of NCNW and NACW to lift while climbing, her message was the same to those throughout the Diaspora. When returning from traveling, she channeled the energy into her writings, where she sought to make African Americans understand the shared struggle for equality among Africans, not just in their country but beyond the United States. As a columnist for the *Chicago Defender,* Bethune used the power of the pen to advocate for Black and Brown people and to bring awareness to her audiences, sharing everything that she learned during her travels. In the years following her retirement Bethune's vision of unifying people of African descent was made complete. She was a trailblazer who carved out a path for future NCNW leaders and the women she mentored to follow and attain even greater heights.

7

The Legacy Continues

From its founding Mary McLeod Bethune led the National Council of Negro Women to incredible heights, becoming an important voice on both national and international affairs. After retiring she continued her work, traveling globally to link Africans throughout the Diaspora and to share her knowledge as a proven leader. Among her accomplishments as president, Bethune established a national headquarters, often hosting international leaders and organizations in the coveted Logan Circle Neighborhood in Washington, DC, and became involved in World War II efforts raising $2 million in war bonds for the launch of the SS *Harriet Tubman* Liberty ship. Under her leadership NCNW traveled to Cuba, served as unofficial observers for the founding of the United Nations, and participated in conferences abroad, taking part in important conversations with global leaders. When Bethune stepped down in 1949, she left huge shoes to fill, but the women who came behind her were not only ready but in many ways had been groomed for success through their prior involvement with NCNW. The following three presidents continued to expand the international scope of the organization, bringing their own unique backgrounds and ideals.

NCNW's second president, Dr. Dorothy Ferebee, served on the executive board prior to becoming president, and she was a well-known medical doctor in the Washington, DC, area (having also been Bethune's physician). In her new role she continued to keep NCNW engaged with the work of the United Nations, urging members to take part in UN Day, while she also began to focus more heavily on involvement in the civil rights movement. Just one year after Bethune's trip to Haiti, NCNW members traveled to the country at the invitation of the Congress of Haitian Women under the leadership of Ferebee. During her tenure she became a sought-after consultant, which resulted in an invitation from the High Commission of Germany to observe postwar conditions. Following Bethune as president was challenging. Bethune had been such a larger-than-life figure to the organization, the nation, and the world, but Ferebee thrived as the second president of NCNW. Ferebee's former national vice president, Vivian Carter Mason, took office as the third president in 1953, and she brought years of administrative skills and experience with the organization to her new role. Mason adopted Bethune's approach of inviting women outside of the United States to become a part of NCNW, and she wrote letters to women in South Africa, Nigeria, and Liberia. She welcomed the First Lady of Haiti by hosting a reception to show support and as a sign of solidarity with the country overall. Mason's presidency came at a time when African Americans were deeply involved in a struggle for civil rights and Africans were engaged in a struggle for liberation from colonialism, and she ensured that the women were active participants who supported both fronts.

The two presidents following Bethune served four-year tenures, but their experiences with the organization had begun years before taking on the highest-ranking position. Dorothy Irene Height, who assumed the presidency in 1957, would go on to serve in the position for more than forty years, making her the longest-serving president. Prior to her tenure she served on various committees under each of the three presidents, continuing the tradition of previous involvement. Following in Bethune's steps, Height led a "European Tour with a Purpose" in 1959. The trip to Europe was one in which NCNW would expand its international awareness while raising Europeans' consciousness about African Americans. Under Height's leadership, members took part in the United Nations Commission on the Status of Women, expanded their travels to Africa, and provided support for student activists protesting racism in the United States. Bethune built a strong foundation as NCNW president, and she mentored women who understood her mission and the importance of continuing to move the organization forward without her.

Dorothy Ferebee

In 1949 Dr. Dorothy Ferebee became the second president of the National Council of Negro Women. A medical doctor, Ferebee was the former personal physician of Bethune, often traveling with her when she took long trips, and Ferebee was heavily backed by the former president to be her successor.[1] In her past leadership experiences she served as the tenth international president of Alpha Kappa Alpha Sorority Inc., where she led an extensive campaign to bring medical assistance to underserved Black communities, spearheading the Mississippi Health Project.[2] Ferebee was no stranger to NCNW, and she was well versed on its inner workings, having served on its executive board as treasurer, vice president, and chair of the national committee on family planning.[3]

Ferebee utilized her previous experience, leadership, and medical background to build on the work of Bethune, with one of the main accomplishments during her four-year tenure being the establishment of the "Nine Point Program." With an emphasis on civil rights, the program fought for antilynching legislation, abolition of poll taxes, more government positions for African Americans, while also leading voter registration campaigns.[4] Continuing her engagement in foreign affairs, she was invited to be on the National Citizens' Committee for United Nations Day to serve as vice chairman in 1950. In the request, Eleanor Roosevelt, chair of the committee, noted "the work of the National Council of Negro Women to increase the knowledge of the American people concerning the achievements, the problems and the purposes of the United Nations is well known. . . . [W]e shall all benefit from your advice and experience in this field."[5] The relationship between the UN and NCNW continued to flourish under Ferebee's leadership, and she relied on UN observer Eunice Hunton to keep the organization abreast of how they could support the goals of the global organization.[6] Hunton's work with the UN became a transformative lifetime affiliation that started with an invitation from Bethune to participate.[7] Ferebee also urged all NCNW members, including Junior Council members, to create programs to celebrate United Nations Day by forming study groups to study the principles of the United Nations or inviting speakers to speak on the topic of the United Nations.

NCNW continued to support Haiti, particularly its women, and in 1950 the organization accepted an invitation from the Congress of Haitian Women to join them for a women's conference. Led by women's rights activist Madeleine Sylvain Bouchereau, women from around the world gathered for the seven-day exposition, which focused on "striving to improve the status of Haitian women."[8] NCNW was urged to send delegates to "meet Latin and Central American women, to discuss common problems, and more particularly to offer the experienced guidance and inspiration that only the women citizens of the United States can offer."[9] NCNW sent four delegates including Dorothy Height, Verda Welcome, Ethel Ramos Harris, and Vivian Carter Mason to attend the conference.[10] They listened to lectures from leading Haitian intellectuals, toured the island, and networked with women from Puerto Rico and India.[11] At the close of the affair the women witnessed a signing of a resolution that challenged Haitian women to take their rightful place as participants in the public life of their country.[12]

Throughout her tenure Ferebee represented NCNW by serving as a delegate to the International Council of Women, attending their conference in Greece.[13] She traveled to Germany at the invitation of the High Commission of Germany, joining other women leaders "to observe postwar conditions."[14] She also encouraged members to continue to educate themselves on international affairs by hosting international relations workshops, United Nations Week, and visits to foreign embassies located in Washington, DC.[15] The four years that she spent leading the organization were challenging, particularly as she was the first to succeed the founder, but she continued to push NCNW to greater heights by ensuring that there was NCNW presence at international gatherings and by maintaining good relations with the newly formed United Nations. Ferebee understood that meeting and building coalitions with world leaders would always be an important part of internationalizing the organization's work. Despite the challenges, upon retirement she stated that it was "one of the most rewarding experiences of my career."[16]

Vivian Carter Mason

In 1953 Mrs. Vivian Carter Mason became the third national president of NCNW. Before becoming president, Mason served as national vice president during Dr. Ferebee's tenure; she was also the president of a local metropolitan council in Norfolk, Virginia. She brought proven leadership abilities demonstrated through her work with the New York City Department of Welfare, where she was the first African American woman to serve as an administrator.[17] The Mary McLeod Bethune National Council House National Historic Site examines Mason's presidency, stating:

> Her administrative skills were beneficial in helping to better organize NCNW's headquarters in Washington, D.C. and connect local chapters to the national office. She also led the organization to amend its constitution to include additional membership categories and incorporated specific items aimed at curtailing the free-wheeling activities of some local councils not sanctioned by the national office, which ended some questionable activities by some local councils and

individuals who were acquiring property, soliciting funds, and engaging in partisan political activities not sanctioned by the national office. Most importantly, as president, she emphasized interracial coalition building and support for grassroots efforts to bring about racial justice. Since her presidency overlapped with some of the major events of the Civil Rights Movement, the movement became one of her top focuses.[18]

Mason's tenure as president came at a critical time when liberation movements in Africa were making great strides, and she sought to make sure that the organization kept themselves abreast of global affairs, particularly through its International Relations Committee. Led by Edith Sampson, former president of Alpha Kappa Alpha Sorority Inc., the committee strengthened the international component of NCNW. By 1954 NCNW was fully involved in United Nations Day, Pan American Day, and World Health Day events.[19] Reaching out to local students from foreign countries and visitors had also become a major part of the responsibilities of the International Relations Committee, also ensuring that NCNW had proper representation at United Nations meetings. During the 1954 NCNW Annual Convention, an International Workshop (hosted by the committee) under the theme "Women United to Understand and Help the Peoples of Africa" was led by Dorothy Porter and Edith Sampson.[20] The workshop also included a keynote address by Dr. Rayford Logan titled "The Picture in Africa Today."

NCNW sent a delegation of members, including President Mason, to the 1955 session of the United Nations Commission on the Status of Women. Discussing topics such as "equal pay for equal work, equal rights in education, equal political rights, and equal rights in marriage and divorce," the women continued to ensure that women's rights were a part of the platform in United Nations efforts.[21] They also continued to welcome international visitors to the Council House, including the wife of Haitian president Paul Magloire. While in Washington, DC, the NCNW hosted a reception for Mrs. Magloire under the leadership of Mason, with Ferebee also attending. At the 1318 Vermont Avenue NW headquarters, Madame Magloire, along with her sister Madame Mauclair Zebhiri, were received by the women of the Council, including future NCNW president Dr. Dorothy Irene Height.[22] In a *Chicago Defender* article discussing the reception and the relationship the organization had built with Haiti, the writer noted that "Haiti is held in especially affectionate regard by the many council women who have visited the country and enjoyed the hospitality of its generous people."[23]

Mason sought to strengthen the organization's relationships with African women by inviting them to join NCNW, just as Bethune had done before. While on her travels, Bethune invited women to join or create their own sections of NCNW or to become affiliate members, resulting in a diverse membership including women from India and Haiti. President Mason shared the international vision of Bethune, and she worked tirelessly to continue her work in Africa. In June 1955 Mason wrote to Ellen Mills Scarborough of Liberia's Department of Public Instruction to revive the Monrovia Council established by Bethune.[24] In response, Scarborough expressed excitement about bringing the women of the College Women's Club into affiliations with NCNW, and she also invited Mason to Liberia. In her guidelines on how to become an affiliate Mason suggested programs such as leadership development, creating an official publication, and developing social service programs while also identifying key ideas and strategies of NCNW that could be useful to meeting the needs of Liberian women.

Continuing to reach out to leading African women, President Mason wrote to Flora Azikiwe to set up a meeting in the United States before she returned to Nigeria. Azikiwe was the wife of Nnamdi Azikiwe; she would go on to become Nigeria's First Lady when her husband became the newly independent country's president in 1963. Mason expressed hope to bring the ideals of NCNW to Nigeria through the establishment of a council, to bring women to the United States to interact with NCNW, and she sought to discuss the problems shared by Black women in the United States and women in Africa.[25] Mason stated that NCNW was "anxious to establish and cement ties of friendship between us."[26] The letter to Azikiwe was the beginning of Mason's efforts to establish NCNW council branches in Nigeria. She also wrote to Edith Nono Msezane of Pretoria, South Africa, seeking information about how NCNW could help existing women's organizations. Offering support, she wrote, "We desire to know about your problems, your activities, your programs, for in so doing we can be helped too by becoming intelligent and more aware of our responsibilities for the women of your country."[27]

Although NCNW was not successful in expanding its influence to Africa in the way that it did in the United States, Mason planted the seeds for future collaborations and projects between the women of Africa and NCNW. When visitors arrived in the United States, it was not uncommon for them to have dinner at the Council House or to be greeted by NCNW members in Washington, DC. In 1956, when Mabel Dove, a member of the Gold Coast Legislative Assembly, was set to visit the United States, NCNW partnered with the local community leaders to host a dinner party in her honor.²⁸ Elected in 1954, Dove was Ghana's first female member of Parliament. At the time navigating segregation was challenging, particularly for those who may not have been familiar with the customs, so having a network of Black women was essential. During Dove's visit NCNW called upon members across the nation to assist in making sure that the dignitary was shown hospitality.

As African countries gained independence, NCNW commended those who fought so valiantly for change. When Ghana received its independence from the British in 1957, President Mason sent a message to the newly freed country through the Ghana News Agency. In wishing the country well, she expressed interest in working with the women of Ghana, writing that NCNW "expresses the hope that a joint conference will be held with the women of Africa and the National Council of Negro Women within the next two years to further mutual aspirations."²⁹ Just as she had done in the beginning of her tenure, Vivian Carter Mason continued to work to unite African American and African women under the banner of NCNW. As she supported African leaders and continued NCNW's global work, she was faced with the challenge of providing equal support for one of the most transformative periods in American history. She rallied NCNW members to become a part of the burgeoning civil rights movement, resulting in fundraisers for the Montgomery Bus Boycott, voter registration drives in collaboration with the Southern Christian Leadership Conference, and she also welcomed Dr. Martin Luther King to speak to the women during their 1957 conference.³⁰ Being president of a leading Black women's organization during the beginning years of the modern civil rights movement while continuing to build international coalitions was no easy task, but Mason did so with grace, building upon her prior years of experience with NCNW while creating her own legacy as a leader.

Dorothy Irene Height

In her memoir, *Open Wide the Freedom Gates,* Dorothy Irene Height reflected on her years of service, including her long affiliation with NCNW:

> In 1977 I retired after thirty-three years on the national YWCA staff. I did not have ten minutes of unused leave. While carrying a full-time job at the YWCA, I had also spent forty years volunteering untold hours at the National Council of Negro Women. Since 1958 I had been

its elected president, devoting almost all of my "free" time to NCNW business.³¹

At NCNW's 1957 convention, Dr. Dorothy Irene Height became the fourth and longest-serving president of the NCNW, ending her tenure in 1998. Rebecca Tuuri discusses Height as being the president who most mirrored Bethune's leadership, given how she "skillfully maneuvered through the white-dominated world of government and private foundations as well as black organizations."³² She brought invaluable leadership experience to the organization, having served as the national president of Delta Sigma Theta Sorority from 1947 to 1956 while working for the national staff of the YWCA. Height was a contributing factor in the integration of the YWCA after she pushed for nationwide integration of the organization's facilities at the 1946 convention. Height also had significant experience with NCNW, having worked with all of the presidents, including the founder. Throughout her years she had been responsible for helping expand the NCNW staff with the hiring of its first executive director, Jeanetta Welch Brown, and she also served on the personnel committee and various other committees under the leadership of both Ferebee and Mason.³³

During her presidency, Height continued NCNW's support of the United Nations, particularly in coordinating and creating United Nations Day events, and participation in the organization's programs. In a memo to NCNW's national affiliate, President Height informed leaders that the organization would participate in the thirteenth session of the United Nations Commission on the Status of Women.³⁴ In that session women from around the world came together to take "the first step in a global study of the access of women to training and employment in the principal professional and technical fields."³⁵ With their participation, NCNW represented women of color from around the world bringing attention to the plight of its constituents.

Following in the steps of Bethune, Height sought to continue to encourage its members to be a part of global conversations by way of travel and networking on behalf of NCNW. In August 1959 NCNW set out on its "European Tour with a Purpose" as a part of its international relations programming. Bethune toured Europe in 1927 before the formation of NCNW with the hope of enlightening the women of NACW, but she was the only one who traveled on behalf of the organization. Now, with NCNW under the leadership of Height, Bethune's vision was coming to pass. The tour would allow the women of NCNW to meet other women's organizations throughout Europe, particularly those affiliated with the International Council of Women. NCNW president Dorothy Height expressed a desire to make the trip a "people-to-people experience" in which women would be able to build relationships with women abroad.[36] While finalizing the plans for the trip, she reached out to the German embassy's women's affairs secretary seeking help with connecting with community service agencies in Bonn and Heidelberg.[37] During the month-long stay, NCNW women would participate in activities and events that focused on four key areas: community relations, women's organizations, educational institutions, and social work/childcare facilities.

On August 5, 1959, ninety-six NCNW delegates left New York for Europe on the "European Tour with a Purpose." In Belgium Queen Mother Elizabeth hosted a reception in honor of their visit and entertained the group. The Council members met the women of the National Council of German Women and were hosted by the lord mayor of Heidelberg. The *Baltimore Afro-American*, a major African American newspaper at the time, captured the trip in its September 1, 1959, issue in an article titled "Queen Mother Elizabeth hosts group from National Council." Not only did the organization make headlines for meeting the queen mother, but they also attended a talk on "modern Italian political, social and economic life"[38] and had an opportunity to visit Monsignor John Patrick Carroll-Abbing's Boys' Towns of Italy. Boys' Towns were established in Italy after World War II when children were left impoverished and homeless because of the war. Throughout their visit the delegates inquired about the education systems in the countries visited, the ways in which Europe dealt with the issue of juvenile delinquency, and the political status of women. Visiting delegates were particularly interested in learning more about how women responded to gaining parliamentary representation in 1948 in the previously male-dominated political realm.

In a news release chronicling the trip, Height remarked, "Assuredly, one can readily understand our hopes for more meetings of this kind, for they certainly build bridges of understanding."[39] The trip to Europe was one in which NCNW would expand its international awareness while raising Europeans' consciousness about African Americans. As the women met with some of Europe's most powerful leaders, there is no doubt that the "bridges of understanding" (as mentioned by Height) included sharing some of the challenges faced by African American women. The trip was also a time for the Council to build allies on the issue of women's rights and meeting members of the National Council of German Women was a major step toward expanding the network of women central to the work of NCNW. Bethune began establishing this network in 1927, and NCNW continued her legacy nearly four years after her death.

Entering her presidency a few years into the modern civil rights movement, Height was determined to make sure that the organization would play a vital role in the movement. In support of students, particularly members of the Student Non-Violent Coordinating Committee, NCNW sponsored several students' educational endeavors. Washington, DC, mayor Marian Berry and Black Power activist Stokely Carmichael were among the students supported by NCNW scholarships, and as the 1963 March on Washington was under way, NCNW served as a meeting place for women to gather, and the organization also helped to coordinate the historic march.[40] Under Height's leadership NCNW became a tax-exempt nonprofit, which made it possible for the organization to receive grants from the Africa Bureau of the United States Agency for International Development (USAID).[41] It was with this funding that the organization expanded its international presence by formally establishing the International Division, hosting the International Women's Year Conference and by launching self-help training programs for women throughout Africa.[42] In honor of Bethune, Height also worked tirelessly to establish a memorial statue in her honor. In 1974 her dream became a reality when Bethune's sculpture was erected, making it the first monument to honor an African American on federal land in Washington, DC. This historic occasion was a direct result of the efficiency and the dedication of Dorothy Height during her tenure as NCNW's fourth president.

* * *

NCNW was birthed out of Bethune's desire to build solidarity among Black women throughout the world. She internationalized the organization through travel abroad, hosting conversations with world leaders and opening membership and affiliation to women outside of the United States. NCNW began its long relationship with the United Nations from Bethune's attendance at its founding, but every president since has continued involvement. Ferebee, Mason, and Height were well positioned to lead NCNW because of the mentorship of Bethune, and their willingness to commit to furthering the organization and to continue the legacy that she left behind. They faced a new era in which barriers of segregation and colonialism were being broken, carefully navigating these challenges by leading the women to engage on all fronts, just as they had done in the past. Welcoming women from African nations to join as members, traveling to Europe to build alliances, solidifying bonds with the women of Haiti, are all ways in which each president uniquely contributed to expanding the international scope of NCNW. Standing upon the shoulders of Bethune, the three women who followed her tenure as president took the organization to even greater heights through their work.

Conclusion

On May 18, 1955, Mary McLeod Bethune passed away quietly in her home. She had spent the day working on projects for her newly established Mary McLeod Bethune Foundation. In the days that followed telegrams and messages from around the world poured into her Daytona home. Clarence L. Simpson, Liberian ambassador to the United States, sent condolences on behalf of the Liberian government and its president.[1] In a letter to Mrs. Bethune's son, Clark M. Eichelberger, executive director of the American Association for the United Nations, recalled the significance of her advocacy for human rights during the San Francisco Conference.[2] In Nigeria, nearly sixty people gathered to pay homage to Bethune after her passing. The group included students, miners, members of the government, and senior civil servants.[3] Newspapers including the *Chicago Defender*, *Daily Tribune* (Nassau, Bahamas), *New York Times*, and *Windsor Star* (Ontario, Canada) recapped her life, noting her accomplishments and her legacy. Although she had once been known as the "First Lady of Negro America," Bethune was beloved by people of African descent throughout the Diaspora.

The response to Bethune's passing is a testament to what she meant to the world. With an undergirding of pride in her African identity, she was a fearless advocate for people of African descent. Her attempt to go to Africa as a missionary at twenty years old indicates an early understanding of her responsibility to bring change to the continent. In that moment she saw religion as the primary means by which she would do so, but throughout her life she evolved from this mindset. As she rose to prominence, she realized that her voice was one of her most powerful assets. Whether at the founding of the United Nations speaking against colonization or writing to show her support for Haitian women's suffrage in the *Chicago Defender*, Bethune lifted her voice to speak for oppressed Africans. She challenged African Americans to understand the plight of other African people and to recognize the similarities in their struggles and to become unified with one another.

* * *

It is imperative that we look beyond Bethune's work as a civil rights pioneer to embrace her role as a Pan-Africanist who internationalized the scope of Black women's organizations to unify people of African descent. She did not limit herself to advocating only for African Americans because she saw herself as a part of the African Diaspora. Although recent scholarship has been more inclusive, Pan-Africanism has largely focused on men. Bethune embodied tenets of Pan-Africanism, and she led NACW and NCNW, with the aim of fostering solidarity, at the forefront of her mission. She encouraged the women to understand the problems of people of African descent and to become a part of the solution. She promoted cultural exchange, travel, and education as ways by which the organization armed themselves to become change agents. Bethune's early years in South Carolina laid a foundation for her leadership, as she learned to embrace her African ancestry. This knowledge raised her awareness to being a part of a Black world that was larger than the United States. As the daughter of Patsy McLeod, she was destined to be a powerful leader. Remembering her mother's pride in her African lineage along with her "will power and drive," Bethune spent her lifetime embodying those same ideas that were imparted to her. Seeing the power of women's leadership in her home and community shaped her understanding that organizing primarily among women would allow her to fulfill her desire to be "a significant link between peoples of color throughout the world."[4]

To further understand Bethune's role as a Pan-Africanist, we must examine how the tenets of the ideology were embodied in her daily life. From the moment she was born into a family that declared its African lineage to be a significant aspect of their lives, Mary was introduced to a facet of Pan-Africanism. As a young woman who was influenced by Pan-Africanist religious leaders who promoted missionary work as a means by which emigration to Africa could be made possible, she came to understand the "Back to Africa" movement, influencing her desire to become a missionary. Although she was unable to fulfill her dream of going to Africa as a missionary, she began to realize that her location did not determine her ability to advocate for the causes impacting people of African descent. Whether she was a delegate at the San Francisco Conference at the founding of the United Nations or writing as a columnist for the *Chicago Defender,* Bethune brought needed attention to issues including but not limited to women's suffrage, colonization, and apartheid. She consistently sought to unify African descendants within her writings, through travel, and, in her later years, as an advisor. For Bethune, Pan-Africanism was a way of life that did not necessitate joining Pan-African organizations and attending conferences because she embodied the tenets of the ideology daily in everything that she did.

Invitations to visit Haiti, awards from Liberia, induction into the Afro-Cuban Society were all important clues into how she was perceived by the Diaspora. In her later years she was sought by Bahamian women for her counsel and celebrated by Afro-Canadian women for her achievements, a further indication of her relationships with African descendants. The mourning of her passing in Nigeria—a place she had never visited and yet one where she was revered and celebrated—is another profound statement of who she was to the Black world. The impact that she had on Black America was great, but understanding Bethune's role as a woman who fostered solidarity among African descendants internationally offers a more accurate assessment of the significance of her work. Her male counterparts have dominated the narrative of Pan-Africanism for too long. It is now time for Mrs. Mary McLeod Bethune to have her say.

Notes

Introduction: Honoring the Africa within Her

Epigraph: Clarence Mitchell, RJB 351, Director, District of Columbia Bureau of the NAACP, December 6, 1968, MS, Ralph J. Bunche Oral Histories Collection on the Civil Rights Movement: Ralph J. Bunche Oral Histories Collection (formerly The Civil Rights Documentation Project), Moorland-Spingarn Research Center, Howard University.

1. In 1945 Bethune was referred to as "First Lady of Negro America" by the *Atlanta Daily World* newspaper (see "'Negro Should Consider World Problems,' Mrs. Bethune Says: Throws Bombshell into Eclectic Thinking of Some Special Pleaders," *Atlanta Daily World*, May 6, 1945).

2. Elaine M. Smith and Audrey Thomas McCluskey, eds., *Mary McLeod Bethune: Building a Better World* (Bloomington: Indiana University Press, 1999), 61.

3. In 1904 Mary McLeod Bethune founded the Daytona Literary and Industrial School for the Training of Negro Girls with $1.50, faith in God, and five little girls. Despite its very humble beginnings, the school grew over the years to become what we know now as Bethune-Cookman University. For more, see Ashley Nichole Robertson, *Mary McLeod Bethune in Florida: Bringing Social Justice to the Sunshine State* (Charleston, SC: Arcadia, 2015), 16.

4. Keisha Blain, Asia Leeds, and Ula Taylor confirm this lack of acknowledgment of Black women as Pan-Africanists: "Despite the proliferation of feminist scholarship over the last several decades, scholarly narratives on Pan-Africanist thought and practice tend to emphasize the contributions of men or overlook the significant relationship between gender and Pan Africanism. Moreover, black women's intellectual and political work remains undertheorized and underrepresented in studies on Pan-Africanism and black internationalism more broadly (for example, Walters 1993; Adi and Sherwood 2003; Edwards 2003; West et al. 2009; Falola and Essein 2014)" (Keisha N. Blain, Asia Leeds, and Ula Y. Taylor, "Women, Gender Politics, and Pan-Africanism," *Women, Gender, and Families of Color* 4, no. 2 [2016]: 139).

5. In the introduction of Reiland Rabaka's text *Handbook of Pan-Africanism*, he speaks of the need to include the contributions of women to Pan-Africanism, noting that Anna Julia Cooper and Fannie Barrier Williams were two of the six women who at-

tended the Pan-African Conference. He also mentions Amy Ashwood Garvey and Amy Jacques Garvey as being significant figures in the Garvey movement. This is notable, but again it discusses these women in reference to male-dominated spaces (Rabaka, *Routledge Handbook of Pan-Africanism* [London: Routledge, 2020], 7).

6. African Diaspora as defined by Joseph E. Harris: "The African Diaspora is a triadic relationship linking a dispersed group of people to the homeland, Africa, and to their host or adopted countries" (Joseph E. Harris, Douglas B. Chambers, Dale T. Graden, Joseph E. Inikori, and Colin A. Palmer, *The African Diaspora* [College Station: published by Texas A&M University Press for the University of Texas at Arlington, 1996], 7).

7. Quoted in Sara Evans, *Born for Liberty* (New York: Free Press, 1997), 208.

8. P. Olisanwuche Esedebe, *Pan-Africanism: The Idea and Movement 1776–1963* (Washington, DC: Howard University Press, 1982), 3.

9. Adi Hakim, *Pan-Africanism: A History* (London: Bloomsbury, 2018), 59.

10. Charles Spurgeon Johnson, 1893–1956, Mary McLeod Bethune Interview Transcript, ca. 1939, State Archives of Florida, Florida Memory.

11. Bethune's Diary, Part 1, Reel 6, Slide 229, Mary McLeod Bethune Foundation Papers, National Archives for Black Women's Records, Washington, DC.

12. Joseph E. Harris and George Shepperson, *Global Dimensions of the African Diaspora,* 2nd ed., ed. Harris (Washington, DC: Howard University Press, 1993), 470.

13. Mary McLeod Bethune, "Bethune Describes Liberia as 'Land of Opportunity' for All," *Chicago Defender,* February 2, 1952, 1.

14. Harris and Shepperson, *Global Dimensions of the African Diaspora,* 465.

15. Oral History Interview with Virginia Foster Durr, October 16, 1975, Interview G-0023-3, Southern Oral History Program Collection (#4007), Southern Historical Collection, Wilson Library, University of North Carolina at Chapel Hill.

16. Quoted in Harris and Shepperson, *Global Dimensions of the African Diaspora,* 465.

Chapter 1. Southern Roots and Evolving African Identity in Bethune's Early Life

1. 1880 United States Census, Lynchburg, Sumter, South Carolina, Roll: 1241, Family History Film: 1255241; Page: 87C; Enumeration District: 115.

2. Ibid.

3. Emma Gelders Sterne, *Mary McLeod Bethune* (New York: Knopf, 1957), 9. Despite limited information on the writing of the text, at the time it was published it was reviewed by several scholars. In a 1958 review in the *Journal of Negro History* Charles Walker Thomas wrote, "*Mary McLeod Bethune* is a book which invites the student of Negro life and history to return to its pages again and again." He also discussed the significance of the book's focus on Bethune's African heritage (Charles Walker Thomas, "Emma Gelders Stone, *Mary McLeod Bethune,*" *Journal of Negro History* 43, no. 1 [1958]: 63).

4. Charles Spurgeon Johnson, 1893–1956, Mary McLeod Bethune Interview Transcript, ca. 1939, State Archives of Florida, Florida Memory.

5. For more on this conversation, see Henry Morton Stanley, *Through the Dark Continent or The Sources of the Nile around the Great Lakes of Equatorial Africa and down the Livingstone River to the Atlantic Ocean* (London: Low, Marston, Searle and Rivington, 1879).

6. Georg Wilhelm Friedrich Hegel, *The Philosophy of History* (Mineola, NY: Dover, 2012), 99.

7. Johnson, Mary McLeod Bethune Interview Transcript, ca. 1939.

8. Ibid.

9. Anneke Helen Stasson, "Bowen, John Wesley Edward (1855–1933) Educator and Theologian," Boston University School of Theology, https://www.bu.edu/missiology/missionary-biography/a-c/bowen-john-wesley-edward-1855-1933/.

10. Gayraud S. Wilmore, *Pragmatic Spirituality: The Christian Faith through an Africentric Lens* (New York: NYU Press, 2004), 289.

11. Congress on Africa, Atlanta, GA, *Africa and the American Negro* (Atlanta: Gammon Theological Seminary, 1896), https://docsouth.unc.edu/church/bowen/bowen.html.

12. Thomas E. Smith, *Emancipation without Equality: Pan-African Activism and the Global Color Line* (Amherst: University of Massachusetts Press, 2018), 43.

13. According to Sylviane A. Diouf, the 1880 census counted 8,099 persons with one or two parents born in Africa, and the numbers are as follows: "The largest number of Africans' children was found in South Carolina, 1,178; Georgia followed with 1,154; Louisiana, 1,041; Alabama, 945; Texas, 924" (Diouf, *Dreams of Africa in Alabama: The Slave Ship Clotilda and the Story of the Last Africans Brought to America* [Oxford: Oxford University Press, 2009], 270).

14. Robert F. W. Allston and J. H. Easterby, *The South Carolina Rice Plantation as Revealed in the Papers of Robert F. W. Allston* (Columbia: University of South Carolina, 2004), 6.

15. Voyages: The Trans-Atlantic Slave Trade Database, Emory University, 2008, www.slavevoyages.org.

16. Judith Carney, "The African Origins of Carolina Rice Culture," *Ecumene* 7, no. 2 (2000): 131.

17. E. Hergesheimer, Map Showing the Distribution of the Slave Population of the Southern States of the United States, Compiled from the Census of 1860, Washington Henry S. Graham, 1861, Library of Congress Geography and Map Division, Washington, DC.

18. "Gullah Geechee Cultural Heritage Corridor," National Park Service, http://www.nps.gov/guge/faqs.htm.

19. Lorenzo Dow Turner, *Africanisms in the Gullah Dialect* (Columbia: University of South Carolina Press, 2002).

20. E. Franklin Frazier argues that the Africans' memories and customs became meaningless in the New World during enslavement. For more on this conversation, see Frazier, *Black Bourgeoisie* (New York: Free Press, 1997).

21. Patrick Manning, Review of *Africa and the African Diaspora: New Directions of Study,* by Kristin Mann, Edna G. Bay, Isidore Okpewho, Carole Boyce Davies, and Ali A. Mazrui, *Journal of African History* 44, no. 3 (2003): 487–506.

22. Melville Jean Herskovits, *The Myth of the Negro Past* (Boston: Beacon, 1990).

23. Michael A. Gomez, *Reversing Sail: A History of the African Diaspora* (Cambridge: Cambridge University Press, 2004), 2.

24. Elaine M. Smith and Audrey Thomas McCluskey, eds., *Mary McLeod Bethune: Building a Better World* (Bloomington: Indiana University Press, 1999), 42.

25. In the text *African Americans and Africa,* Nemata Amelia Ibitayo Blyden discusses African American missionaries and their desire to return to Africa to "maintain a connection with Africa through missionary, humanitarian and philanthropic work" (Blyden, *African Americans and Africa: A New History* [New Haven, CT: Yale University Press, 2019], 114).

26. Dr. Sylvia Jacobs discussed the significance of the work of Black women missionaries in Africa in the article "African American Women Missionaries," where she examines the experiences of women who served between 1882 and 1951. In her overall analysis of their work, she wrote: "These women missionaries often sacrificed comfortable lives in America to travel to an unknown land, where they would confront a culture with features both admired and despised. Nevertheless, they remained committed and dedicated workers and left Africa probably having made a more positive, albeit limited, contribution than a negative one to African society through their contact with African girls and women" (Rosalyn Terborg-Penn and Andrea Benton Rushing, eds., *Women in Africa and the African Diaspora: A Reader,* 2nd ed. [Washington, DC: Howard University Press, 1996], 98).

27. Johnson, Mary McLeod Bethune Interview Transcript, ca. 1939.

28. In her article "African American Women Missionaries," Dr. Sylvia Jacobs states that "Black Americans represented an infinitesimal percentage" of total missionaries, noting that only about 800 of the roughly 450,000 American missionaries were Black (Jacobs, "African American Women Missionaries," 90).

29. In Bettye Collier-Thomas's text *Jesus, Jobs, and Justice: African American Women and Religion,* she explains that the number of African American missionaries sharply declined in the early 1900s partly due to the "the rise of the 'New Negro' consciousness, Pan-Africanism, Marcus Moziah Garvey, and the Universal Negro Improvement Association's Back to Africa Movement, and other ideologies among African Americans, were threatening to European colonial powers" (Collier-Thomas, *Jesus Jobs and Justice: African American Women and Religion* [New York: Knopf, 2010], 208).

30. P. Olisanwuche Esedebe, *Pan-Africanism: The Idea and Movement 1776–1963* (Washington, DC: Howard University Press, 1982), 3.

31. Quoted in Sara Evans, *Born for Liberty* (New York: Free Press, 1997), 208.

32. Michael J. K. Bokor, "When the Drum Speaks: The Rhetoric of Motion, Emotion, and Action in African Societies," *Rhetorica: A Journal of the History of Rhetoric* 32, no. 2 (2014): 165–94.

33. Mary McLeod Bethune, "A Yearning and Longing Appeased," Mary McLeod

Bethune Foundation Collection, Part 1, Reel 1, National Archives for Black Women's Records, Washington, DC.

34. Marika Sherwood, *Origins of Pan-Africanism: Henry Sylvester Williams, Africa, and the African Diaspora* (New York: Taylor and Francis, 2012).

35. Y. G. M. Lulat, *United States Relations with South Africa: A Critical Overview from the Colonial Period to the Present* (New York: Peter Lang, 2008), 439.

36. Toyin Falola and Raphael Chijioke Njoku, "American Missionaries in Africa, 1780–1920S," in *United States and Africa Relations, 1400s to the Present* (New Haven, CT: Yale University Press, 2020).

37. In Colin Grant's text *Negro with a Hat: The Rise and Fall of Marcus Garvey* he notes that the much of Garvey's rhetoric encouraging Africans to go back to Africa in the early twentieth century mirrored the words of Turner, demonstrating his importance as an early influence on the Pan-African movement.

38. Keisha N. Blain, Asia Leeds, and Ula Y. Taylor, "Women, Gender Politics, and Pan-Africanism," *Women, Gender, and Families of Color* 4, no. 2 (2016): 140.

39. Audrey Thomas McCluskey, *A Forgotten Sisterhood: Pioneering Black Women Educators and Activists in the Jim Crow South* (London: Rowman and Littlefield, 2014), 55.

40. Johnson, Mary McLeod Bethune Interview Transcript, ca. 1939.

41. Ashley N. Robertson, *Mary McLeod Bethune in Florida: Bringing Social Justice to the Sunshine State* (Charleston, SC: Arcadia, 2015).

42. Ibid.

43. For more information on the history of Bethune-Cookman College, see Sheila Y. Flemming, *Bethune-Cookman College, 1904–1994: The Answered Prayer to a Dream* (Virginia Beach, VA: Donning, 1995).

44. Stephanie Y. Evans, *Black Women in the Ivory Tower, 1850–1954: An Intellectual History* (Gainesville: University Press of Florida, 2008), 152.

45. Mary McLeod Bethune, "Clarifying Our Vision with the Facts," *Journal of Negro History* 23, no. 1 (1938): 12.

Chapter 2. Global Citizenship and the Influence of the Black Clubwomen's Movement

1. In Reiland Rabaka's book *Handbook on Pan-Africanism,* the work of Bethune and several of her clubwomen's movement contemporaries is recognized. Bethune would be mentored by, collaborate with, and encounter many of the women that Rabaka names as those whose work gives us a deeper understanding of Pan-Africanism. Rabaka states: "It would be virtually impossible to adequately grasp and grapple with Pan-Africanism without critically engaging the incomparable contributions of the National Association of Colored Women (NACW), the Universal African Black Cross Nurses, the Women's International Circle for Peace and Foreign Relations, The Universal Association of Ethiopian Women, Anna Julia Cooper, Mary Church Terrell, Fannie Barrier Williams, Margaret Murray Washington, Constance Cummings-John, Ida Gibbs Hunt, Amy Ashwood Garvey, Amy Jacques Garvey, Henrietta Vinton Davis, Claudia Jones, Jessie Fauset, Ad-

die Waites Hunton, Addie Dickerson, and Mary McLeod Bethune among others" (Rabaka, *Routledge Handbook of Pan-Africanism* [London: Routledge, 2020], 6).

2. Paula Giddings, *When and Where I Enter: The Impact of Black Women on Race and Sex in America* (New York: William Morrow, 1985), 200. Although Giddings states that the meeting took place in 1909, NACW records indicate that the speech was given in 1912. It was during this time that she gave a speech about her early life and the founding of the school and $21.06 was collected (NACW Convention Notes, 1912, Hampton, Virginia, Conventions [1895–1992], Records of the National Association of Colored Women's Clubs [1895–1992]).

3. Mary McLeod Bethune, "Last Will and Testament," *Ebony Magazine* August 1955.

4. John H. Bracey Jr. and August Meir, *Records of the National Association of Colored Women's Clubs, 1895–1992*, Part 1 (Bethesda: University Publications of America, 1994), viii.

5. Giddings, *When and Where I Enter*, 82.

6. Deborah Gray White, *Too Heavy a Load: Black Women in Defense of Themselves, 1894–1994* (New York: Norton, 1999), 27.

7. Bracey and Meir, *Records of the National Association of Colored Women's Clubs, 1895–1992*, Part 1, ix.

8. For more information on the National Association of Colored Women, see Karen J. Blair, *The Clubwoman as Feminist: True Womanhood Redefined, 1868–1914* (New York: Holmes and Meier, 1980). See also Sophonisba P. Breckinridge, *Women in the Twentieth Century: A Study of their Political, Social, and Economic Activities* (New York: Arno, 1972); Evelyn Brooks Higginbotham, *Righteous Discontent: The Women's Movement in the Black Baptist Church, 1880–1929* (Cambridge, MA: Harvard University Press, 1993); Sharon Harley and Rosalyn Terborg-Penn, *The Afro-America Woman: Struggles and Images* (Baltimore, MD: Black Classic Press, 1997); and Stephanie Shaw, "Black Club Women and the Creation of the National Association of Colored Women," *Journal of Women's History* 3 (fall 1991): 10–25.

9. White, *Too Heavy a Load*, 33–35.

10. Bracey and Meir, *Records of the National Association of Colored Women's Clubs, 1895–1992*, Part 1, x.

11. Alison M. Parker, *Unceasing Militant: The Life of Mary Church Terrell* (Chapel Hill: University of North Carolina Press, 2020), 4.

12. For more, see Michelle Rief, "Thinking Locally, Acting Globally: The International Agenda of African American Clubwomen, 1880–1940," *Journal of African American History* 89, no. 3 (2004): 203–22.

13. Mary Church Terrell, *A Colored Woman in a White World* (Amherst, NY: Humanity Books, 2005), 244–45.

14. Mary Church Terrell, Mary Church Terrell Papers: Speeches and Writings, 1866–1953; 1904, June 13, Address to Be Delivered at the International Congress of Women in Berlin, Germany (also German translation, 1904), Manuscript/Mixed Material, https://www.loc.gov/item/mss425490363/.

15. Ibid.

16. Terrell, *A Colored Woman in a White World*, 244.

17. Ibid., 375.

18. Elaine M. Smith and Audrey Thomas McCluskey, eds., *Mary McLeod Bethune: Building a Better World* (Bloomington: Indiana University Press, 1999), 84.

19. Parker, *Unceasing Militant*, 225.

20. Part 1, Reel 6, Slide 456, Records of the National Association for Colored Women, National Archives for Black Women's History, Washington, DC.

21. Part 1, Reel 6, Slide 458, Records of the National Association for Colored Women, National Archives for Black Women's History, Washington, DC.

22. Joyce A. Hanson, *Mary McLeod Bethune and Black Women's Political Activism* (Columbia: University of Missouri Press, 2003), 98.

23. Smith and McCluskey, *Mary McLeod Bethune*, 133.

24. Addie W. Hunton and Kathryn Magnolia Johnson, *Two Colored Women with the American Expeditionary Forces* (New York: AMS, 1971).

25. For more information on Madam Casely Hayford's activism, see Adelaide M. Cromwell, *An African Victorian Feminist: The Life and Times of Adelaide Smith Casely Hayford 1868–1960* (Washington, DC: Howard University Press, 1992).

26. Rina Okonkwo, "Adelaide Casely Hayford Cultural Nationalist and Feminist," *Phylon* 42, no. 1 (1981): 43.

27. Part 1, Reel 1, Slide 649, Records of the National Association for Colored Women, National Archives for Black Women's History, Washington, DC.

28. Okonkwo, "Adelaide Casely Hayford," 44.

29. Ibid.

30. Smith and McCluskey, *Mary McLeod Bethune*, 157.

31. Nikki Brown, *Private Politics and Public Voices: Black Women's Activism from World War I to the New Deal* (Bloomington: Indiana University Press, 2006), 89.

32. Part 1, Reel 1, Slide 770, Records of the National Association for Colored Women, National Archives for Black Women's History, Washington, DC.

33. Smith and McCluskey, *Mary McLeod Bethune*, 161.

34. Ibid., 163.

35. For more, see Roy Kay, *The Ethiopian Prophecy in Black American Letters* (Gainesville: University Press of Florida, 2011).

36. Smith and McCluskey, *Mary McLeod Bethune: Building a Better World*, 164.

37. Ibid., 162.

38. "Noted Figures Sign for European Trip," *Chicago Defender*, May 7, 1927.

39. Dr. D. M. Miller, "Williams Party in Visit to Lord Mayor of London: Physicians and Wives Cordially Received by Notables while Touring British Isles," *Chicago Defender*, July 16, 1927.

40. Ibid.

41. Smith and McCluskey, *Mary McLeod Bethune*, 83.

42. Jacqueline Anne Rouse, "Out of the Shadow of Tuskegee: Margaret Murray Washington, Social Activism, and Race Vindication," *Journal of Negro History* 81 (winter-autumn 1996): 40.

43. Mary Church Terrell, Mary Church Terrell Papers: Subject File, 1962, International Council of the Darker Races of the World, 1962, 1884, Manuscript/Mixed Material.

44. "Booker T.'s Wife Heads World Order," *Chicago Defender,* August 26, 1922.

45. Folder 238, International Council of the Women of the Darker Races, Mary Church Terrell Papers, Moorland-Spingarn Research Center, Washington, DC.

46. Lerone Bennett, "What's in a Name? Negro vs. Afro-American vs. Black," *ETC: A Review of General Semantics* 26, no. 4 (1969): 402.

47. Mary Church Terrell, Mary Church Terrell Papers: Subject File, 1962, International Council of the Darker Races of the World, 1962, 1884, Manuscript/Mixed Material.

48. Sheena Harris, *Margaret Murray Washington: The Life and Times of a Career Clubwoman* (Knoxville: University of Tennessee Press, 2021), 131.

49. Rouse, "Out of the Shadow of Tuskegee," 40.

50. William Edward Burghardt Du Bois, *The Souls of Black Folk* (Chicago: A. C. McClurg, 1904), 13.

51. Richard Wright, Gunnar Myrdal, and Amritjit Singh, T*he Color Curtain: A Report on the Bandung Conference* (Jackson: University Press of Mississippi, 1995), 13.

52. Ibid., 12.

53. Washington to Hope, September 15, 1922, Folder 239, International Council of the Women of the Darker Races Correspondence A–H, Mary Church Terrell Papers, Moorland-Spingarn Research Center, Washington, DC.

54. Pero Gaglo Dagbovie, *The Early Black History Movement, Carter G. Woodson, and Lorenzo Johnston Greene* (Urbana: University of Illinois Press, 2007), 229. For more information on the origins of Negro History Week, see C. G. Woodson, "Negro History Week." *Journal of Negro History* 11, no. 2 (1926): 238–42.

55. Rief, "Thinking Locally, Acting Globally," 215.

56. Sheila Y. Flemming, *Bethune-Cookman College, 1904–1994: The Answered Prayer to a Dream* (Virginia Beach, VA: Donning, 1995), 28.

57. Rief, "Thinking Locally, Acting Globally," 216.

58. Mary Church Terrell, Mary Church Terrell Papers: Subject File, 1962, International Council of the Darker Races of the World, 1962, 1884, Manuscript/Mixed Material.

59. Ibid.

60. Mrs. Booker T. Washington and Mrs. H. L. McCrory, "International Council Elects at Convention: Gathering of Darker Women's Conference in Washington Comes to an End," *Chicago Defender,* August 18, 1923.

61. Ibid.

62. Folder 238, International Council of the Women of the Darker Races, Mary Church Terrell Papers, Moorland-Spingarn Research Center, Washington, DC.

63. Brenda Gayle Plummer discusses the response to Haitian occupation, stating: "The reaction of black Americans to the Haitian occupation is significant because it reflects the great change during this era in blacks' self-assessment, and in their view of kindred peoples of African descent in other parts of the world. Well-known race leaders led the way in responding to the Haitian controversy, but once it became familiar to the public, ordinary black Americans reacted to the racial injustices they believed were happening in Haiti" (Plummer, "The Afro-American Response to the Occupation of Haiti, 1915–1934," *Phylon* 43, no. 2 [1982]: 125).

64. Mary A. Renda, *Taking Haiti: Military Occupation and the Culture of U.S. Imperialism, 1915–1940* (Chapel Hill: University of North Carolina Press, 2001), 267.

65. "Council of Darker Races in Session at Hot Springs," *Chicago Defender,* August 2, 1930.

Chapter 3. The Founding and Internationalizing of the National Council of Negro Women

1. Laura Micheletti Puaca, *Searching for Scientific Womanpower: Technocratic Feminism and the Politics of National Security, 1940–1980* (Chapel Hill: University of North Carolina Press, 2014), 20.

2. "Mrs. Bethune Back from Bermuda Trip," *New York Amsterdam News,* August 19, 1931.

3. Mary McLeod Bethune, "The Lure of Bermuda," *New York Amsterdam News,* September 23, 1931.

4. Ibid. Details surrounding Bethune's trip to Bermuda are limited. However, she drew criticism for some of her comments about Bermudians. In her analysis of the visit, she called their education system "backwards," criticized citizens of color for lack of business development, and called for race consciousness as the solution. Being the guest of colonial officials did not give Bethune the full picture of the Bahamian people, which is apparent in her writings. For more, see Bethune, "The Lure of Bermuda."

5. "Mrs. Bethune: Spingarn Medalist," *Crisis,* July 1935, 202.

6. Elaine M. Smith and Audrey Thomas McCluskey, eds., *Mary McLeod Bethune: Building a Better World.* (Bloomington: Indiana University Press, 1999), 169–70.

7. Series 2, Box 1, Folder 1, Minutes 1935, National Council of Negro Women Papers, National Archives for Black Women's History, Washington, DC.

8. Elaine M. Smith, *Mary McLeod Bethune and the National Council of Negro Women: Pursuing a True and Unfettered Democracy* (Washington, DC: Alabama State University, for the Mary McLeod Bethune Council House, National Historic Site, National Park Service, 2003).

9. Paula J. Giddings, *When and Where I Enter: The Impact of Black Women on Race and Sex in America* (New York: William Morrow, 1996), 202.

10. Smith and McCluskey, *Mary McLeod Bethune,* 173.

11. Ibid.

12. Ida Jones, *Mary McLeod Bethune in Washington, D.C.: Activism and Education in Logan Circle* (Charleston, SC: History Press, 2013), 56.

13. Ibid.

14. In the book *Mary McLeod Bethune in Washington, DC,* Dr. Ida Jones discusses the uniqueness of this concept: "Unlike earlier groups, the NCNW sought to attract membership from Negro women's organizations as well as individuals. The organizations were not solely collegiate or professional groups; they included religious, masonic and neighborhood/regional clubs. She welcomed grassroots organizations whose purpose served the larger black community" (ibid., 57).

15. Mary C. McComb, *Great Depression and the Middle Class: Experts, Collegiate Youth and Business Ideology, 1929–1941* (New York: Routledge, 2006), 22.

16. Joyce A. Hanson, *Mary McLeod Bethune and Black Women's Political Activism* (Columbia: University of Missouri Press, 2003), 135.

17. Jill Watts, *The Black Cabinet: The Untold Story of African Americans and Politics during the Age of Roosevelt* (New York: Grove Atlantic, 2020), xii.

18. Hanson, *Mary McLeod Bethune,* 146. (In the text Hanson calls the Division of Negro Affairs the Office of Minority Affairs.)

19. Series 1, Box 1, Folder 1, Constitutions and By-Laws, National Council of Negro Women Papers, National Archives for Black Women's History, Washington, DC.

20. Ibid.

21. "Mrs. F. D. Receives 40 Women: Delegates from Many States Confer at White House," April 9, 1938.

22. For more on the Hunton family, see Yun Li and Marilyn Greenwald, *Eunice Hunton Carter: A Lifelong Fight for Social Justice* (New York: Fordham University Press, 2021).

23. For more on Eunice Hunton Carter's work as a lawyer, see Stephen L. Carter, *Invisible: The Forgotten Story of the Black Woman Lawyer Who Took down America's Most Powerful Mobster* (New York: Henry Holt, 2018).

24. Sadie T. M. Alexander, *Democracy, Race, and Justice: The Speeches and Writings of Sadie T. M. Alexander* (New Haven, CT: Yale University Press, 2021), xvii.

25. Cheryl Townsend Gilkes, "'Together and in Harness': Women's Traditions in the Sanctified Church," *Signs* 10, no. 4 (1985): 688.

26. Anthea D Butler, *Women in the Church of God in Christ: Making a Sanctified World* (Chapel Hill: University of North Carolina Press, 2012), 124.

27. Mabel Alston, "368 Women Have Tea at White House," *Afro-American,* November 2, 1940.

28. Rebecca Stiles Taylor, "Activities of Women's National Organizations: The National Council of Negro Women Registered Seventeen Organizations," *Chicago Defender,* December 2, 1939.

29. Sarah Azaransky, *This Worldwide Struggle: Religion and the International Roots of the Civil Rights Movement* (Oxford: Oxford University Press, 2017), 28.

30. Peter R. Eisenstadt and Quinton Hosford Dixie, *Visions of a Better World: Howard Thurman's Pilgrimage to India and the Origins of African American Nonviolence* (Boston: Beacon, 2011) 87–89.

31. Ibid., 101, 109.

32. "Sue Bailey Thurman's Lecture in Florida Stimulates Group," *Atlanta Daily World,* June 19, 1936.

33. Smith and McCluskey, *Mary McLeod Bethune,* 161.

34. Takkara K. Brunson, *Black Women, Citizenship, and the Making of Modern Cuba* (Gainesville: University of Florida Press, 2021), 107.

35. Ibid.

36. Ibid.

37. Frank Andre Guridy, *Forging Diaspora: Afro-Cubans and African Americans in a World of Empire and Jim Crow* (Chapel Hill: University of North Carolina, 2010), 184.

38. Mary Bethune, "Mrs. Bethune Says," *Baltimore Afro-American,* June 1, 1940.

39. St. Clair Drake defines "Small p" Pan Africanist methods as those that "ha[ve] ends that are not political and [are] part of a people-to-people approach to transatlantic relations among black people" (quoted in Joseph E. Harris and George Shepperson, *Global Dimensions of the African Diaspora,* 2nd ed., ed. Harris [Washington, DC: Howard University Press, 1993], 465).

40. Sue Bailey Thurman, "The Seminar in Cuba," *Aframerican Woman's Journal* 1, nos. 2–3 (summer-fall 1940), Series 13, Box 1, Folder 6, National Council of Negro Women Records, National Archives for Black Women's Records, Washington, DC.

41. Dr. Ana Echegoyen de Canizares, "Cuban Social Life and the Negro Woman," *Aframerican Woman's Journal* 1, nos. 2–3 (summer-fall 1940), Series 13, Box 1, Folder 6, National Council of Negro Women Records, National Archives for Black Women's Records, Washington, DC.

42. Second National Conference on Problems of the Negro and Negro Youth, 1939; Proceedings, January 12, 1939, 164 pp., Mary McLeod Bethune Papers: The Bethune Foundation Collection, Part 1: Writings, Diaries, Scrapbooks, Biographical Materials, and Files on the National Youth Administration and Women's Organizations, 1918–1955, Mary McLeod Bethune Papers, Bethune-Cookman College Archives, Daytona Beach, FL, https://congressional.proquest.com/histvault?q=001387-012-0443&accountid=11490.

43. Angel C. Pinto, "The Negro in the Cuban Political Order," *Aframerican Woman's Journal* 1, nos. 2–3 (summer-fall 1940), Series 13, Box 1, Folder 6, National Council of Negro Women Records, National Archives for Black Women's Records, Washington, DC.

44. Ibid.

45. Portuondo Cala, "Brilliant Homage Paid the Ladies of Washington by the Governor," "El Pais," *Havana Daily,* August 22 1940, reprinted in *Aframerican Woman's Journal* 1, nos. 2–3 (summer-fall 1940), Series 13, Box 1, Folder 6, National Council of Negro Women Records, National Archives for Black Women's Records, Washington, DC.

46. *Aframerican Woman's Journal* 1, nos. 2–3 (summer-fall 1940), Series 13, Box 1, Folder 6, National Council of Negro Women Records, National Archives for Black Women's Records, Washington, DC.

47. "Brilliant Homage," *Aframerican Woman's Journal* 1, nos. 2–3 (summer-fall 1940), Series 13, Box 1, Folder 6, National Council of Negro Women Papers, National Archives for Black Women's History, Washington, DC.

48. "Editor-in-Chief," *Chicago Defender,* June 8, 1940.

49. Mary McLeod Bethune, "From the President," *Aframerican Woman's Journal* 1 (spring 1940), Series 13, Box 1, Folder 5, National Council of Negro Women Papers, National Archives for Black Women's History, Washington, DC.

50. "The National Council of Negro Women of the United States of America, Inc.," *Aframerican Woman's Journal* 1 (spring 1940), Series 13, Box 1, Folder 5, National Council of Negro Women Papers, National Archives for Black Women's History, Washington, DC.

51. Sarah Hodges, *Contraception, Colonialism and Commerce: Birth Control in South India, 1920–1940* (Burlington, VT: Ashgate, 2008), 51.

52. Ibid.

53. Mary McLeod Bethune, *Aframerican Woman's Journal* 1, no. 4 (1941), Series 13, Box 1, Folder 7, National Council of Negro Women Papers, National Archives for Black Women's History, Washington, DC.

54. Smith and McCluskey, *Mary McLeod Bethune*, 238.

55. "Conference Reports," *Aframerican Woman's Journal* 1, no. 4 (1941), Series 13, Box 1, Folder 7, National Council of Negro Women Papers, National Archives for Black Women's History, Washington, DC.

56. "Conference Reports," *Aframerican Woman's Journal* 1, no. 4 (1941), Series 13, Box 1, Folder 7, National Council of Negro Women Papers, National Archives for Black Women's History, Washington, DC.

57. "*Aframerican Woman's Journal* Wins Praise," *Philadelphia Tribune*, December 5, 1942.

58. Ibid.

59. Ibid.

60. Mary G. Rolinson, *Grassroots Garveyism: The Universal Negro Improvement Association in the Rural South, 1920–1927* (Chapel Hill: University of North Carolina Press, 2012), 1.

61. Part 1, Reel 11, Slide 46, Mary McLeod Bethune Foundation Papers, National Archives for Black Women's Records, Washington, DC.

62. Devyn Spence Benson discusses the challenges of the Cuban Revolution's antiracism agenda, particularly its impact on Afro-Cubans. In the introduction she examines Fidel Castro's promises "to fulfill late nineteenth-century aspirations to build a raceless and unified Cuba" (Devyn Spence Benson, *Antiracism in Cuba: The Unfinished Revolution* [Chapel Hill: University of North Carolina Press, 2016], 2).

63. Part 1, Reel 11, Slide 44, Mary McLeod Bethune Foundation Papers, National Archives for Black Women's Records, Washington, DC.

64. "Elect Mrs. Bethune to Cuban Society," *Chicago Defender*, May 29, 1943.

65. Frank Andre Guridy, *Forging Diaspora: Afro-Cubans and African Americans in a World of Empire and Jim Crow* (Chapel Hill: University of North Carolina, 2010), 158.

66. William Pickens to Stimson, 27 August 1930, sc micro r-4463, reel 11, William Pickens Papers, Schomburg Center for Research in Black Culture, New York.

67. This incident is mentioned in Guridy's *Forging Diaspora*; and Gerald Horne's *Race to Revolution: The U.S. and Cuba during Slavery and Jim Crow* (New York: NYU Press, 2014).

68. Ada Ferrer, *Insurgent Cuba: Race, Nation and Revolution, 1868–1898* (Chapel Hill: University of North Carolina Press, 1999), 3.

69. William Pickens to Stimson, 27 August 1930, sc micro r-4463, reel 11, William Pickens Papers, Schomburg Center for Research in Black Culture, New York.

70. For a further examination of the relationships between African Americans and Cubans, see Lisa Brock and Digna Castenada-Fuertes, *Between Race and Empire: Afri-*

can-Americans and Cubans before the Cuban Revolution (Philadelphia: Temple University Press, 1998).

71. "Cuba Seeks to Stop American Tourists," *Chicago Defender*, September 13, 1930, sec. 4–4.

72. Guridy, *Forging Diaspora*, 159.

73. John A. Gronbeck-Tedesco, *Cuba, the United States, and Cultures of the Transnational Left, 1930–1975* (Cambridge: Cambridge University Press, 2015), 253.

74. Mary McLeod Bethune to Urrutia, September 15, 1930, Aug., sc micro r-4463, reel 11, William Pickens Papers, Schomburg Center for Research in Black Culture, New York.

75. Mary McLeod Bethune to Urrutia, September 15, 1930, Aug., sc micro r-4463, reel 11, William Pickens Papers, Schomburg Center for Research in Black Culture, New York.

76. Frank Guridy notes that "NCNW organized receptions for the Afro-Cuban delegation during their stopovers in 1947, 1948 and 1949 and probably beyond" (Guridy, *Forging Diaspora*, 190).

77. Ralph Matthews, "President Edwin Barclay Arrives from Africa: Liberian Chief and Successor in Washington, *Baltimore Afro-American*, May 29, 1943.

78. Ibid.

79. Mary McLeod Bethune to The Women of the Republic of Liberia, 28 May 1943, Series 5, Box 5, Folder 84, National Council of Negro Women Papers, National Archives for Black Women's History, Washington, DC.

80. Ibid.

81. "800 Attend N.Y. Barclay Dinner," *Chicago Defender*, 19 June 1943, 1.

82. Series 5, Box 12, Folder 205, Ethiopia 1944, National Council of Negro Women Papers, National Archives for Black Women's History, Washington, DC.

83. Ibid.

84. Dorothy McAllister, "Notes on an East African Journey," *Crisis* 79, no. 9 (November 1972): 306.

85. Mary McLeod Bethune to Princess Tenagnework, April 1944, Series 5, Box 12, Folder 205, Ethiopia 1944, National Council of Negro Women Papers, National Archives for Black Women's History, Washington, DC.

Chapter 4. World War II and the Challenge of Decolonization

1. *Free World*, October 30, 1943, Part 1, Reel 2, Slide 124 Mary McLeod Bethune Foundation Papers, National Archives for Black Women's Records, Washington, DC.

2. John H. Morrow, "Black Africans in World War II: The Soldiers' Stories," *Annals of the American Academy of Political and Social Science* 632 (2010): 12.

3. Sifiso Ndlovu, Mammo Muchie, and Chris Landsberg, "Summary of Presentations by the Main Speakers," *The Influence of the ANC on South Africa's Foreign Policy*, Institute for Global Dialogue, 2012, http://www.jstor.org/stable/resrep07776.6.

4. T. Michael Parrish and Thomas Cutrer, *Doris Miller, Pearl Harbor, and the Birth of the Civil Rights Movement* (College Station: Texas A&M University Press, 2018), xii–xiii.

5. James G. Thompson, letter to editor, *Pittsburgh Courier,* originally printed January 31, 1942; reprinted April 11, 1942, 5.

6. Ibid.

7. David Copeland, *The Media's Role in Defining the Nation: The Active Voice* (New York: Peter Lang, 2010), 207.

8. "'No Fight Against Fascism in World War II'—Du Bois," *Chicago Defender,* June 8, 1946, 7.

9. W. E. B. Du Bois, "Close Ranks," *Crisis* 16, no. 3 (July 1918): 111.

10. W. E. B. Du Bois, "Returning Soldiers," *Crisis* 18, no. 1 (May 1919): 13.

11. Elaine M. Smith and Audrey Thomas McCluskey, eds., *Mary McLeod Bethune: Building a Better World* (Bloomington: Indiana University Press, 1999), 247.

12. Matthew Andrew Wasniewski, *Women in Congress, 1917–2006* (Washington, DC: US Government Printing Office, 2006), 73.

13. Katie McCabe and Dovey Johnson Roundtree, *Justice Older Than the Law: The Life of Dovey Johnson Roundtree* (Jackson: University Press of Mississippi, 2009), 52.

14. Smith and McCluskey, *Mary McLeod Bethune,* 202.

15. Col. Oveta Culp Hobby, "WAAC's at Work," *Chicago Defender,* September 26, 1942, 1.

16. McCabe and Roundtree, *Justice Older Than the Law,* 57.

17. Ibid.

18. McCabe and Roundtree, *Justice Older Than the Law,* 56.

19. "The WAAC—The Girl Who Wouldn't Be Left Behind," *Aframerican Woman's Journal* 3, nos. 1–2 (summer-fall 1942).

20. Smith and McCluskey, *Mary McLeod Bethune,* 174–75.

21. Stephanie Y. Evans, Andrea D. Domingue, and Tania D. Mitchell, *Black Women and Social Justice Education: Legacies and Lessons* (Albany: State University of New York Press, 2019), 316.

22. Ibid.

23. "$3,452,000 Bonds for S.S. *Tubman,*" *Baltimore Afro-American,* September 9, 1944, 23.

24. "S.S. *Tubman* Bond Drive Oversubscribed on Coast," *Chicago Defender,* August 5, 1944, 9.

25. Frederick N. Rasmussen, "Liberty Ships Honored Black in U.S. History," *Baltimore Sun,* March 6, 2004.

26. Lindsey R. Swindall, *The Path to the Greater, Freer, Truer World: Southern Civil Rights and Anticolonialism, 1937–1955* (Gainesville: University Press of Florida, 2014), 61.

27. Ibid., 49.

28. Ibid., 56.

29. Council on African Affairs, *New Africa* 2, no. 1 (August 1943), W. E. B. Du Bois Papers (MS 312), Special Collections and University Archives, University of Massachusetts Amherst Libraries.

30. Ibid.

31. Ibid.

32. Nora Holt, "Paul Robeson Party Honoree: 5000 Attend Fete Marking "Othello's"

46th Birthdate: Thousands Pay Birthday Tribute to Paul Robeson," *New York Amsterdam News*, April 22, 1944.

33. "Mrs. Bethune Has a Birthday Party," *New York Amsterdam News*, July 28, 1945.

34. Swindall, *The Path to the Greater, Freer, Truer World*, 52.

35. Ibid., 54.

36. Conference Agenda on Africa—*New Perspectives*, April 14, 1944, Series 5, Box 10, Folder 1, National Council of Negro Women Papers, National Archives for Black Women's History, Washington, DC.

37. Swindall, *The Path to the Greater, Freer, Truer World*, 90.

38. Ibid. Bethune's attendance is mentioned in the Max Yergan biography (see David Henry Anthony III, *Max Yergan: Race Man, Internationalist, Cold Warrior* [New York: New York University Press, 2006], 213).

39. Conference Agenda on Africa—*New Perspectives*, April 14, 1944, Series 5, Box 10, Folder 1, National Council of Negro Women Papers, National Archives for Black Women's History, Washington, DC.

40. Yergan and Robeson to Bethune, November 29, 1944, Series 5, Box 10, Folder 1, National Council of Negro Women Papers, National Archives for Black Women's History, Washington, DC.

41. "Robeson Urges U.S. Aid for Africa's Starving Millions," *Chicago Defender*, March 23, 1946, 7.

42. "Starving Africans Sent Food, Cash by N.Y. Council," *Chicago Defender*, February 2, 1946.

43. Ibid.

44. Penny Marie Von Eschen, *Race against Empire: Black Americans and Anti-Colonialism 1937–1957* (Ithaca, NY: Cornell University Press, 1997), 104.

45. "African Council Meeting Asks End to Imperialism," *Chicago Defender*, June 22, 1946, 8.

46. Ibid.

47. Council on African Affairs, *New Africa* 5, no. 7 (July 1946), W. E. B. Du Bois Papers (MS 312), Special Collections and University Archives, University of Massachusetts Amherst Libraries.

48. Eschen, *Race against Empire*, 104.

49. Ibid.

50. Carol Anderson, *Eyes off the Prize: The United Nations and the African American Struggle for Human Rights, 1944–1955* (Cambridge: Cambridge University Press, 2003), 163.

51. Ibid.

52. "23 Dropped from African Council: Mrs. Bethune Elected to Succeed Robeson," *Baltimore Afro-American*, May 1, 1948.

53. Mary McLeod Bethune to Robeson and Yergan, June 14, 1948, Max Yergan Papers, Series C, Correspondence Collection 206-3, Folder 12, Mary McLeod Bethune, Moorland Spingarn Research Center, Washington, DC.

54. Anderson, *Eyes off the Prize*, 164–65.

55. "Dr. Bethune Barred from New Jersey School," *Jet* magazine, May 8, 1952, 5.

56. Tony Perucci, *Paul Robeson and the Cold War Performance Complex: Race, Madness, Activism* (Ann Arbor: University of Michigan Press, 2012), 50–51.

57. Carole Boyce Davies, *Left of Karl Marx: The Political Life of Black Communist Claudia Jones* (Durham, NC: Duke University Press Books, 2008), 41.

58. Bethune to White, June 22, 1943, Part 1, Reel 11, Slide 125, Mary McLeod Bethune Foundation Papers, National Archives for Black Women's Records, Washington, DC.

59. Walter White, *A Rising Wind* (Garden City, NY: Doubleday, Doran, 1945), 144.

60. David Levering Lewis, *W. E. B. Dubois: The Fight for Equality and the American Century, 1919–1963* (New York: Henry Holt, 2000), 504.

61. Department of State Press Release, April 10, 1945, Series 5, Box 34, Folder 6, National Council of Negro Women Records, National Archives for Black Women's Records, Washington, DC.

62. Brown to Macleish, Series 5, Box 34, Folder 6, National Council of Negro Women Records, National Archives for Black Women's Records, Washington, DC.

63. Telegram from National Council of Negro Women to NAACP, April 16, 1945, W. E. B. Du Bois Papers (MS 312), Special Collections and University Archives, University of Massachusetts Amherst Libraries.

64. Rebecca Stiles Taylor, "Federated Clubs: National Council Negro Women Selects April as 'World Security Month,'" *Chicago Defender,* April 14, 1945.

65. Anderson, *Eyes off the Prize*, 41.

66. United States Delegation, United Nations Conference on International Organization, 1945, San Francisco, California, United Nations Conference on International Organization consultants and associates, ca. May 1945, W. E. B. Du Bois Papers (MS 312), Special Collections and University Archives, University of Massachusetts Amherst Libraries.

67. Metz T. P. Lochard, "Parley Ducks Colonial Issue: Delegates Juggle Colonial Question: White, Du Bois Ask Equality of Races," *Chicago Defender,* May 5, 1945.

68. National Association for the Advancement of Colored People Press Release, May 8, 1945, W. E. B. Du Bois Papers (MS 312), Special Collections and University Archives, University of Massachusetts Amherst Libraries.

69. Ibid.

70. Sue Bailey Thurman, "Dress Circle Affairs Highlighted Parley," *Chicago Defender,* June 16, 1945.

71. Bethune to Friends, May 10, 1945, Series 5, Box 34, Folder 6, National Council of Negro Women Records, National Archives for Black Women's History, Washington, DC.

72. Bethune to Friends, May 10, 1945, Series 5, Box 34, Folder 6, National Council of Negro Women Records, National Archives for Black Women's History, Washington, DC.

73. "Hit U.S. Stand on Colonies," *Chicago Defender,* May 19, 1945, 4.

74. "Hit U.S. Opposition to Colonial Independence," *Chicago Defender,* May 26, 1945.

75. Ibid.

76. Ibid.

77. Ibid.

78. Ibid.

79. Walter White, "People, Politics and Places," *Chicago Defender,* May 19, 1945, 13.

80. Ibid.

81. Grace V. Leslie and Michael O. West, "'United, We Build a Free World': The Internationalism of Mary McLeod Bethune and the National Council of Negro Women," in *To Turn the Whole World Over: Black Women and Internationalism*, ed. Keisha N. Blain and Tiffany M. Gill (Urbana: University of Illinois Press, 2019), 203.

82. Barbara Ransby, *Eslanda: The Large and Unconventional Life of Mrs. Paul Robeson* (New Haven, CT: Yale University Press, 2014), 147.

83. Brenda Gayle Plummer, *Rising Wind: Black Americans and U.S. Foreign Affairs, 1935–1960* (Chapel Hill: University of North Carolina Press, 2000), 135–36.

84. Lewis, *W. E. B. Dubois*, 510.

85. W. E. B. (William Edward Burghardt) Du Bois, 1868–1963, W. E. B. Du Bois to Mary M. Bethune, December 17, 1929, W. E. B. Du Bois Papers (MS 312), Special Collections and University Archives, University of Massachusetts Amherst Libraries.

86. Mary McLeod Bethune, 1875–1955, Mary McLeod Bethune to W. E. B. Du Bois, January 2, 1930, W. E. B. Du Bois Papers (MS 312), Special Collections and University Archives, University of Massachusetts Amherst Libraries.

87. "Dr. Bethune Brings Frisco Confab Story to Daytona Beach," *Daytona Beach Morning Journal*, June 9, 1945, 1.

88. Ibid.

89. Ibid.

90. L. J. Patterson, "National Leaders Meet to Formulate United Platform, to Fight for FEPC," *Baltimore Afro-American*, June 30, 1945.

91. Ibid.

92. Ibid.

93. Ibid.

94. Brief Analysis of San Francisco Conference United Nations Charter and Related Problems, 1945, Series 5, Box 3, Folder 6, National Council of Negro Women Records, National Archives for Black Women's History, Washington, DC.

95. Ibid.

96. "Indian Women Join Council," *Baltimore Afro-American*, June 19, 1945.

97. Bethune to Friends, May 10, 1945, Series 5, Box 34, Folder 6, National Council of Negro Women Records, National Archives for Black Women's History, Washington, DC.

98. Series 5, Box 34, Folder 6, United Nations 1944–47, National Council of Negro Women Papers, National Archives for Black Women's History, Washington, DC.

99. Ibid.

100. Ibid.

101. Marika Sherwood, "There Is No New Deal for the Blackman in San Francisco," *International Journal of African Historical Studies* 29 (1996): 94.

102. "Education: Prince with a Purpose," *Time* magazine, January 1, 1945.

103. American Council on African Education, American Council on African Education pamphlet, ca. 1945, W. E. B. Du Bois Papers (MS 312), Special Collections and University Archives, University of Massachusetts Amherst Libraries.

104. Ibid.

105. "5 Additional Students here from Africa," *Baltimore Afro-American*, April 24, 1948.

106. "African Benefit Program Slated for Concord Church," *New York Amsterdam News,* September 11, 1948.

107. "Bethune to Acquah, 1950" Africa—General, 1944–1954, 48 pp., Mary McLeod Bethune Papers: The Bethune Foundation Collection, Part 3: Subject Files, 1939–1955, Mary McLeod Bethune Foundation Archive, Bethune-Cookman College campus, Daytona Beach, Florida. Copyright, 2011: Bethune-Cookman College, Inc.

Chapter 5. National Council of Negro Women's Postwar Leadership Abroad

1. Series 5, Box 18, Folder 14, International Relations 1944–46, National Council of Negro Women Papers, National Archives for Black Women's History, Washington, DC.

2. Ida E. Jones, *Mary McLeod Bethune in Washington, D.C.: Activism and Education in Logan Circle* (Charleston, SC: Arcadia, 2013), 56.

3. Clifford L. Muse Jr., "Howard University and U.S. Foreign Affairs during the Franklin D. Roosevelt Administration, 1933–1945," *Journal of African American History* 87 (fall 2002): 403–15.

4. Series 5, Box 18, Folder 14, International Relations 1944–46, National Council of Negro Women Papers, National Archives for Black Women's History, Washington, DC.

5. "Cover: Margaret Just Butcher Biographical Note," *Negro History Bulletin* 20, no. 1 (1956): 15.

6. Janet Sims-Wood, *Dorothy Porter Wesley at Howard University: Building a Legacy of Black History* (Charleston, SC: History Press, 2014).

7. Maurice C. Woodard, "Merze Tate," *PS: Political Science and Politics* 38, no. 1 (2005): 101.

8. Robert P. Smith, "An Exemplary Life: A Tribute to Will Mercer Cook (1903–1987)," *CLA Journal* 31, no. 2 (1987): 246.

9. Series 5, Box 18, Folder 14, International Relations 1944–46, National Council of Negro Women Papers, National Archives for Black Women's History, Washington, DC.

10. Nancy Raquel Mirabal, *Suspect Freedoms: The Racial and Sexual Politics of Cubanidad in New York, 1823–1957* (New York: NYU Press, 2017), 201.

11. Lula Jones Garrett, "Baltimoreans off to Trinidad for Social Work Conference," *Baltimore Afro-American,* April 27, 1946, 13.

12. Series 5, Box 9, Folder 18, Coterie of Social Workers of Trinidad and Tobago 1946, National Council of Negro Women Papers, National Archives for Black Women's History, Washington, DC.

13. Ibid.

14. Helen Rappaport, *Encyclopedia of Women Social Reformers,* vol. 1 (Santa Barbara, CA: ABC-CLIO, 2001), 335.

15. Series 5, Box 9, Folder 18, Coterie of Social Workers of Trinidad and Tobago 1946, National Council of Negro Women Papers, National Archives for Black Women's History, Washington, DC.

16. Ibid.

17. Sarah Simpson George to Bethune, May 1945, Series 5, Box 18, Folder 301, International Relations, National Council of Negro Women Papers, National Archives for Black Women's History, Washington, DC.

18. Eleanor Roosevelt, "My Day October 27, 1944," Eleanor Roosevelt Papers Project.

19. Series 5, Box 18, Folder 301, International Relations, National Council of Negro Women Papers, National Archives for Black Women's History, Washington, DC.

20. William V. S. Tubman Papers, 1904–1992: The National Liberian Women's Social and Political Movement, 1946–1969, (undated Civic, Social and Political Organizations, Civil Society-Related Materials), Indiana University Digital Library Program, Bloomington.

21. Ashley N. Robertson, "'The Drums of Africa Still Beat in My Heart': The Internationalism of Mary McLeod Bethune and the National Council of Negro Women (1895–1960)" (PhD diss., Howard University, 2013).

22. Series 5, Box 12, Folder 208, National Council of Negro Women Papers, National Archives for Black Women's History, Washington, DC.

23. William V. S. Tubman Papers, 1904–1992: The National Liberian Women's Social and Political Movement, 1946–1969, (undated Civic, Social and Political Organizations, Civil Society-Related Materials), Indiana University Digital Library Program, Bloomington.

24. Ekekwe Obiora to Bethune, December 30, 1946, Part 2, Reel 4, Mary McLeod Bethune Foundation Papers, National Archives for Black Women's Records, Washington, DC.

25. Joe Columbus Wobil to Bethune, July 4, 1947, Part 2, Reel 4, Slide 432, Mary McLeod Bethune Foundation Papers, National Archives for Black Women's Records, Washington, DC.

26. Felix U. Zeh to Bethune, December 12, 1947, Part 2, Reel 4, Slide 434, Mary McLeod Bethune Foundation Papers, National Archives for Black Women's Records, Washington, DC.

27. Joseph E Harris, "Expanding the Scope of African Diaspora Studies: The Middle East and India, a Research Agenda," *Radical History Review*, no. 87 (2003): 157–58.

28. Folder 238, International Council of the Women of the Darker Races, Mary Church Terrell Papers, Moorland-Spingarn Research Center, Washington, DC.

29. Gerald Horne, *The End of Empires: African Americans and India* (Philadelphia: Temple University Press, 2009), 58.

30. Peter Eisenstadt and Quinton Dixie, *Visions of a Better World: Howard Thurman's Pilgrimage to India and the Origins of African American Nonviolence* (Boston: Beacon, 2011), 85–117.

31. Elaine M. Smith and Audrey Thomas McCluskey, eds., *Mary McLeod Bethune: Building a Better World* (Bloomington: Indiana University Press, 1999), 85.

32. *Telefact*, January 1947, Part 1, Reel 19, Slide 621, Mary McLeod Bethune Foundation Papers, National Archives for Black Women's Records, Washington, DC.

33. Mary McLeod Bethune, "Two Young Guests Give Insight of Woman's New Status in India," *Chicago Defender*, September 24, 1949, 6.

34. Kenton J. Clymer, "Jawaharlal Nehru and the United States: The Preindependence Years," *Diplomatic History* 14, no. 2 (1990): 144.

35. Clymer, "Jawaharlal Nehru and the United States," 151.

36. Lillian Scott, "Cut Negroes from Nehru Visit here," *Chicago Defender,* October 15, 1949.

37. Courier New York Bureau, "NEHRU . . . Leaders: Prime Minister of India Faces Top Leadership," *Pittsburgh Courier,* November 12, 1949.

38. Ibid.

39. Singh to Bethune, Part 2, Reel 4, Slide 415, Mary McLeod Bethune Foundation Papers, National Archives for Black Women's Records, Washington, DC.

40. Singh to Bethune, Part 2, Reel 4, Slide 422, Mary McLeod Bethune Foundation Papers, National Archives for Black Women's Records, Washington, DC.

41. Mary McLeod Bethune, "In Token of a Common Humanity We Must Give Grain to India," *Chicago Defender,* April 28, 1951, 6.

42. Canadian Association for South Asian Studies, *Contributions to Asian Studies 1977* (Leiden, Netherlands: Brill Archives, 1997), 89.

43. Bethune, "In Token of a Common Humanity," 6.

44. Robert J. McMahon, "Food as a Diplomatic Weapon: The India Wheat Loan of 1951," *Pacific Historical Review* 56 (August 1987): 355.

45. McMahon, "Food as a Diplomatic Weapon," 373.

46. Ibid., 359.

47. Bethune, "In Token of a Common Humanity," 6.

48. *The Department of State Bulletin* (Washington, DC: Office of Public Communication, Bureau of Public Affairs, 1956), 204.

49. Mary McLeod Bethune, "Calls Haiti Symbol of Attainable Freedom for Thousands of Blacks," *Chicago Defender,* July 23, 1949.

50. Ibid.

51. C. L. R. James, *The Black Jacobins* (New York: Vintage, 1989).

52. Matt D. Childs, *The 1812 Aponte Rebellion in Cuba and the Struggle against Atlantic Slavery* (Chapel Hill: University of North Carolina Press, 2009), 169; Brandon R. Byrd, *The Black Republic: African Americans and the Fate of Haiti* (Philadelphia: University of Pennsylvania Press, 2019), 3.

53. Bethune, "Calls Haiti Symbol of Attainable Freedom."

54. Lindsay J. Twa, *Visualizing Haiti in U.S. Culture, 1910–1950* (Burlington, VT: Ashgate, 2014), 210.

55. Charles to Bethune, June 9, 1949, Part 2, Reel 5, Slide 430, Mary McLeod Bethune Foundation Papers, National Archives for Black Women's Records, Washington, DC.

56. Bethune Diary, July 12, 1949, Part 1, Reel 5, Slide 714, Mary McLeod Bethune Foundation Papers, National Archives for Black Women's Records, Washington, DC.

57. "Mrs. Bethune Decorated by Haitian Government: Back in U.S. after Conferences for Haitian Women," *Atlanta Daily World,* July 24, 1949.

58. Bethune Diary, July 13, 1949, Part 1, Reel 5, Slide 716, Mary McLeod Bethune Foundation Papers, National Archives for Black Women's Records, Washington, DC.

59. "U.S. Ambassador to Haiti Resigns," *Los Angeles Sentinel,* July 5, 1951.

60. Bethune Diary, July 1949, Part 1, Reel 5, Slide 718, Mary McLeod Bethune Foundation Papers, National Archives for Black Women's Records, Washington, DC.

61. Ibid.

62. Bethune Diary, July 1949, Part 1, Reel 5, Slide 721, Mary McLeod Bethune Foundation Papers, National Archives for Black Women's Records, Washington, DC.

63. Ibid.

64. Mary McLeod Bethune, "Constructive Action in Haiti Depends on Unity among People," *Chicago Defender,* June 3, 1950, 6.

65. Bethune Diary, July 1949, Part 1, Reel 5, Slide 723, Mary McLeod Bethune Foundation Papers, National Archives for Black Women's Records, Washington, DC.

66. Bethune Diary, July 1949, Part 1, Reel 5, Mary McLeod Bethune Foundation Papers, National Archives for Black Women's Records, Washington, DC.

67. Ibid.

68. Bethune Diary, July 20, 1949, Part 1, Reel 5, Slide 737, Mary McLeod Bethune Foundation Papers, National Archives for Black Women's Records, Washington, DC.

69. Ibid.

70. "Mrs. Bethune Decorated by Haitian Government," July 24, 1949.

71. Beverly Bell, *Fault Lines: Views across Haiti's Divide* (Ithaca, NY: Cornell University Press, 2013), 44.

72. Chantalle F. Verna and Paulette Poujol Oriol, "The Ligue Feminine d'Action Sociale: An Interview with Paulette Poujol Oriol," *Journal of Haitian Studies* 17, no. 1 (2011): 248.

73. Ibid., 249.

74. Grace Louise Sanders, "La voix des femmes: Haitian Women's Rights, National Politics and Black Activism in Port-au-Prince and Montreal, 1934–1986" (PhD diss., University of Michigan, 2013), 96.

75. For more information on the Haitian Exposition, see Michael J. Smith, *Red and Black in Haiti: Radicalism, Conflict, and Political Change, 1934–57* (Chapel Hill: University of North Carolina Press, 2009).

76. Bethune Diary, July 1949, Part 1, Reel 5, Slide 749–50, Mary McLeod Bethune Foundation Papers, National Archives for Black Women's Records, Washington, DC.

77. "Mrs. Bethune Decorated by Haitian Government," July 24, 1949.

78. Joseph E. Harris and George Shepperson, *Global Dimensions of the African Diaspora,* 2nd ed., ed. Harris (Washington, DC: Howard University Press, 1993), 463.

79. Ruth Clement-Bond to Bethune, January 21, 1947, from Port-au-Prince, NCNW Papers, Box 5, Folder 2, National Archives for Black Women's History, Washington, DC.

80. Bethune to Daniel, August 8, 1949, Part 1, Reel 5, Slide 434, Mary McLeod Bethune Foundation Papers, National Archives for Black Women's Records, Washington, DC.

81. Bethune to Daniels, August 18, 1949, Part 1, Reel 16, Slide 438, Mary McLeod Bethune Foundation Papers, National Archives for Black Women's Records, Washington, DC.

82. "Mrs. Bethune Heads Drive of Women to Aid Haiti Orphans," *Atlanta Daily World,* September 30, 1949.

83. Mary McLeod Bethune, "Constructive Action in Haiti Depends on Unity among People," *Chicago Defender,* June 3, 1950, 6.

84. Bethune to Estimé, September 15, 1949, Part 2, Reel 5, Slide 436, Mary McLeod Bethune Foundation Papers, National Archives for Black Women's Records, Washington, DC.

85. Bethune to Estimé, September 15, 1949, Part 2, Reel 5, Slide 445, Mary McLeod Bethune Foundation Papers, National Archives for Black Women's Records, Washington, DC.

86. Joyce A. Hanson, *Mary McLeod Bethune and Black Women's Political Activism* (Columbia: University of Missouri Press, 2003), 145.

87. Bethune to Estimé, September 15, 1949, Part 2, Reel 5, Slide 438, Mary McLeod Bethune Foundation Papers, National Archives for Black Women's Records, Washington, DC.

88. Bethune to Estimé, September 15, 1949, Part 2, Reel 5, Slide 441, Mary McLeod Bethune Foundation Papers, National Archives for Black Women's Records, Washington, DC.

89. Frederick Douglass, *Life and Times of Frederick Douglass,* Documenting the American South (De Wolfe and Fiske, 1892), 752, https://docsouth.unc.edu/neh/dougl92/dougl92.html#p752.

90. Ibid.

Chapter 6. Bethune Advances Her Global Agenda beyond Retirement

1. "Our Opinions: Mrs. Bethune Steps Down, but Not Out," *Chicago Defender,* November 26, 1949.

2. Ibid.

3. Ibid.

4. Series 5, Box 35, Folder 5, US Department of Labor 1946–47, National Council of Negro Women Papers, National Archives for Black Women's History, Washington, DC.

5. Letter from the Ladies Welfare Group (Junta Femenine de Beneficencia) of Panama to Bethune, June 6, 1945, Part 2, Reel 4, Slide 448, Mary McLeod Bethune Foundation Papers, National Archives for Black Women's Records, Washington, DC.

6. Estrella De Costa Rica to Bethune, November 15, 1948, Part 2, Reel 4, Slide 438, Mary McLeod Bethune Foundation Papers, National Archives for Black Women's Records, Washington, DC.

7. William V. S. Tubman Papers, 1904–1992: The National Liberian Women's Social and Political Movement, 1946–1969 (undated Civic, Social and Political Organizations, Civil Society–Related Materials), Indiana University Digital Library Program, Bloomington.

8. Frank Andre Guridy, *Forging Diaspora: Afro-Cubans and African Americans in a World of Empire and Jim Crow* (Chapel Hill: University of North Carolina, 2010), 191.

9. "We Need Love—Mrs. Bethune," *Baltimore Afro-American,* November 25, 1950.

10. Ibid.

11. Evelio Grillo, *Black Cuban, Black American: A Memoir* (Houston, TX: Arte Publico, 2000), 24.

12. Bethune Cookman University, *The Wildcat, 1930*, Digital Services unit of the University of Central Florida Libraries, Central Florida Memory Digital Archives, http://digitalcollections.lib.ucf.edu/cdm-CFM/document.php?CISOROOT=/CFM&CISOPTR=83477&CISOSHOW=83434.

13. Grillo, *Black Cuban*, 24.

14. Bethune Cookman University Photograph Collection, Digital Services unit of the University of Central Florida Libraries, Central Florida Memory Digital Archives, http://digitalcollections.lib.ucf.edu/cdm-CFM/document.php?CISOROOT=/CFM&CISOPTR=68214.

15. Part 1, Reel 16, Slide 653, Mary McLeod Bethune Foundation Papers, National Archives for Black Women's Records, Washington, DC.

16. Part 1, Reel 16, Slide 654, Mary McLeod Bethune Foundation Papers, National Archives for Black Women's Records, Washington, DC.

17. Takkara K. Brunson, *Black Women, Citizenship, and the Making of Modern Cuba* (Gainesville: University of Florida Press, 2021), 151.

18. Claude A. Barnett, "Peaceful Inauguration, Election Mark Progress in Liberia: Republic Installs Reelected Tubman as Nation's President," *Atlanta Daily World*, January 9, 1952.

19. Mary McLeod Bethune, "Trip to Africa Stirs Memory of the Founding of Liberia in 1822," *Chicago Defender*, January 5, 1952, 10.

20. Miles Mark Fisher, "Lott Cary, the Colonizing Missionary," *Journal of Negro History* 7, no. 4 (1922): 380–418.

21. Lynchburg (Va.) Free Negro and Slave Records, 1784–1864, Local Government Records Collection, Lynchburg Court Records, Library of Virginia, Richmond, 23219, http://ead.lib.virginia.edu/vivaxtf/view?docId=lva/vi04311.xml.

22. Toyin Falola and Raphael Chijioke Njoku, *United States and Africa Relations, 1400s to the Present* (New Haven, CT: Yale University Press, 2020), 86.

23. Fisher, "Lott Cary," 389.

24. Mary McLeod Bethune, "Trip to Africa Stirs Memory of the Founding of Liberia in 1822," *Chicago Defender*, January 5, 1952, 10.

25. Bethune's Diary, Part 1, Reel 6, Slide 229, Mary McLeod Bethune Foundation Papers, National Archives for Black Women's Records, Washington, DC.

26. Brenna Wynn Greer, *Represented: The Black Imagemakers Who Reimagined African American Citizenship* (Philadelphia: University of Pennsylvania Press, 2019), 119.

27. Carl Murphy, "From Varied Fields: Many Americans Attend Inauguration in Liberia," *Baltimore Afro-American*, January 26, 1952.

28. Bethune's Diary, Part 1, Reel 6, Slide 229, Mary McLeod Bethune Foundation Papers, National Archives for Black Women's Records, Washington, DC.

29. Jonathan Zimmerman, *Innocents Abroad: American Teachers in the American Century* (Cambridge, MA: Harvard University Press, 2009), 71–72.

30. Bethune's Diary, Part 1, Reel 6, Slide 239, Mary McLeod Bethune Foundation Papers, National Archives for Black Women's Records, Washington, DC.

31. Part 2, Reel 3, File 280, Mary McLeod Bethune Foundation Papers, National Archives for Black Women's Records, Washington, DC.

32. Part 2, Reel 3, File 280, Mary McLeod Bethune Foundation Papers, National Archives for Black Women's Records, Washington, DC.

33. Part 2, Reel 3, File 280, Mary McLeod Bethune Foundation Papers, National Archives for Black Women's Records, Washington, DC.

34. "Liberia Pays Final Tribute to Mrs. Maude Morris," *Baltimore Afro-American*, December 9, 1961.

35. "Maude Morris, Prominent Liberian, Guest in Windy City," *Chicago Defender*, September 6, 1947, 17.

36. Part 2, Reel 3, Slide 281, Mary McLeod Bethune Foundation Papers, National Archives for Black Women's Records, Washington, DC.

37. Part 1, Reel 6, Slide 245, Mary McLeod Bethune Foundation Papers, National Archives for Black Women's Records, Washington, DC.

38. James Oliver Horton, *Landmarks of African American History* (New York: Oxford University Press, 2005), 165.

39. Henry B. Cole, "Life's Reports: March of the Brongs," *Life* magazine, March 23, 1942, 12.

40. "Bishop W. Sampson Brooks Is Dead: Death Ends Career of Bishop Brooks [...]," *Chicago Defender*, July 21, 1934.

41. "Star of Africa to 2 Delegates: President Tubman Confers Honors," *Baltimore Afro-American*, January 26, 1952.

42. Part 1, Reel 6, Slide 247, Mary McLeod Bethune Foundation Papers, National Archives for Black Women's Records, Washington, DC.

43. "Mrs. Bethune Stricken: Trip to Liberia Sapped Strength," *Chicago Defender*, January 26, 1952.

44. Mary McLeod Bethune, "Bethune Describes Liberia as 'Land of Opportunity' for All," *Chicago Defender*, February 2, 1952, 1.

45. Ibid.

46. Ibid.

47. Vincent J. Browne, "Economic Development in Liberia," *Journal of Negro Education* 24 (Spring 1955): 117.

48. Bethune, "Bethune Describes Liberia," February 2, 1952.

49. Ibid.

50. Ibid.

51. This notion of returning to Africa was not new, in fact there were many Black leaders who were successful in doing so. As early as 1787, Prince Hall, founder of the Black Freemasons, petitioned the Massachusetts legislature for funds to immigrate to Africa. (For more on this, see Harry A. Reed, "Financing an Early Back-to-Africa Scheme," *Proceedings of the Massachusetts Historical Society* 90 [1978]: 103–5). In 1816, a little over a century before Garvey, Seaman Paul Cuffee used his resources to assist a group of thirty-eight African Americans emigrate to Sierra Leone in search of true independence. In his attempts to take as many people to Sierra Leone as possible, he traveled to Baltimore, Philadelphia, and New York City spreading his ideals about the benefits of

returning to Africa. (For more on this, see "To James Madison from Paul Cuffe, 16 June 1813," Founders Online, National Archives, https://founders.archives.gov/documents/Madison/03-06-02-0375.) In 1852 Martin Delaney published *The Condition, Elevation, Emigration, and Destiny of the Colored People of the United States, Politically Considered*, which encouraged Black people to immigrate to Africa to gain liberation from the oppression they faced in the United States. In 1859 he traveled to an area near the Niger River to locate a site for the new nation he hoped to establish.

52. Lamar Fort to Bethune, June 10, 1947, Part 2, Reel 4, Mary McLeod Bethune Foundation Papers, National Archives for Black Women's Records, Washington, DC.

53. "Liberian Farm Expert Coming Home on Visit," *St. Petersburg (FL) Times*, November 28, 1956, 22.

54. Mary McLeod Bethune, "U.S. Democracy and Mrs. Bethune have Reached Another Milestone," *Chicago Defender*, July 19, 1952, 10.

55. Ibid.

56. Anthony Phalen, "South Africans Disobey Apartheid Laws (Defiance of Unjust Laws Campaign), 1952–1953," Global Nonviolent Action Database, June 11, 2009, https://nvdatabase.swarthmore.edu/content/south-africans-disobey-apartheid-laws-defiance-unjust-laws-campaign-1952-1953.

57. Mary McLeod Bethune, "Words of South African Racists Are Compared with Hitler's "Mein Kampf,'" *Chicago Defender*, July 26, 1952, 10.

58. Ibid.

59. Mary McLeod Bethune, "Cuba to Celebrate 100th Birthday of Martyred Apostle of Liberty," *Chicago Defender*, January 24, 1953.

60. For more information on Martí, see Alfonso W. Quiroz, *The Cuban Republic and José Martí: Reception and Use of a National Symbol* (Lanham, MD: Lexington, 2006).

61. Bethune, "Cuba to Celebrate 100th Birthday of Martyred Apostle of Liberty."

62. Ibid.

63. Ibid.

64. Kwame Botwe-Asamoah, *Kwame Nkrumah's Politico-Cultural Thought and Policies: An African-Centered Paradigm for the Second Phase of the African Revolution* (New York: Routledge, 2005), 79.

65. Mary McLeod Bethune, "Writer Looks at Africa through Its Great Leader, Kwame Nkrumah," *Chicago Defender*, April 4, 1953.

66. Ibid.

67. Ibid.

68. Sylvia M. Jacobs, "James Emman Kwegyir Aggrey: An African Intellectual in the United States," *Journal of Negro History* 81, no. 1/4 (1996): 47.

69. Bethune, "Writer Looks at Africa through Its Great Leader."

70. Jim C. Harper, *Western-Educated Elites in Kenya, 1900–1963: The African American Factor* (New York: Routledge, 2005), 104.

71. Mary McLeod Bethune, "Writer Pays Tribute to Negro Beauticians as Ambassadors," *Chicago Defender*, May 15, 1954.

72. Tiffany M. Gill, *Beauty Shop Politics: African American Women's Activism in the Beauty Industry* (Urbana: University of Illinois Press, 2010), 87–88.

73. "Vet Businessmen Hear College President," *Daytona Beach Morning Journal*, October 27, 1948, 2.

74. "Clubs and Societies," *Tribune* (Nassau, Bahamas), March 20, 2015, http://m.tribune242.com/news/2015/mar/20/clubs-and-societies-march-20-2015/.

75. Christina Greene, *Our Separate Ways: Women and the Black Freedom Movement in Durham, North Carolina* (Chapel Hill: University of North Carolina Press, 2006), 98.

76. Jennifer Abbassi and Sheryl L. Lutjens, *Rereading Women in Latin America and the Caribbean: The Political Economy of Gender* (Lanham, MD: Rowman and Littlefield, 2002), 138.

77. "Suffrage Women," LibGuide on Woman Suffrage, University of Bahamas, September 19, 2020, https://cob-bs.libguides.com/wsb.

78. Gail Saunders, *Race and Class in the Colonial Bahamas, 1880–1960* (Gainesville: University Press of Florida, 2016), 274.

79. Ibid.

80. Mary McLeod Bethune, "Mrs. Bethune Gives an Inspiring Word or Two to the People of Nassau," *Chicago Defender*, May 9, 1953.

81. Ibid.

82. Ibid.

83. Saunders, *Race and Class in Colonial Bahamas*, 275.

84. Kim Williams-Pulfer, "'When Bain Town Woman Catch a Fire, Even the Devil Run': The Bahamian Suffrage Movement as National and Cultural Development," *Voluntas: International Journal of Voluntary and Nonprofit Organizations* 27, no. 3 (2016): 1487.

85. Charles Spurgeon Johnson, *Mary McLeod Bethune Interview Transcript, ca. 1939*, State Archives of Florida M95-2, Florida Memory.

86. "Florida Citizens Stage Emancipation Celebration," *Chicago Defender*, January 19, 1929.

87. Ibid.

88. Mary McLeod Bethune, "We Look Forward to Democracy and Brotherhood," *Chicago Defender*, January 15, 1949.

89. "No World Peace in World of Hate: Arrives in Canada," *Chicago Defender*, July 6, 1946.

90. Natasha L. Henry, *Emancipation Day: Celebrating Freedom in Canada* (Toronto: Dundurn, 2010), 101.

91. Jeffrey Kerr-Ritchie discusses the diversity of the emancipation ceremonies in his book *Rites of August First* (see Kerr-Ritchie, *Rites of August First: Emancipation Day in the Black Atlantic World* [Baton Rouge: Louisiana State University Press, 2007], 156).

92. Henry, *Emancipation Day*, 26.

93. "Canadians Plan Big Anniversary Fete in Windsor," *Pittsburgh Courier*, August 3, 1935.

94. Mary McLeod Bethune, "Visits Historic Sites during Canadian Freedom Celebration," *Chicago Defender*, August 14, 1954.

95. Ibid.

96. "Dr. Bethune Views Dawn of New Age," *Windsor Star*, August 3, 1954, 3.

97. Julie Kotsis, "Urban Design Expert Addresses Anti-Black Racism across City Landscapes," *Windsor Star,* September 24, 2020, A4.

98. Elise Harding-Davis to the author, January 21, 2022.

99. Bethune, "Visits Historic Sites," August 14, 1954.

100. Ibid.

101. Natasha L. Henry, *Talking about Freedom: Celebrating Emancipation Day in Canada* (Toronto: Dundurn, 2012), 88.

102. Henry, *Emancipation Day,* 200.

103. "Expect 600 at Function," *Windsor Star,* July 6, 1954, 12.

104. Angus Munro, "Count Your Blessings, Emancipator Tells All," *Windsor Star,* August 4, 1954, 6.

Chapter 7. The Legacy Continues

1. In 1945, when Bethune traveled to the founding of the UN in San Francisco, Dr. Ferebee was by her side (see Stephen L. Carter, *Invisible: The Forgotten Story of the Black Woman Lawyer Who Took down America's Most Powerful Mobster* [New York: Henry Holt, 2018], 231).

2. Diane Kiesel, *She Can Bring Us Home: Dr. Dorothy Boulding Ferebee, Civil Rights Pioneer* (Lincoln: University of Nebraska Press, 2015), 54.

3. Ibid., 104.

4. Nina Mjagkij, ed., *Organizing Black America: An Encyclopedia of African American Associations* (New York: Routledge, 2001), 389.

5. Series 7, Box 15, Folder 11, United Nations 1950–52, National Council of Negro Women Papers, National Archives for Black Women's History, Washington, DC.

6. "Dr. Ferebee Urges Women to Fight for Brotherhood, Freedom: Women Must Achieve Ideals of Democracy, Says NCNW Head," *Baltimore Afro-American,* June 3, 1950.

7. Marilyn S. Greenwald and Yun Li, *Eunice Hunton Carter: A Lifelong Fight for Social Justice* (New York: Fordham University Press, 2021), 151.

8. "World's Women Study Mutual Problems in Haiti," *Norfolk (VA) Journal and Guide,* April 29, 1950.

9. Series 7, Box 9, Folder 1, International Relations, 1950–1951, National Council of Negro Women Papers, National Archives for Black Women's History, Washington, DC.

10. Series 7, Box 9, Folder 1, International Relations, 1950–1951, National Council of Negro Women Papers, National Archives for Black Women's History, Washington, DC.

11. "World's Women Study Mutual Problems in Haiti."

12. Ibid.

13. "Dr. Ferebee to Step down for Incoming NCNW President," *Pittsburgh Courier,* November 14, 1953.

14. Kiesel, *She Can Bring Us Home,* 188.

15. "NCNW Votes Dr. Ferebee Second Term," *Chicago Defender,* November 3, 1951.

16. Pastsy Graves, "Dr. Ferebee Quits NCNW Post, Many Gains Cited," *Chicago Defender,* November 28, 1953.

17. Elsa Barkley Brown, Rosalyn Terborg-Penn, and Darlene C. Hine, *Black Women in America: An Historical Encyclopedia* (New York: Carlson, 1993), 755.

18. Veronica La Du, "Vivian Carter Mason," Mary McLeod Bethune Council House, National Park Service, last modified February 25, 2021, https://www.nps.gov/mamc/learn/historyculture/vivian-carter-mason.htm.

19. Series 7, Box 9 Folder 3, International Relations Department–NCNW, 1952–1959, National Council of Negro Women Papers, National Archives for Black Women's History, Washington, DC.

20. Ibid.

21. Series 7, Box 15, Folder 12, United Nations 1953–1959, National Council of Negro Women Papers, National Archives for Black Women's History, Washington, DC.

22. "NCNW Reception for Mrs. Magloire Brilliant," *Chicago Defender* February 12, 1955, 20.

23. Ibid.

24. Series 7, Box 1, Folder 2, Africa, 1953–1959, National Council of Negro Women Papers, National Archives for Black Women's History, Washington, DC.

25. Ibid.

26. Ibid.

27. Ibid.

28. Kenneth Little, *African Women in Towns: An Aspect of Africa's Social Revolution* (Cambridge: Cambridge University Press, 1973), 212; "Sixty Toast Gold Coast Legislator," *Los Angeles Sentinel,* August 2, 1956.

29. Series 7, Box 9, Folder 3, International Relations Department–NCNW, 1952–1959, National Council of Negro Women Papers, National Archives for Black Women's History, Washington, DC.

30. Ralph E. Luker and Christopher M. Richardson, *Historical Dictionary of the Civil Rights Movement* (Lanham, MD: Rowman and Littlefield, 2014), 340.

31. Dorothy Height, *Open Wide the Freedom Gates: A Memoir* (New York>: PublicAffairs, 2003), 155.

32. Rebecca Tuuri, *Strategic Sisterhood: The National Council of Negro Women in the Black Freedom Struggle* (Chapel Hill: University of North Carolina Press, 2018), 22–23.

33. Ibid., 156

34. Series 7, Box 15, Folder 12, United Nations 1953–1959, National Council of Negro Women Papers, National Archives for Black Women's History, Washington, DC.

35. Ibid.

36. Series 7, Box 6, Folder 11, European Tour, 1959 Jan–May, National Council of Negro Women Papers, National Archives for Black Women's History, Washington, DC.

37. Ibid.

38. "Queen Mother Elizabeth Hosts Group from National Council," *Baltimore Afro-American,* September 1, 1959, 12.

39. Series 7, Box 6, Folder 13, European Tour, 1959 Jul–Aug, National Council of Negro Women Papers, National Archives for Black Women's History, Washington, DC.

40. Ashley Robertson, "The Backbone of the Civil Rights Movement: National Council of Negro Women's Role in the Struggle," in *In Spite of the Double Drawbacks: African American Women in History and Culture*, ed. Lopez Matthews, Marshanda Smith, Kenvi Phillips, and Ida E. Jones, 66–74 (Charleston, SC: CreateSpace Independent Publishing Platform, 2012).

41. Tuuri, *Strategic Sisterhood*, 177.

42. Tuuri, *Strategic Sisterhood*, 178.

Conclusion

1. "Thousands Send Wires of Tribute to Bethune Home: Notables Mourn Dr. Bethune," *Chicago Defender*, May 28, 1955.

2. Death of Mary McLeod Bethune, 1955, Folder 001387-009-0610, Newsclippings by Topic, Death of Mary McLeod Bethune, 1955, 71 pp., Mary McLeod Bethune Papers: The Bethune Foundation Collection, Part 1: Writings, Diaries, Scrapbooks, Biographical Materials, and Files on the National Youth Administration and Women's Organizations, 1918-1955, Bethune-Cookman College Archives, Daytona Beach, FL.

3. "Sixty Gather to Honor Mrs. Mary Bethune," *Atlanta Daily World*, May 25, 1955.

4. Elaine M. Smith and Audrey Thomas McCluskey, eds., *Mary McLeod Bethune: Building a Better World* (Bloomington: Indiana University Press, 1999), 161.

Bibliography

Archives

Central Florida Memory Digital Archives
 Bethune Cookman University Photograph Collection. Digital Services Unit of the University of Central Florida Libraries.
Indiana University Digital Library
 William V. S. Tubman Papers, 1904–1992. Liberian Collections. Indiana University Bloomington.
Library of Congress Digital Library
 Mary Church Terrell Papers
Moorland-Spingarn Research Center. Washington, DC.
 Mary Church Terrell Papers
 Max Yergan Papers
National Archives and Records Administration. College Park, Maryland.
 Records of the National Youth Administration
National Archives for Black Women's History. Washington, DC.
 Mary McLeod Bethune Foundation Papers
 National Council of Negro Women Records
 Records of the National Association for Colored Women
The Eleanor Roosevelt Papers Project
Schomburg Center for Research in Black Culture. New York City.
State Archives of Florida Digital Archive
 Charles Spurgeon Johnson Interview of Mary McLeod Bethune
University of Massachusetts Amherst Libraries. Special Collections and University Archives.
 W. E. B. Du Bois Papers
Woodrow Wilson Presidential eLibrary. Staunton, Virginia.
 http://www.woodrowwilson.org

Newspapers and Magazines

Atlanta Daily World
Baltimore (MD) Afro-American
Chicago Defender (national edition)
Crisis
Daytona Beach (FL) Morning Journal
Ebony
Jet
Los Angeles (CA) Sentinel
Michigan Chronicle
New York Amsterdam News
New York Times
Norfolk (VA) Journal and Guide
Philadelphia (PA) Tribune
Pittsburgh (PA) Courier
St. Petersburg (FL) Times
Time
Transition
Tribune (Nassau, Bahamas)
Washington Afro-American
Windsor Star (Ontario, Canada)

Published Sources

Abbassi, Jennifer, and Sheryl L. Lutjens. *Rereading Women in Latin America and the Caribbean: The Political Economy of Gender*. Lanham, MD: Rowman and Littlefield, 2002.

Adi, Hakim. *Pan-Africanism: A History*. London: Bloomsbury, 2018.

"*Aframerican Woman's Journal* Wins Praise." *Philadelphia Tribune*, December 5, 1942.

"African Benefit Program Slated for Concord Church." *New York Amsterdam News*, September 11, 1948.

Alexander, *Sadie T. M. Democracy, Race, and Justice: The Speeches and Writings of Sadie T. M. Alexander*. New Haven, CT: Yale University Press, 2021.

Allston, Robert F. W., and J. H. Easterby. *The South Carolina Rice Plantation as Revealed in the Papers of Robert F. W. Allston*. Columbia: University of South Carolina, 2004.

Alston, Mabel. "368 Women Have Tea at White House." *Baltimore Afro-American*, November 2, 1940.

American Council on African Education. American Council on African Education pamphlet, ca. 1945. W. E. B. Du Bois Papers (MS 312). Special Collections and University Archives, University of Massachusetts Amherst Libraries.

Anderson, Carol. *Eyes off the Prize: The United Nations and the African American Struggle for Human Rights, 1944–1955*. Cambridge: Cambridge University Press, 2003.

———. "Symposium: African Americans and U.S. Foreign Relations from Hope to Disil-

lusion: African Americans, the United Nations, and the Struggle for Human Rights, 1944–1947." *Diplomatic History* 20 (October 1996): 531–64.
Anthony, David Henry, III. *Max Yergan: Race Man, Internationalist, Cold Warrior*. New York: New York University Press, 2006.
Asante, Molefi K. *The History of Africa*. New York: Routledge, 2007.
Azaransky, Sarah. *This Worldwide Struggle: Religion and the International Roots of the Civil Rights Movement*. Oxford: Oxford University Press, 2017.
Barnett, Claude A. "Peaceful Inauguration, Election Mark Progress in Liberia: Republic Installs Reelected Tubman as Nation's President." *Atlanta Daily World*, January 9, 1952.
Bell, Beverly. *Fault Lines: Views across Haiti's Divide*. Ithaca, NY: Cornell University Press, 2013.
Bennett, Carolyn LaDelle. *No Room for Despair: Mary McLeod Bethune's Cold War Integration-Era Commentary*. Baltimore, MD: privately printed, 2006.
Bennett, Lerone. "What's in a Name? Negro vs. Afro-American vs. Black." *ETC: A Review of General Semantics* 26, no. 4 (1969): 399–412.
Benson, Devyn Spence. *Antiracism in Cuba: The Unfinished Revolution*. Chapel Hill: University of North Carolina Press, 2016.
Bertram, Peggy Brooks, and Barbara A. Seals Nevergold. *Uncrowned Queen: African American Women Community Builders*. Buffalo, NY: Petit Printing, 2005.
Bethune, Mary McLeod. "Calls Haiti Symbol of Attainable Freedom for Thousands of Blacks." *Chicago Defender*, July 23, 1949.
———. "Clarifying Our Vision with the Facts." *Journal of Negro History* 23, no. 1 (1938): 10–15.
———. "Last Will and Testament." *Ebony* magazine, August 1955.
———. Mary McLeod Bethune to W. E. B. Du Bois, January 2, 1930. W. E. B. Du Bois Papers (MS 312). Special Collections and University Archives, University of Massachusetts Amherst Libraries.
———. "Mrs. Bethune Gives an Inspiring Word or Two to the People of Nassau." *Chicago Defender*, May 9, 1953.
———. "Mrs. Bethune Says." *Baltimore Afro-American*, June 1, 1940.
———. "Visits Historic Sites during Canadian Freedom Celebration." *Chicago Defender*, August 14, 1954.
———. "We Look Forward to Democracy and Brotherhood." *Chicago Defender*, January 15, 1949.
———. "Writer Looks at Africa through Its Great Leader, Kwame Nkrumah." *Chicago Defender*, April 4, 1953.
———. "Writer Pays Tribute to Negro Beauticians as Ambassadors." *Chicago Defender*, May 15, 1954.
"Bethune to Acquah, 1950." Africa—General. 1944–1954. 48 pp. Mary McLeod Bethune Papers: The Bethune Foundation Collection. Part 3: Subject Files, 1939–1955, Mary McLeod Bethune Foundation Archive, Bethune-Cookman College campus, Daytona Beach, Florida. Copyright, 2011: Bethune-Cookman College, Inc.
"Birthday Party for Mrs. Bethune a Large Affair: Seventieth Anniversary Celebration

"One of Many Held throughout Nation: Mrs. Bethune Has a Birthday Party." *New York Amsterdam News,* July 28, 1945.
"Bishop W. Sampson Brooks Is Dead: Death Ends Career of Bishop Brooks Passes Away." *Chicago Defender,* July 21, 1934.
Blackwell, Joyce. *No Peace without Freedom: Race and the Women's International League for Peace and Freedom,* 1915–1975. Carbondale: Southern Illinois University Press, 2004.
Blain, Keisha N., Asia Leeds, and Ula Y. Taylor. "Women, Gender Politics, and Pan-Africanism." *Women, Gender, and Families of Color* 4, no. 2 (2016): 139–45.
Blair, Karen J. *The Clubwoman as Feminist: True Womanhood Redefined, 1868–1914.* New York: Holmes and Meier, 1980.
Blyden, E. W. *Selected Works of Dr. Edward Wilmont Blyden.* Robertsport: Tubman Center of African Culture, 1976.
Blyden, Nemata Amelia Ibitayo. *African Americans and Africa: A New History.* New Haven, CT: Yale University Press, 2019.
Bokor, Michael J. K. "When the Drum Speaks: The Rhetoric of Motion, Emotion, and Action in African Societies." *Rhetorica: A Journal of the History of Rhetoric* 32, no. 2 (2014): 165–94.
"Booker T.'s Wife Heads World Order." *Chicago Defender,* August 26, 1922.
Botwe-Asamoah, Kwame. *Kwame Nkrumah's Politico-Cultural Thought and Policies: An African-Centered Paradigm for the Second Phase of the African Revolution.* New York: Routledge, 2005.
Bracey, John H., Jr., and August Meir. *Records of the National Association of Colored Women's Clubs, 1895–1992.* Part 1. Bethesda, MD: University Publications of America, 1994.
Breckinridge, Sophonisba P. *Women in the Twentieth Century: A Study of their Political, Social, and Economic Activities.* New York: Arno, 1972.
Bressey, Dr. Caroline. "A Strange and Bitter Crop: Ida B Wells' Anti-Lynching Tours, Britain 1893 and 1894." *Centre for Capital Punishment Studies Occasional Papers* 1 (December 2003): 8–28.
Brock, Lisa, and Digna Castenada-Fuertes. *Between Race and Empire: African-Americans and Cubans before the Cuban Revolution.* Philadelphia: Temple University Press, 1998.
Brown, Elsa Barkley, Rosalyn Terborg-Penn, and Darlene C. Hine. *Black Women in America: An Historical Encyclopedia.* New York: Carlson, 1993.
Brown, Nikki. *Private Politics and Public Voices: Black Women's Activism from World War I to the New Deal.* Bloomington: Indiana University Press, 2006.
Brunson, Takkara K. *Black Women, Citizenship, and the Making of Modern Cuba.* Gainesville: University Press of Florida, 2021.
Buick, Kirsten. *Child of the Fire: Mary Edmonia Lewis and the Problem of Art History's Black and Indian Subject.* Durham, NC: Duke University Press, 2010.
Butler, Anthea D. *Women in the Church of God in Christ: Making a Sanctified World.* Chapel Hill: University of North Carolina Press, 2012.
Byrd, Brandon R. *The Black Republic: African Americans and the Fate of Haiti.* Philadelphia: University of Pennsylvania Press, 2019.

"Canadians Plan Big Anniversary Fete in Windsor." *Pittsburgh Courier*, August 3, 1935.
Carney, Judith. "The African Origins of Carolina Rice Culture." *Ecumene* 7, no. 2 (2000): 125–49.
Carson, Clayborne ed. *The Papers of Martin Luther King, Jr.* Vol 5: *Threshold of a New Decade*. Berkeley: University of California Press, 2005
Carter, Stephen L. *Invisible: The Forgotten Story of the Black Woman Lawyer Who Took down America's Most Powerful Mobster*. New York: Henry Holt, 2018.
Childs, Matt D. *The 1812 Aponte Rebellion in Cuba and the Struggle against Atlantic Slavery*. Chapel Hill: University of North Carolina Press, 2009.
Clark-Lewis, Elizabeth, and Ida Elizabeth Jones, eds. *Emerging Voices and Paradigms: Black Women's Scholarship*. Washington, DC: Association for Black Women Historians, 2008.
"Clubs and Societies." *Tribune* (Nassau, Bahamas), March 20, 2015. http://m.tribune242.com/news/2015/mar/20/clubs-and-societies-march-20-2015/.
Clymer, Kenton J. "Jawaharlal Nehru and the United States: The Preindependence Years." *Diplomatic History* 14, no. 2 (1990): 143–61.
Cole, Henry B. "Life's Reports: March of the Brongs." *Life* magazine, March 23, 1942.
Congress on Africa, Atlanta, Georgia. *Africa and the American Negro*. Atlanta: Gammon Theological Seminary, 1896. https://docsouth.unc.edu/church/bowen/bowen.html.
Council on African Affairs. *New Africa* 2, no. 1, August 1943. W. E. B. Du Bois Papers (MS 312). Special Collections and University Archives, University of Massachusetts Amherst Libraries.
———. *New Africa* 5, no. 7, July 1946. W. E. B. Du Bois Papers (MS 312). Special Collections and University Archives, University of Massachusetts Amherst Libraries.
Courier New York Bureau. "NEHRU . . . Leaders: Prime Minister of India Faces Top Leadership." *Pittsburgh Courier*, November 12, 1949.
"Cover: Margaret Just Butcher Biographical Note." *Negro History Bulletin* 20, no. 1 (1956): 15–15.
Cromwell, Adelaide M. *An African Victorian Feminist: The Life and Times of Adelaide Smith Casely Hayford 1868–1960*. Washington, DC: Howard University Press, 1992.
Dagbovie, Pero Gaglo. *The Early Black History Movement, Carter G. Woodson, and Lorenzo Johnston Greene*. Urbana: University of Illinois Press, 2007.
Davies, Carole Boyce, ed. *Encyclopedia of the African Diaspora*. Vol. 1: *Origins, Experiences and Culture*. Santa Barbara, CA: ABC-CLIO, 2008.
———. *Left of Karl Marx: The Political Life of Black Communist Claudia Jones*. Durham, NC: Duke University Press, 2008.
Dees, Jesse Walter. *The College Built on Prayer: Mary McLeod Bethune*. Daytona Beach, FL: Bethune-Cookman College, 1953.
The Department of State Bulletin. Washington, DC: Office of Public Communication, Bureau of Public Affairs, 1956.
Diouf, Sylviane A. *Dreams of Africa in Alabama: The Slave Ship* Clotilda *and the Story of the Last Africans Brought to America*. Oxford: Oxford University Press, 2009.
Douglass, Frederick. *Life and Times of Frederick Douglass*. Documenting the American

South. De Wolfe and Fiske, 1892. https://docsouth.unc.edu/neh/dougl92/dougl92.html#p752.

Drake, St. Clair. *Black Folk Here and There: An Essay in History and Anthropology.* Los Angeles: Center for Afro-American Studies, University of California, 1990.

"Dr. Bethune Views Dawn of New Age." *Windsor Star* (Ontario), August 3, 1954, 3.

"Dr. Ferebee to Step down for Incoming NCNW President." *Pittsburgh Courier,* November 14, 1953.

"Dr. Ferebee Urges Women to Fight for Brotherhood, Freedom: Women Must Achieve Ideals of Democracy, Says NCNW Head." *Baltimore Afro-American,* June 3, 1950.

Driskell, David C., et al. *The Other Side of Color: African American Art in the Collection of Camille O. and William H. Cosby, Jr.* San Francisco: Pomegranate, 2001.

Du Bois, W. E. B. (William Edward Burghardt). "Close Ranks." *Crisis* 16, no. 3 (July 1918).

———. "Returning Soldiers." *Crisis* 18, no. 1 (May 1919).

———. *The Souls of Black Folk.* Chicago: A. C. McClurg, 1904.

———. W. E. B. Du Bois to Mary M. Bethune, December 17, 1929. W. E. B. Du Bois Papers (MS 312). Special Collections and University Archives, University of Massachusetts Amherst Libraries.

"Editor-in-Chief." *Chicago Defender,* June 8, 1940.

"Education: Prince with a Purpose." *Time* magazine, January 1, 1945.

1880 United States Census. University of Virginia Historical Census Browser. http://mapserver.lib.virginia.edu.

Eisenhower, Dwight D. "Letter to Secretary Dulles Regarding Transfer of the Affairs of the Foreign Operations Administration to the Department of State." Online by Gerhard Peters and John T. Woolley. American Presidency Project. http://www.presidency.ucsb.edu/ws/?pid=10454.

Eisenstadt, Peter R., and Quinton Hosford Dixie. *Visions of a Better World: Howard Thurman's Pilgrimage to India and the Origins of African American Nonviolence.* Boston: Beacon, 2011.

"Elect Mrs. Bethune to Cuban Society." *Chicago Defender,* May 29, 1943.

Ellis, Stephen. "Colonial Conquest in Central Madagascar: Who Resisted what?" In *Rethinking Resistance: Revolt and Violence in African History.* Leiden, Netherlands: Brill, 2003.

Engel, Elisabeth. *Encountering Empire: African American Missionaries in Colonial Africa, 1900–1939.* Stuttgart, Germany: Franz Steiner, 2015.

Eschen, Penny Marie Von. *Race against Empire: Black Americans and Anti-Colonialism 1937–1957.* Ithaca, NY: Cornell University Press, 1997.

Esedebe, P. Olisanwuche. *Pan-Africanism: The Idea and Movement 1776–1963.* Washington, DC: Howard University Press, 1982.

Evans, Sara. *Born for Liberty.* New York: Free Press, 1997.

Evans, Stephanie Y. *Black Women in the Ivory Tower, 1850–1954: An Intellectual History.* Gainesville: University Press of Florida, 2008.

Evans, Stephanie Y., Andrea D. Domingue, and Tania D. Mitchell. *Black Women and Social Justice Education: Legacies and Lessons.* Albany: State University of New York Press, 2019.

"Expect 600 at Function." *Windsor Star* (Ontario), July 6, 1954, 12.
Falola, Toyin, and Raphael Chijioke Njoku. "American Missionaries in Africa, 1780–1920S." In *United States and Africa Relations, 1400s to the Present*, 107–28. New Haven, CT: Yale University Press, 2020.
———. *United States and Africa Relations, 1400s to the Present*. New Haven, CT: Yale University Press, 2020.
Ferrer, Ada. *Insurgent Cuba: Race, Nation and Revolution, 1868–1898*. Chapel Hill: University of North Carolina Press, 1999.
Fisher, Miles Mark. "Lott Cary, the Colonizing Missionary." *Journal of Negro History* 7, no. 4 (1922): 380–418.
Flemming, Sheila Y. *Bethune-Cookman College, 1904–1994: The Answered Prayer to a Dream*. Virginia Beach, VA: Donning, 1995.
"5 Additional Students Here from Africa." *Baltimore Afro-American*, April 24, 1948.
"Florida Citizens Stage Emancipation Celebration." *Chicago Defender*, January 19, 1929.
Frazier, E. Franklin. *Black Bourgeoisie*. New York: Free Press, 1997.
Frazier, Michael, and David Walton, eds. *An Anthology of Contending Views on International Security*. Hauppauge, NY: Nova Science, 2012.
Garvey, Amy Jacques, ed. *The Philosophy and Opinions of Marcus Garvey: Africa for the Africans*. New York: Routledge, 1978.
Garvey, Marcus. *Message to the People: The Course of African Philosophy*. Edited by Tony Martin. Dover, MA: Majority, 1986.
Giddings, Paula J. *Ida: A Sword among Lions: Ida B. Wells and the Campaign against Lynching*. New York: HarperCollins, 2008.
———. *When and Where I Enter: The Impact of Black Women on Race and Sex in America*. New York: William Morrow, 1985, 1996.
Gilkes, Cheryl Townsend. "'Together and in Harness': Women's Traditions in the Sanctified Church." *Signs* 10, no. 4 (1985): 678–99.
Gill, Tiffany M. *Beauty Shop Politics: African American Women's Activism in the Beauty Industry*. Urbana: University of Illinois Press, 2010.
Gomez, Michael A. *Diasporic Africa: A Reader*. New York: New York University Press, 2006.
———. *Reversing Sail*. Cambridge: Cambridge University Press, 2005.
Grant, Colin. *Negro with a Hat: The Rise and Fall of Marcus Garvey*. New York: Oxford University Press, 2010.
Graves, Patsy. "Dr. Ferebee Quits NCNW Post, Many Gains Cited." *Chicago Defender*, November 28, 1953.
Greene, Christina. *Our Separate Ways: Women and the Black Freedom Movement in Durham, North Carolina*. Chapel Hill: University of North Carolina Press, 2006.
Greenwald, Marilyn S., and Yun Li. *Eunice Hunton Carter: A Lifelong Fight for Social Justice*. New York: Fordham University Press, 2021.
Greer, Brenna Wynn. *Represented: The Black Imagemakers Who Reimagined African American Citizenship*. Philadelphia: University of Pennsylvania Press, 2019.
Gronbeck-Tedesco, John A. *Cuba, the United States, and Cultures of the Transnational Left, 1930–1975*. New York: Cambridge University Press, 2015.

"Gullah Geechee Cultural Heritage Corridor." National Park Service. Available at http://www.nps.gov/guge/faqs.htm.

Guridy, Frank Andre. *Forging Diaspora: Afro-Cubans and African Americans*. Chapel Hill: University of North Carolina Press, 2010.

Hanson, Joyce A. *Mary McLeod Bethune and Black Women's Political Activism*. Columbia: University of Missouri Press, 2003.

Harley, Sharon, and Rosalyn Terborg-Penn. *The Afro-America Woman: Struggles and Images*. Baltimore, MD: Black Classic Press, 1997.

Harper, Jim C. *Western-Educated Elites in Kenya, 1900–1963: The African American Factor*. New York: Routledge, 2005.

Harris, Joseph E. *The African Presence in Asia*. Evanston, IL: Northwestern University Press, 1971.

———. "Expanding the Scope of African Diaspora Studies: The Middle East and India, a Research Agenda." *Radical History Review* 87, no. 87 (2003): 157–68.

Harris, Joseph E., and George Shepperson. *Global Dimensions of the African Diaspora*. 2nd ed. Washington, DC: Howard University Press, 1993.

Harris, Joseph E., Douglas B. Chambers, Dale T. Graden, Joseph E. Inikori, and Colin A. Palmer. *The African Diaspora*. College Station: published by Texas A&M University Press for the University of Texas at Arlington, 1996.

Harris, Sheena. *Margaret Murray Washington: The Life and Times of a Career Clubwoman*. Knoxville: University of Tennessee Press, 2021.

Hegel, Georg Wilhelm Friedrich. *The Philosophy of History*. Mineola, NY: Dover, 2012.

Height, Dorothy. *Open Wide the Freedom Gates: A Memoir*. New York: PublicAffairs, 2009.

Henry, Natasha L. *Emancipation Day: Celebrating Freedom in Canada*. Toronto: Dundurn, 2010.

———. *Talking about Freedom: Celebrating Emancipation Day in Canada*. Toronto: Dundurn, 2012.

Hergesheimer, E. Map Showing the Distribution of the Slave Population of the Southern States of the United States. Compiled from the Census of 1860. Entered according to Act of Congress A.D. 1861. Library of Congress Map & Geography Division. Washington, DC.

Herskovits, Melville Jean. *The Myth of the Negro Past*. Boston: Beacon, 1990.

Higginbotham, Evelyn Brooks. *Righteous Discontent: The Women's Movement in the Black Baptist Church, 1880–1929*. Cambridge, MA: Harvard University Press, 1993.

Hine, Darlene Clark, Wilma King, and Linda Reed, eds. *We Specialize in the Wholly Impossible: A Reader in Black Women's History*. Brooklyn, NY: Carlson, 1995.

"Hit U.S. Opposition to Colonial Independence." *Chicago Defender*, May 26, 1945.

Hodges, Sarah. *Contraception, Colonialism and Commerce: Birth Control in South India, 1920–1940*. Burlington, VT: Ashgate, 2008.

Holt, Nora. "Paul Robeson Party Honoree: 5000 Attend Fete Marking "Othello's" 46th Birthdate: Thousands Pay Birthday Tribute to Paul Robeson." *New York Amsterdam News*, April 22, 1944.

Holt, Rackham. *Mary McLeod Bethune: A Biography*. New York: Doubleday, 1964.

Hooker, J. R. "The Pan-African Conference 1900." *Transition* 46 (October-December 1974): 20–24.

Horne, Gerald. *The End of Empires: African Americans and India*. Philadelphia: Temple University Press, 2009.

———. *Race to Revolution: The U.S. and Cuba during Slavery and Jim Crow*. New York: NYU Press, 2014.

Horton, James Oliver. *Landmarks of African American History*. New York: Oxford University Press, 2005.

Hotchkiss, Cryssie A. *Mary McLeod Bethune: A Great Negro Woman Leader*. New York: Macfadden-Bartell, 1966.

Hunton, Addie W., and Kathryn Magnolia Johnson. *Two Colored Women with the American Expeditionary Forces*. New York: AMS Press, 1971.

"Indian Women Join Council." *Baltimore Afro-American*, June 19, 1945.

Jackson, Maurice, and Jacqueline Bacon. *African Americans and the Haitian Revolution: Selected Essays and Historical Documents*. New York: Routledge, 2009.

Jacobs, Sylvia M. "James Emman Kwegyir Aggrey: An African Intellectual in the United States." *Journal of Negro History* 81, no. 1/4 (1996): 47–61.

James, C. L. R. *The Black Jacobins*. 2nd ed. New York: Vintage, 1989.

Johnson, Charles Richard, and Patricia Smith. *Africans in America: America's Journey through Slavery*. San Diego: Harcourt Brace, 1999.

Johnson, Charles Spurgeon, 1893–1956. Mary McLeod Bethune Interview Transcript, ca. 1939. State Archives of Florida, Florida Memory.

Johnson, Karen Ann. *Uplifting the Women and the Race: The Educational Philosophies and Social Activism of Anna Julia Cooper and Nannie Helen Burroughs*. New York: Routledge, 2000.

Jones, Ida. *Mary McLeod Bethune in Washington, D.C.: Activism & Education in Logan Circle*. Charleston, SC: History Press, 2013.

Jones, Jacqueline. *Labor of Love, Labor of Sorrow: Black Women, Work, and the Family, from Slavery to Present*. New York: Basic, 1985.

Kay, Roy. *The Ethiopian Prophecy in Black American Letters*. Gainesville: University Press of Florida, 2011.

Kerr-Ritchie, Jeffrey R. *Rites of August First: Emancipation Day in the Black Atlantic World*. Baton Rouge: Louisiana State University Press, 2007.

Kiesel, Diane. *She Can Bring Us Home: Dr. Dorothy Boulding Ferebee, Civil Rights Pioneer*. Lincoln: University of Nebraska Press, 2015.

Kotsis, Julie. "Urban Design Expert Addresses Anti-Black Racism across City Landscapes." *Windsor Star* (Ontario), September 24, 2020, A4.

La Du, Veronica. "Vivian Carter Mason." Mary McLeod Bethune Council House. National Park Service. Last modified February 25, 2021. https://www.nps.gov/mamc/learn/historyculture/vivian-carter-mason.htm.

Leslie, Grace V., and Michael O. West. "'United, We Build a Free World': The Internationalism of Mary McLeod Bethune and the National Council of Negro Women." In *To Turn the Whole World Over: Black Women and Internationalism*, ed. Keisha N. Blain and Tiffany M. Gill, 192–218. Urbana: University of Illinois Press, 2019.

Lewis, David Levering. *W. E. B. Du Bois: The Fight for Equality and the American Century, 1919–1963*. New York: Henry Holt, 2000.

Li, Yun., Greenwald, Marilyn. *Eunice Hunton Carter: A Lifelong Fight for Social Justice*. New York: Fordham University Press, 2021.

"Liberia Pays Final Tribute to Mrs. Maude Morris." *Baltimore Afro-American*, December 9, 1961.

Little, Kenneth. *African Women in Towns: An Aspect of Africa's Social Revolution*. Cambridge: Cambridge University Press, 1973.

Lochard, Metz T. P. "Parley Ducks Colonial Issue: Delegates Juggle Colonial Question: White, Du Bois Ask Equality of Races." *Chicago Defender*, May 5, 1945.

Luker, Ralph E., and Christopher M. Richardson. *Historical Dictionary of the Civil Rights Movement*. London: Rowman and Littlefield, 2014.

Lulat, Y. G. M. *United States Relations with South Africa: A Critical Overview from the Colonial Period to the Present*. New York: Peter Lang, 2008.

Lynchburg (Va.) Free Negro and Slave Records, 1784–1864. Local Government Records Collection, Lynchburg Court Records. Library of Virginia, Richmond. http://ead.lib.virginia.edu/vivaxtf/view?docId=lva/vi04311.xml.

Manning, Patrick. *The African Diaspora: A History through Culture*. New York: Colombia University Press, 2009.

———. Review of *Africa and the African Diaspora: New Directions of Study*, by Kristin Mann, Edna G. Bay, Isidore Okpewho, Carole Boyce Davies, and Ali A. Mazrui, *Journal of African History* 44, no. 3 (2003): 487–506.

Matthews, Ralph. "President Edwin Barclay Arrives from Africa." *Baltimore Afro-American*, May 29, 1943.

McCabe, Katie, and Dovey Johnson Roundtree. *Justice Older Than the Law: The Life of Dovey Johnson Roundtree*. Jackson: University Press of Mississippi, 2009.

McCluskey, Audrey Thomas. *A Forgotten Sisterhood: Pioneering Black Women Educators and Activists in the Jim Crow South*. London: Rowman and Littlefield, 2014.

McComb, Mary C. *Great Depression and the Middle Class: Experts, Collegiate Youth and Business Ideology, 1929–1941*. New York: Routledge, 2006.

Miller, Dr. D. M. "Williams Party in Visit to Lord Mayor of London: Physicians and Wives Cordially Received by Notables while Touring British Isles." *Chicago Defender*, July 16, 1927.

Mirabal, Nancy Raquel. *Suspect Freedoms: The Racial and Sexual Politics of Cubanidad in New York, 1823–1957*. New York: NYU Press, 2017.

Mitchell, Clarence, RJB 351, Director, District of Columbia Bureau of the National Association for the Advancement of Colored People (NAACP). December 6, 1968. MS, Ralph J. Bunche Oral Histories Collection on the Civil Rights Movement: Ralph J. Bunche Oral Histories Collection (formerly The Civil Rights Documentation Project). Moorland-Spingarn Research Center, Howard University.

Mjagkij, Nina, ed. *Organizing Black America: An Encyclopedia of African American Associations*. New York: Routledge, 2001.

Morrow, John H. "Black Africans in World War II: The Soldiers' Stories." *Annals of the American Academy of Political and Social Science* 632 (2010): 12–25.

"Mrs. Bethune Decorated by Haitian Government: Back in U.S. after Conferences for Haitian Women." *Atlanta Daily World*, July 24, 1949.

"Mrs. Bethune Heads Drive of Women to Aid Haiti Orphans." *Atlanta Daily World*, September 30, 1949.

"Mrs. Bethune: Spingarn Medalist." *Crisis* magazine, July 1935.

"Mrs. Bethune Stricken: Trip to Liberia Sapped Strength." *Chicago Defender*, January 26, 1952.

"Mrs. F. D. Receives 40 Women: Delegates from Many States Confer at White House." *Baltimore Afro-American*, April 9, 1938.

Munro, Angus. "Count Your Blessings, Emancipator Tells All." *Windsor Star* (Ontario), August 4, 1954, 6.

Murphy, Carl. "From Varied Fields: Many Americans Attend Inauguration in Liberia." *Baltimore Afro-American*, January 26, 1952.

Muse, Clifford L. "Howard University and U.S. Foreign Affairs during the Franklin D. Roosevelt Administration, 1933–1945." *Journal of African American History* 87 (Fall 2002): 403–15.

Nathaniel, Ras. *50th Anniversary of his Imperial Majesty Emperor Haile Selassie I: First Visit to the United States (1954–2004)*. Victoria, BC, Canada: Trafford, 2004.

"NCNW Votes Dr. Ferebee Second Term." *Chicago Defender*, November 3, 1951.

Ndlovu, Sifiso, Mammo Muchie, and Chris Landsberg. "Summary of Presentations by the Main Speakers." Edited by Fritz Nganje. *The Influence of the ANC on South Africa's Foreign Policy*. Institute for Global Dialogue, 2012.

"'Negro Should Consider World Problems,' Mrs. Bethune Says: Throws Bombshell into Eclectic Thinking of Some Special Pleaders." *Atlanta Daily World*, May 6, 1945.

Newman, Debra L. *Black History: A Guide to Civilian Records in the National Archives*. Washington, DC: National Archives Trust Fund Board, 1984.

"No World Peace in World of Hate: Arrives in Canada." *Chicago Defender*, July 6, 1946.

"Noted Figures Sign for European Trip." *Chicago Defender*, May 7, 1927.

Okonkwo, Rina. "Adelaide Casely Hayford: Cultural Nationalist and Feminist." *Phylon* 42, no. 1 (1981): 41–51.

Parker, Alison M. *Unceasing Militant: The Life of Mary Church Terrell*. Chapel Hill: University of North Carolina Press, 2020.

"Oral History Interview with Virginia Foster Durr." October 16, 1975. Interview G-0023-3. Southern Oral History Program Collection (#4007) in the Southern Oral History Program Collection, Southern Historical Collection, Wilson Library, University of North Carolina at Chapel Hill.

"Our Opinions: Mrs. Bethune Steps Down, but Not Out." *Chicago Defender*, November 26, 1949.

Parrish, T. Michael, and Thomas W. Cutrer. *Doris Miller, Pearl Harbor, and the Birth of the Civil Rights Movement*. College Station: Texas A&M University Press, 2018.

Patterson, L. J. "National Leaders Meet to Formulate United Platform, to Fight for FEPC." *Baltimore Afro-American*, June 30, 1945.

Plummer, Brenda Gayle. "The Afro-American Response to the Occupation of Haiti, 1915–1934." *Phylon* 43, no. 2 (1982): 125–43.

———. *Rising Wind: Black Americans and U.S. Foreign Affairs, 1935–1960.* Chapel Hill: University of North Carolina Press, 2000.

Phalen, Anthony. "South Africans Disobey Apartheid Laws (Defiance of Unjust Laws Campaign), 1952–1953." Global Nonviolent Action Database. June 11, 2009. https://nvdatabase.swarthmore.edu/content/south-africans-disobey-apartheid-laws-defiance-unjust-laws-campaign-1952-1953.

Puaca, Laura Micheletti. *Searching for Scientific Womanpower: Technocratic Feminism and the Politics of National Security, 1940–1980.* Chapel Hill: University of North Carolina Press, 2014.

Quiroz, Alfonso W. *The Cuban Republic and José Martí: Reception and Use of a National Symbol.* Lanham, MD: Lexington, 2006.

Rabaka, Reiland. *Routledge Handbook of Pan-Africanism.* New York: Routledge, 2020.

Ransby, Barbara. *Eslanda: The Large and Unconventional Life of Mrs. Paul Robeson.* New Haven, CT: Yale University Press, 2014.

Rappaport, Helen. *Encyclopedia of Women Social Reformers.* Vol. 1. Santa Barbara, CA: ABC-CLIO, 2001.

Rasmussen, Frederick N. "Liberty Ships Honored Black in U.S. History." *Baltimore Sun,* March 6, 2004.

Reed, Harry A. "Financing an Early Back-to-Africa Scheme." *Proceedings of the Massachusetts Historical Society* 90 (1978): 103–5.

Renda, Mary A. *Taking Haiti: Military Occupation and the Culture of U.S. Imperialism, 1915–1940.* Chapel Hill: University of North Carolina Press, 2001.

Rief, Michelle. "Thinking Locally, Acting Globally: The International Agenda of African American Clubwomen, 1880–1940." *Journal of African American History* 89, no. 3 (2004): 203–22.

Robertson, Ashley N. "'The Drums of Africa Still Beat in My Heart': The Internationalism of Mary McLeod Bethune and the National Council of Negro Women (1895–1960)." PhD diss., Howard University, 2013.

Robertson, Ashley N. "The Backbone of the Civil Rights Movement: National Council of Negro Women's Role in the Struggle." In *In Spite of the Double Drawbacks: African American Women in History and Culture,* edited by Lopez Matthews, Marshanda Smith, Kenvi Phillips, and Ida E. Jones, 66–74. Charleston, SC: CreateSpace Independent Publishing Platform, 2012.

———. *Mary McLeod Bethune in Florida: Bringing Social Justice to the Sunshine State.* Charleston, SC: Arcadia, 2015.

"Role of Women in National Development." United Nations Economic Commission for Africa (UNECA) Institutional Repository. http://repository.uneca.org/bitstream/handle/10855/13114/Bib-54341.pdf?sequence=1.

Rolinson, Mary G. *Grassroots Garveyism: The Universal Negro Improvement Association in the Rural South, 1920–1927.* Chapel Hill: University of North Carolina, 2007.

Roosevelt, Eleanor. "My Day October 27, 1944." Eleanor Roosevelt Papers Project.

Rouse, Jacqueline Anne. "Out of the Shadow of Tuskegee: Margaret Murray Washington, Social Activism, and Race Vindication." *Journal of Negro History* 81 (winter-autumn 1996): 31–46.

Sanders, Grace Louise. "La voix des femmes: Haitian Women's Rights, National Politics and Black Activism in Port-au-Prince and Montreal, 1934–1986." PhD diss., University of Michigan, 2013.
Saunders, Gail. *Race and Class in the Colonial Bahamas, 1880–1960*. Gainesville: University Press of Florida, 2016.
Scott, Lillian. "Cut Negroes from Nehru Visit Here." *Chicago Defender*, October 15, 1949.
Shaw, Stephanie. "Black Club Women and the Creation of the National Association of Colored Women." *Journal of Women's History* 3 (fall 1991): 10–25.
"Senegal and Guinea, Freedom, The Making of African American Identity: Volume I, 1500–1865." National Humanities Center Toolbox Library: Primary Resources in U.S. History and Literature.
Sherwood, Marika. *Origins of Pan-Africanism: Henry Sylvester Williams, Africa, and the African Diaspora*. London: Routledge, 2012.
Sims-Wood, Janet. *Dorothy Porter Wesley at Howard University: Building a Legacy of Black History*. Charleston, SC: History Press, 2014.
"Sixty Gather to Honor Mrs. Mary Bethune." *Atlanta Daily World*, May 25, 1955.
"Sixty Toast Gold Coast Legislator." *Los Angeles Sentinel*, August 2, 1956.
Smith, Amanda. *An Autobiography: The Story of the Lord's Dealings with Mrs. Amanda Smith, the Colored Evangelist: Containing an Account of Her Life Work of Faith, and Her Travels in America, England, Ireland, Scotland, India, and Africa as an Independent Missionary*. Chicago: Meyer and Brother, 1893.
Smith, Elaine M., and Audrey Thomas McCluskey, eds. *Mary McLeod Bethune: Building a Better World*. Bloomington: Indiana University Press, 1999.
Smith, Michael J. *Red and Black in Haiti: Radicalism, Conflict, and Political Change, 1934–57*. Chapel Hill: University of North Carolina Press, 2009.
Smith, Robert P. "An Exemplary Life: A Tribute to Will Mercer Cook (1903–1987)." *CLA Journal* 31, no. 2 (1987): 246–49.
Smith, Thomas E. *Emancipation without Equality: Pan-African Activism and the Global Color Line*. Amherst: University of Massachusetts Press, 2018.
Spencer, John H. *Ethiopia at Bay: A Personal Account of the Haile Selassie Years*. Hollywood, CA: Tsehai, 2006.
Stanley, Henry Morton. *Through the Dark Continent or The Sources of the Nile around the Great Lakes of Equatorial Africa and down the Livingstone River to the Atlantic Ocean*. London: Low, Marston, Searle and Rivington, 1879.
Stasson, Anneke Helen. "Bowen, John Wesley Edward (1855–1933) Educator and Theologian." Boston University School of Theology. https://www.bu.edu/missiology/missionary-biography/a-c/bowen-john-wesley-edward-1855-1933/.
"Star of Africa to 2 Delegates: President Tubman Confers Honors." *Baltimore Afro-American*, January 26, 1952.
"Starving Africans Sent Food, Cash by N.Y. Council." *Chicago Defender*, February 2, 1946.
Sterne, Emma Gelders. *Mary McLeod Bethune*. New York: Knopf, 1957.
"Sue Bailey Thurman's Lecture in Florida Stimulates Group." *Atlanta Daily World*, June 19, 1936.

"Suffrage Women." LibGuide on Woman Suffrage. University of Bahamas, September 19, 2020. https://cob-bs.libguides.com/wsb

Swan, Quito J. "Bermuda Looks to the East: Marcus Garvey, The UNIA, and Bermuda, 1920–1931." *Wadabagei: A Journal of the Caribbean and Its Diaspora* 13 (spring 2010): 29.

Swindall, Lindsey R. *The Path to the Greater, Freer, Truer World: Southern Civil Rights and Anticolonialism, 1937–1955*. Gainesville: University Press of Florida, 2014.

Taylor, Rebecca Stiles. "Activities of Women's National Organizations: The National Council of Negro Women Registered Seventeen Organizations." *Chicago Defender*, December 2, 1939.

———. "Federated Clubs: National Council Negro Women Selects April as 'World Security Month.'" *Chicago Defender*, April 14, 1945.

Taylor, Ula Yvette. *The Veiled Garvey: The Life and Times of Amy Jacques Garvey*. Chapel Hill: University of North Carolina Press, 2001.

Terborg-Penn, Rosalyn, and Andrea Benton Rushing. *Women in Africa and the African Diaspora: A Reader*. 2nd ed. Washington, DC: Howard University Press, 1996.

Terrell, Mary Church. *A Colored Woman in a White World*. Amherst, NY: Humanity Books, 2005.

Terrell, Mary Church. Mary Church Terrell Papers: Speeches and Writings, -1953; June 13, 1904, Address to be Delivered at the International Congress of Women in Berlin, Germany also German translation. 1904. Manuscript/Mixed Material.

———. Mary Church Terrell Papers: Subject File, -1962; International Council of the Darker Races of the World. -1962, 1884. Manuscript/Mixed Material.

Thomas, Bettye Collier. *Jesus Jobs and Justice: African American Women and Religion*. New York: Knopf, 2010.

Thomas, Charles Walker. *Journal of Negro History* 43, no. 1 (1958): 62–64.

"Thousands Send Wires of Tribute to Bethune Home: Notables Mourn Dr. Bethune." *Chicago Defender*, May 28, 1955.

Thurman, Sue Bailey. "Dress Circle Affairs Highlighted Parley." *Chicago Defender*, June 16, 1945.

"To James Madison from Paul Cuffe, 16 June 1813." Founders Online, National Archives, https://founders.archives.gov/documents/Madison/03-06-02-0375.

Tolbert, Emory J., ed. *Perspectives on the African Diaspora*. 3rd ed. Boston: Houghton Mifflin, 2001.

———. *UNIA and Black Los Angeles: Ideology and Community in the American Garvey Movement*. Los Angeles: Center for Afro-American Studies, University of California, 1980.

Turner, Lorenzo Dow. *Africanisms in the Gullah Dialect*. Columbia: University of South Carolina Press, 2002.

Tuuri, Rebecca. *Strategic Sisterhood: The National Council of Negro Women in the Black Freedom Struggle*. Chapel Hill: University of North Carolina Press, 2018.

Twa, Lindsay J. *Visualizing Haiti in U.S. Culture, 1910–1950*. Burlington, VT: Ashgate, 2014.

"23 Dropped from African Council: Mrs. Bethune Elected to Succeed Robeson." *Baltimore Afro-American*, May 1, 1948.
United States Delegation, United Nations Conference on International Organization. 1945, San Francisco, California. United Nations Conference on International Organization consultants and associates, ca. May 1945. W. E. B. Du Bois Papers (MS 312). Special Collections and University Archives, University of Massachusetts Amherst Libraries.
Verna, Chantalle F., and Paulette Poujol Oriol. "The Ligue Feminine d'Action Sociale: An Interview with Paulette Poujol Oriol." *Journal of Haitian Studies* 17, no. 1 (2011): 246–57.
"U.S. Ambassador to Haiti Resigns." *Los Angeles Sentinel*, July 5, 1951.
Voyages: The Trans-Atlantic Slave Trade Database. Emory University, 2008. www.slavevoyages.org.
"The WAAC—The Girl Who Wouldn't Be Left Behind." *Aframerican Woman's Journal* 3, nos. 1–2 (summer-fall 1942).
Walters, Ronald. *Pan-Africanism in the African Diaspora: An Analysis of Modern Afrocentric Movements*. Detroit, MI: Wayne State University Press, 1993.
Washington, Mrs. Booker T., and Mrs. H. L. McCrory. "International Council Elects at Convention: Gathering of Darker Women's Conference in Washington Comes to an End." *Chicago Defender*, August 18, 1923.
Wasniewski, Matthew Andrew. *Women in Congress, 1917–2006*. Washington, DC: US Government Printing Office, 2006.
Watts, Jill. *The Black Cabinet: The Untold Story of African Americans and Politics during the Age of Roosevelt*. New York: Grove Atlantic, 2020.
"We Need Love—Mrs. Bethune." *Baltimore Afro-American*, November 25, 1950.
White, Deborah Gray. *Too Heavy a Load: Black Women in Defense of Themselves, 1894–1994*. New York: Norton, 1999.
White, Walter. *A Rising Wind*. Garden City, NY: Doubleday, Doran, 1945.
Williams-Pulfer, Kim. "'When Bain Town Woman Catch a Fire, Even the Devil Run': The Bahamian Suffrage Movement as National and Cultural Development." *Voluntas: International Journal of Voluntary and Nonprofit Organizations* 27, no. 3 (2016): 1472–93.
Wilmore, Gayraud S. *Pragmatic Spirituality: The Christian Faith through an Africentric Lens*. New York: NYU Press, 2004.
Woodard, Maurice C. "Merze Tate." *PS: Political Science and Politics* 38, no. 1 (2005): 101–2.
"World's Women Study Mutual Problems in Haiti." *Norfolk Journal and Guide*, April 29, 1950.
Wright, Richard, Gunnar Myrdal, and Amritjit Singh. *The Color Curtain: A Report on the Bandung Conference*. Jackson: University Press of Mississippi, 1995.
Zimmerman, Jonathan. *Innocents Abroad: American Teachers in the American Century*. Cambridge, MA: Harvard University Press, 2009.

Index

Achimota School, James Aggrey, 121
Acquah, Joseph, 86
Ad Hoc Committee of Great Floridians, 5
Addams, Jane, 37
Aframerican Woman's Journal, 7, 37, 46, 47–50, 53, 54, 71, 92; China, 49; and Cuba, 49; Cuba trip, 45, 46, 50, 51, 89; Division of Cultural Relations (State Department), 49; from the President, 47; Haiti, 7, 49; Hubert Herring Seminar, 48; India, 7, 49; International Program of Negro Women, 48; Latin America, 7; McCrorey, Mary, 49; Philippines, 7, 49; Puerto Rico, 49; Simmons, Virginia, 48; Smith College, 49; Thurman, Sue Bailey, 4, 43–52, 89; Virgin Islands, 49; Wesley, Dorothy Porter, 8, 49, 70; Women's National Press Club, 49; World War II, 69
Africa, 7, 32, 34, 41, 44, 78, 83, 134, 138, 140; Cameroon, 120; Colonization, 3, 10, 16, 22, 31, 32, 65, 66, 72, 78, 80; Council on African Affairs (CAA), 66, 72–76; Dark Continent, 12; Decolonization, 65, 74, 78, 84, 86; Gold Coast, 86, 110; Liberia, 8; Trip to Africa, 112
African Academy of Arts and Research, 109
African Cuban Society, 142
African Food Fund, 74
African Methodist Episcopal (AME) Church, 17–18
African National Congress, 67; Defiance of Unjust Laws Campaign, 119
Afro American, 112
Afro-Canadians, 126, 127, 142
Afro Cuban Society, 142
Afro Cubans, 7, 44–47, 50, 91, 110, 112

Aggrey, James, 120; Achimota School, 121; "Father of African Education," 121
Alabama, 14
Alexander, Sadie T. M., 37, 42
All-India Women's Congress (AIWC), 47, 48
Alpha Kappa Alpha Sorority, 39; Ferebee, Dorothy, as member, 131; Hunton, Addie, as member, 39; Sampson, Edith, as member, 133
Amanda Smith Club, 27
American Association for the United Nations and Eichelberger, Clark M, 140
American Association of University Women, 79
American Colonization Society, 112; Falola, Toyin, 113; Njoku, Raphael Chijioke, 113
American Council on African Education, 86; founded by Orizu, Nwafor, 85
American Council on Race Relations, 81
Amherstburg Freedom Museum, 6
Anderson, Marian, 74
Apartheid, 119, 142
Aponte Rebellion, 46, 99
Ashanti, 110
Ashburn, Eudora, 39
Asians, 33, 94
Asociación Cultural Femenina (ACF Women's Cultural Association), founded by Echegoyen, Ana and Serro, Consuela, 44
Associated Negro Press, 114
Association for the Study of Negro Life and History, 20, 33–34, 50
Astolfi, Valdes, 46
Atlanta Daily World, 70

Atlantic Charter, 67, 72
Atlantic slave trade, 94
Awards: Haitian Medal of Honor and Merit, 8, 89, 99, 104; Spingarn Award, 38, 78
Azikiwe, Flora, 134
Azikiwe, Nnamdi, Nigeria, 134

Back to Africa movement, 117, 141
Bahamas, 4, 8; Carver Garden Club, 122–124; *Daily Tribune,* 140; Daughters of the Improved Benevolent and Protective Order of Elks of the World, 123; House of Assembly, 123; Industrial Home for Boys, 123; Ingraham, Mary, 123; Johnson, Doris, 123, 124; Lockhart, Eugenia, 123; National Council of Women, 12, 39, 114, 124; Neville, Robert Arthur Ross, 123; Sands, Stafford, 123; Suffrage, 123, 142; Symonette, Georgiana, 123; Toote, Thaddeus, 123; Walker, Mabel, 123
Baltimore Afro-American, 44, 76, 137
Bandung Conference, 33
Barbados, 8, 88, 123
Barclay, Edwin, 52
Barnett, Claude E., 95, 114, 115
Barry, Marion, 138
Battle, Samuel J., 52
Belgium, Queen Mother Elizabeth, 137
Berlin Conference, 16, 65
Bermuda, 38
Bethune, Albert McLeod, 19
Bethune, Albert McLeod, Jr., 5, 50
Bethune, Albertus, 19
Bethune, Donald, 111
Bethune Beach, 5
Bethune-Cookman College, 5, 43, 50, 83, 84, 86, 93, 96, 111, 114, 117, 118, 121; Southeastern Conference, 105; Spirit of Freedom pageant, 125
Big Three Unity for Colonial Freedom Rally, 75
Blair House, 52
Black Cabinet, 107; National Youth Administration, 40, 41
Black Liberation, 89
Bond, Max, 117
Bond, Ruth Clement, 104
Booker T. Washington Institute, Wynn, Walter C., 114

Bouchereau, Madeleine Sylvain, Congress of Haitian Women, 131
Bowen, Irene Smallwood, 13
Bowen, John Wesley Edward, 12; Congress on Africa, 13; Gammon Theological Seminary, 13; Methodist Episcopal Church, 13; Smith, Thomas E., 13; Stewart Missionary Foundation for Africa, 13
Boy's Towns of Italy, 137
Brazil, 23, 33
British American Association of Colored Brothers, Canada, 125; International Women's Committee, 127
British Guiana, 8, 88, 91
Brooks, Elizabeth Carter, 29
Brooks, W. Sampson, 115
Brown, Charlotte Hawkins, 32; National Conference of Negro Leaders, 84; National Council of Negro Women, 39, 84
Brown, Hallie Q., 29, 37
Brown, Jeanetta Welch, 53, 79, 136
Brunson, Takkara, 44, 111
Brutus, Timoleon, 100
Bunche, Ralph, 5, 52, 90, 95, 100, 109
Burma, 43, 78
Burroughs, Nannie Helen, 32; International Council of Women of the Darker Races, 34
Butcher, Margaret Just. See Wormly, Margaret Just
Butler, Nicholas Murray, 52

Cala, Portuondo, 46
Cameroon, 120
Canada, 110, 122, 124–128; Afro-Canadians, 126, 127; British American Association of Colored Brothers, 125, 127; Emancipation Day celebration, 124–125, 127; Hour-a-Day Study Club, 126, 127; Harding-Davis, Elise, 126, 127; Prince Edward Hotel, 126; Sandwich First Baptist Church, 126; Twenty-Second Annual Emancipation Parade, 126–127; Underground Railroad monuments, 126; Windsor Emancipation Day, 125; *Windsor Star,* 140
Canadian Association for the Advancement of Colored People (CAACP), Jenkins, James, 125

Canadians of African descent, 124
Cape Town, South Africa, 74
Caribbean, 40
Carmichael, Stokely, 138
Carney, Judith, 14
Carroll-Abbing, John Patrick, 137
Carter, Elizabeth C., 34; International Council of Women of the Darker Races (ICWDR), 14
Carter, Eunice H., *See* Hunton, Eunice H.
Carver, George Washington, 38, 122
Carver Garden Club, 122–123
Cary, Lott, 112, 113
Central America, 95
Ceylon, *See* Sri Lanka
Charles, Joseph D., 99, 104
Charter for African Freedom, 75
Chicago Conference on Africa, 18
Chicago Defender, 2, 4, 32, 50, 51, 52, 68, 76, 80, 81, 82, 97, 98, 101, 104, 105, 110, 112, 116, 117, 118, 120, 122, 124, 125, 126, 128, 133, 140, 141
Chicago Exposition, Women's Archives Exhibition, 49
Childrens' Breakfast Centres, Trinidad, 92
China, 49, 54, 78, 85
Citizens of New York City, 52
Civil Improvement Club, 27
Civil Rights Movement, 7, 133
Clark, Tom, 76
Clark-Lewis, Elizabeth, 4
Clayton, William L., 79
Club Cubano Inter-Americano, 91
Coasley, (Mrs.) John, 91
Cold War, 97, 98, 116, 120
Cole, Henry B., 115
College Women's Club, Liberia, 134
Colonialism, 77, 97
Colonization, 7, 10, 16, 22, 32, 65, 78, 81, 113, 142
Colored Women's League of Washington, DC (CWL), 24
Communism, 76, 77
Communist Party, and Jones, Claudia, 77; Robeson, Paul, 76, 77; *The Worker,* 77
Congress of Haitian Women, 129, 131
Congress on Africa, 13
Convention People's Party, Ghana, 120; Nkrumah, Kwame, 120
Cook, Mercer, 91
Cooper, Anna Julia, 1, 24
Cooper, Jeanette L., Liberian Women's Social and Political Movement, 93
Costa Rica Star (Estrella de Costa Rica), 109
Costigan-Wagner Anti-Lynching Bill, 40
Coterie of Social Workers of Trinidad & Tobago, 91; Childrens' Breakfast Centres, 92; Jeffers, Audrey, 92; Saint Mary's Home for Blind Girls and Women, 92
Council of Jewish and Catholic Women, 79
Council on African Affairs (CAA), 66, 72–76, 77, 78, 84, 87; Big Three Unity for Colonial Freedom Rally, 75; Charter for African Freedom, 75; Conference on Africa—New Perspectives, 73; Help Africa Day, 74; Hunton, William A., 72; *New Africa,* 72; Robeson, Paul, 72, 76; Subversive organization, 76, 77; Yergan, Max, 72, 76–77
Council on Foreign Relations, 49
Crisis Magazine, 38, 68
Cuba, 4, 38, 49, 50–54, 91, 110, 129; Aponte Rebellion, 46, 99; Astolf, Valdes, 46; Club Cubano Inter-Americano, 91, 110–112; Echegoyen, Ana, 46, 47; Gomez, Maximo, 119; Grillo, Evelio, 111; Grillo, Sylvia, 45; Grillo, Raphael, 111; Grinan, Jose, 45; Hughes, Langston, 51; Maceo, Antonio, 119; Martí, José, 119; 100th Birthday, 119; Ortiz, Fernando, 50; Ostend Manifesto, 119; Partido Revolucionario Cubano, 119; Pinto, Angel, 46; Platt Amendment, 120; Seminar on Goodwill to Cuba, 49; Society of Afro-Cubans, 37, 50, 142; Society of Afro-Cuban Studies, 50; Thurman, Sue Bailey, 44; Tucker, Nora R., 110; Urrutia, Gustavo, 51
Cuban American Goodwill Association, 44; Grillo, Calá Henry, 110–111; Planos, Celia, 111; Portuondo, Pedro, 110–111
Cuban Society of Letters, 110, 111
Curtis, Helen, Liberia, 29, 30
Curtis, James L., Liberia, 29

Daily Tribune (Nassau, Bahamas), 140
Daniel, Constance E. H., 99, 105

Dark Continent, 12
Daughters of the Improved Benevolent and Protective Order of Elks of the World, 123
Davis, Mamie, 80
Davis, Sr., Benjamin O., 115
Daytona Beach Morning Journal, 122
Daytona Literary and Industrial School for the Training of Negro Girls, 19
Death, 140
Declaration on the Granting of Independence to Colonial Countries and Peoples, 84
Decolonization, 1, 3, 7
DeCourcy, William E., 100
Defiance of Unjust Laws Campaign, African National Congress, 119
Delany, Martin, 31
Delinquent Home for Colored Girls, Ocala, Florida, 27, 102
Delta Sigma Theta Sorority, members: Alexander, Sadie T.M., 37, 42; Brown, Hallie Q., 37; Height, Dorothy Irene, 136; Murphy, Vashti Turley, 37; Terrell, Mary Church, 37
De Priest, Oscar, 52
Diaspora, 2, 3, 6, 7–10, 15, 19, 22, 26, 30, 34, 35, 45, 65, 66, 67, 94, 98, 101, 107–110, 117, 118, 120, 122, 127, 128, 129, 140, 141, 142
Dickerson, Addie, 32, 35
Dies, Martin, 77
Discrimination, 81
Division of Negro Affairs, 7; National Youth Administration, 40, 41, 102, 106
Double V campaign, 71; Hoover, J. Edgar, 68
Douglass, Frederick, 70; Haiti, 106–107
Dove, Mabel, 134; Parliament, 135
Drake, St. Clair, 8, 45
Du Bois, W. E. B., 31, 33, 38, 68, 74, 75; Father of Pan Africanism, 3; NAACP Director of Special Research, 78; Pan-African congresses, 3; San Francisco Conference, 3; University of Massachusetts Amherst Libraries, 6; United Nations Charter, 7, 78, 80–83, 85
Dudley, Edward, Liberia, 112, 115
Dudley, Rae, 115
Dunham, Katherine, 75

Eastern bloc, 97
Echegoyen, Ana, 44, 46, 47; Cuban Negro Problem, 45

Eichelberger, Clark M., American Association for the United Nations, 140
Emancipation Day, Canada, 124–125
Emancipation Proclamation, 125
England, 31
Esedebe, P. Olisanwuche, 2, 17
Espionage and Smith Acts, 68
Estimé, Dumarsais, 101, 106; Haitian International Exposition, 99
Estimé, Lucienne H., 99, 100, 102, 103, 105
Ethiopia, 31, 38, 40, 54, 72, 74, 75, 109; Brown, Jeanette Welch, 53; Charter for African Freedom, 75; Selassie, Tenagnework, 53; Tesemma, Gatahoun, 53
Ethiopian Legation, 53
Ethiopian women, 7
Europe, 2, 18, 31, 35, 78, 122, 130, 136, 137
European Tour with a Purpose, 130, 136, 137
Evans, Stephanie, 20
Evanti, Lillian, 114

Fafunwa, Babs, 121
Falola, Toyin, 113
Family, 10–21, 23; McLeod, Beauregord (brother), 11; McLeod, Julia (sister), 11; McLeod, Kissie (sister), 11; McLeod, Patsy McIntosh (mother), 11; McLeod, Samuel (father); McLeod, William T. (brother), 11
Father of African American Education, 121
Ferebee, Dorothy, 129–132, 136; Alpha Kappa Alpha Sorority, 131; High Commission of Germany, 130, 132; International Council of Women, 132; Mississippi Health Project, 131; National Council of Negro Women, 80; Nine Point Program, 131; United Nations Day, 129, 131; United Nations Week, 132
First Black Republic, Haiti, 35
First Lady of Negro America, 1, 42, 140
First Pan-African Christian Church Conference, 13
Fiske, Mary McCritty, Liberian Women's Social and Political Movement, 93
Flemming, Sheila, 34
Florida, 15, 27; Ad Hoc Committee of Great Floridians, 5; Daytona Literary and Industrial School for the Training of Negro Girls, 19; Kirby, Edmund, 5; McLeod Hospital, 19; Statuary Hall, 5

Florida Federation of Colored Women, 27, 102
Floyd, Addie Hunton, *See* Hunton, Addie
Fordham University, 86
Fort, Lamar, United States Economic Mission, 117–118
Fowler, John, 5
France, 31, 109
Frazier, E. Franklin, 15
Free World, 65
Freeman, Benjamin Green, 93
French Revolution, 98

Gammon Theological Seminary, 13
Gandhi, Mahatma, 94, 96, 118; Nonviolent Resistance Movement, 43
Garoute, Augustine, 105
Garvey, Amy Ashwood, 2, 74
Garvey, Amy Jacques, 2
Garvey, Marcus, 31, 94; Back to Africa movement, 4, 18; *Negro World*, 49
Gatheru, Reuel John Mugo, 121
General Agreement for Technical Assistance and Cooperation, 116
General Federation of Women's Clubs, 79
George, Sarah Simpson, 92, 93, 107, 114; Liberian Women's Social and Political Movement, 89
Georgia, 14, 15, 19
Germany, 31; Ferebee, Dorothy, 130, 132; High Commission of Germany, 130, 132; National Council of German Women, 137
Ghana (Gold Coast), 135; Convention People's Party, 110, 120; Nkrumah, Kwame, 110, 120
Ghana News Agency, 135
Giddings, Paula, 22
Girls' Vocation School, 29; Hayford, Adelaide Smith Casely, 28, 30
Gold Coast (Ghana), 86, 93, 110, 120, 86
Gold Coast Legislative Assembly, Dove, Mabel, 134
Gomez, Maximo, 119
Gomez, Michael, 15
Good Will and Investigation Tour to Europe, 30
Great Depression, 39, 40
Greece, 132
Grillo, Calá Henry, 44, 110, 111
Grillo, Evelio, 111

Grillo, Rafael, 111
Grillo, Sylvia, 45
Grinan, Jose, 45
Gullah/Geechee Cultural Heritage Corridor, 3, 15
Gullah language, baby talk or broken English, 15

Haines Normal and Industrial School, 18
Haiti, 3, 4, 22, 24; Bond, Ruth Clement, 104; Brutus, Timoleon, 100; Charles, Joseph D., 99, 104; Congress of Haitian Women, 129, 131; Cook, Mercer, 91; DeCourcy, William E., 100; Ecole République d'Argentine, 101; Estime, Dumarsais, 99, 101, 106; Estime, Lucienne H., 99, 100, 102, 103, 105; First Black Republic, 35; Garoute, Augustine, 105; International Council of Women of the Darker Races, 7, 32, 33, 34, 49, 89, 91, 98–107, 109, 122, 129, 130, 132, 133, 134, 142; Lescot, Elie, 48; Ligue Feminine d'Action Sociale, 102, 103, 105, 106, 107; Magloire, (Mrs.) Paul, 133; McCrorey, Mary L., 48; Oriole, Paulette, 103; Refuge Home for Orphan Children, 105; School Republique of Venezuela, 102; Sunshine Orphanage, 102; Verna, Chantalle, 203; Vieux, Andre, 102; Zebhiri, Mauclair, 133
Haitian International Exposition, 104; Estimé, Dumarsais, 99, 101, 106
Haitian Medal of Honor and Merit, 8, 89, 99, 104
Haitian Revolution, 98, 99, 104
Haitian women, 102, 103, 104, 132, 140; voting rights, 2, 105, 106
Handy, W. C., 126
Hansberry, William Leo, 52
Harding, Rachel Madison, 126
Harding-Davis, Elise, 126, 127
Harold V. Lucas Foundation, 5
Harper, Frances, 24
Harriet Tubman Club of Boston, 24
Harriman, J. Borden, 48
Harris, Ethel Ramos, 48; National Council of Negro Women, 131
Harris, Joseph E., 94
Harris, Sheena, 33
Hatcher, (Mrs.) Bernard, 91

Havana Daily, 46
Hayford, Adelaide Smith Casely, 30; Girls' Vocation School, 28, 29; International Council of Women of the Darker Races, 32; Sierra Leone, 28; United Negro Improvement Association, 28
Hayford, J. E. Casely, 28
Haynes, William, New England Baptist Convention, 75
Hegel, Georg, 12
Height, Dorothy Irene, 133, 135–138; Delta Sigma Theta Sorority, 136; European Tour with a Purpose, 130, 136, 137; National Council of Negro Women, 131 133, 135–138; *Open Wide the Freedom Gates*, 135; Young Women's Christian Association, 135, 136
Help Africa Day, 74
Herskovits, Melville J., 15
Higgins, Cleo, 5
Higgins, Mame Mason, 92, 93
High Commission of Germany, 130, 132
Hitler, Adolf, 67
Hobby, Oveta Culp, 69, 70
Hoover, J. Edgar, Espionage and Smith Acts, 68; Double V Campaign, 68
Hope, Lugenia, International Council of Women of the Darker Races, 33
Horne, Lena, 74
Hospitalization, 44
Hour-a-Day Study Club, Canada, 126
House Un-American Activities Committee (HUAC), 76, 77
Houston, Charles Hamilton, 77; National Conference of Negro Leaders, 84
Howard University, 4, 86, 89; Bunche, Ralph, 5, 52, 90, 95, 100, 109; Cook, Mercer, 90, 91; Hansberry, William Leo, 52; Houston, Charles Hamilton, 77, 84; Johnson, Mordecai, 84, 95; Locke, Alaine, 90; Logan, Rayford, 52, 84, 133; Moorland-Spingarn Research Center, 90; Rocabruna, Angel Suarez, 91; Slowe, Lucy Diggs, 40, 90; Tate, Merze, 8, 90; Thurman, Howard, 43, 44; Thurman, Sue Bailey, 4, 37, 43–52, 89; Wesley, Dorothy Porter, 7, 8, 49, 70, 90, 133; Wormly, Margaret, 8, 90
Hubert Herring Seminar, Mexico, 48
Hughes, Langston, 51

Hunton, Addie: Black troops, 42; France, 28; International Council of Women of the Darker Races, 32, 34, 35; Johnson, Kathryn Magnolia, 28; National Association for the Advancement of Colored People, 28; National Association of Colored Women, 28; National Council of Negro Women, 28, 39, 42; World War I, 28
Hunton, Eunice, 74; National Council of Negro Women, 7, 41, 80, 131; United Nations Observer, 131
Hunton, William Alphaeus, Sr.: Council on African Affairs, 72; Young Men's Christian Association, 42

Illness, 44, 116
Imperialism, 78, 90, 95, 97
The Independent, 24
Independent India, 95–96
India, 7, 43, 49, 78, 89, 94–98, 132, 134; All-India Women's Congress (AIWC), 47, 48; India Emergency Food Aid Act, 98; Nehru, Jawaharlal, 95, 96; Non-Aligned Movement, 97
Indian Independence movement, 72
Indiana University Archives, William V. S. Tubman Papers, 6
Industrial Home for Boys, Bahamas, 123
Ingraham, Mary, 123
International Council of Women of the Darker Races (ICWDR), 6, 22, 23, 24, 32–36, 44, 137; Africa, 7, 34; Brazil, 23, 33; Brown, Charlotte Hawkins, 32; Burroughs, Nanie Helen, 32, 34; Carter, Elizabeth C., 34; Cuba, 3; Dickerson, Addie, 32, 35; Haiti, 3, 7, 24, 33–35; Hayford, Adelaide Casely, 32; Hope, Lugenia, 33; Hunton, Addie, 32, 34, 35; India, 3, 7, 43, 85, 94, 96; Liberia, 3, 23, 33; Nannie Helen Burroughs National Training School, 32, 34; Philippines, 7, 23, 33; South Africa, 23; Sri Lanka (Ceylon), 32; Talbert, Mary, 29, 32, 35; Terrell, Mary Church, 32; Washington, Margaret Murray, 32, 35; West Indies, 32; Women's International League for Peace and Freedom, 35
International Congress of Women Congress, Berlin, Germany, and Terrell, Mary Church, 26

International Council of Women of the World, 31, 137; Ferebee, Dorothy, 132
International Program of Negro Women, 48
International Relations Committee, 8, 89, 90, 98, 133
International Women's Committee, Canada, and British American Association of Colored Brothers, Canada, 125
International Women's Year Conference, 138
Internationalism, 90
Israel, 109
Italy, 31, 40, 137

Jacks, James W., Missouri Press Association, 24
Jamaica, 8, 88, 91, 94, 123
James, C. L. R., 98
Jeffers, Audrey, 92; Coterie of Social Workers of Trinidad and Tobago, 91
Jenkins, James, Canada, 125
Jim Crow, 20, 26, 47, 67, 68, 96, 97, 117, 118
Johnson, Charles Spurgeon, 12, 13, 124
Johnson, Doris, 123
Johnson, James Weldon, 68
Johnson, Kathryn Magnolia, 28
Johnson, Mordecai, 84, 95
Jones, Claudia, and Communist Party, 77; Deportation, 77; McCarran Act, 77
Joyner, Marjorie, 121–122
Junta Femenine de Beneficencia, Panama, and Ladies Welfare Group, 109

Keller, Helen, 37
Kendall Institute, 19
Kenya, and Mau Mau movement, 72
Kinard, Joy, 4
King, Charles D.B., 5, 52
King, Jr., Martin Luther, 135
Kirby, Edmund, 5
Ku Klux Klan, 19

La Asociación Cultural Femenina, 46, 47
Ladies Welfare Group, 109
Lady Astor, 2
LaGuardia, Fiorello H., 52, 53
Lampkin, Daisy, 39, 77
Laney, Lucy Craft, Haines Normal and Industrial School, 18–19

Latin America, 7, 47, 49, 54
Lescot, Elie, 48
Lewis, David Levering, 82
Liberia, 3, 4, 7, 8, 14, 17, 23, 30, 33, 74, 85, 92, 109, 112–118, 122, 130, 134, 142; Ambassador to, 110, 113; American Colonization Society, 112–113; Barclay, Edwin, 52; Bond, Max, 117; Booker T. Washington Institute, 114; Brooks, W. Sampson, 115; College Women's Club, 134; Department of Public Instruction, 134; Dudley, Edward, 112, 115; Dudley, Rae, 115; Fort, Lamar, 117–118; General Agreement for Technical Assistance and Cooperation, 116; George, Sarah Simpson, 89, 92, 93, 107, 114; King, C.D.V., 52; Land of Opportunity, 116; Monrovia, 29, 113, 114, 115; Monrovia College, 115; National Council of Women of Liberia, 114; Order of the Star of Africa Commander Cross (Star of Africa), 115; Powell, Jr., Adam Clayton, 53; Simpson, Clarance L., 140; Stokes, Anson Phelps, 53; Tolbert, William R., 113; Tubman, Antoinette, 113; Tubman William V. S., 52, 53, 112–114, 115, 116; United States Economic Mission, 115; University of Liberia, 117; West, John, 117; Yergan, Max, 53
Liberian Women's Social and Political Movement, 115; Cooper, Jeanette L., 93; George, Sarah Simpson, 89, 93, 107, 114; Fiske, Mary McCritty, 93
Liberty ships, Douglass, Frederick, 70; SS *Harriet Tubman*, 70, 71, 129; Washington, Booker T., 70
Library of Congress, 6
Lifting as We Climb, National Association of Colored Women (NACW), 24, 30, 103
Ligue Feminine d'Action Sociale, 102, 106, 107; Garoute, Augustine, 105; Oriole, Paulette, 103
Lincoln University, 86, 121
Livingstone College, 121
Locke, Alaine, 90
Lockhart, Eugenia, 123
Locklear, Senorita, 5
Logan, Rayford, 52, 133; National Conference of Negro Leaders, 84
Louisiana, 14
Lucas, Harold V., 5

Maceo, Antonio, 119
MacLeish, Archibald, 79
MacLeod, Edith, 31
Madam C. J. Walker's School of Beauty Culture, 93
Magloire, (Mrs.) Paul, 133
Malaysia, 78
Mallory, Arenia, 42
Manning, Patrick, 15
March on Washington, 138
Martí, José, Partido Revolucionario Cubano, 119
Marxism, 77
Mary McLeod Bethune Council House National Historic Site (DC), 4, 5, 134; Mason, Vivian Carter, 132
Mary McLeod Bethune Foundation National Historic Site (FL), 5, 140
Mary McLeod Bethune Statue, 5, 138
Mason, Vivian Carter, 132–135, 136, 138; Civil Rights Movement, 133; National Council of Negro Women, 90, 130, 131, 132–135; International Relations Committee, 133; New York City Department of Welfare, 132
Maxwell, Irene E, 39
Mau Mau movement, 72
Mbadiwe, Kingsley Ozuomba, African Academy of Arts and Research, 109
McCarran Act, 77
McCrorey, Mary L., 49
McLeod, Beauregord (brother), 11
McLeod, Julia (sister), 11
McLeod, Kissie (sister), 11
McLeod, Patsy McIntosh (mother), 11, 14, 141
McLeod, Samuel (father), 11
McLeod, Samuel (brother), Jr., 124
McLeod, Satira (sister), 124
McLeod, William T. (brother), 11
McLeod Hospital, 19
Medal of Honor and Merit, 8, 89, 99, 104
Methodist Episcopal Church, 13
Mexico, 48
Miles, Margaret, 5
Miller, Doris "Dorie," 67
Ming, Wei Tae, 85
Mississippi, 27, 131
Mississippi Health Project, National Council of Negro Women, 131

Missouri Press Association, Jacks, James W., 24
Monrovia, Liberia, 113, 114
Monrovia College, 115
Monrovia Council, 134
Montgomery Bus Boycott, 135
Moody, Harold, 72
Moody Bible College, 16, 108, 112
Moorland-Spingarn Research Center, 6, 90
Morehouse, College, 86
Morris, Maude A., 114
Morrow, John H., 66
Msezane, Edith Nono, South Africa, 134
Murphy, Carl, 112, 115
Murphy, Vashti Turley, 37
My Day, Roosevelt, Eleanor, 93

Nannie Helen Burroughs National Training School, 32, 34
National Archives for Black Women's History, 5, 6
National Association for the Advancement of Colored People, 28, 39, 125; Board of Directors, 78; San Francisco Conference, 78, 79, 80, 81, 84, 85; Spingarn Award, 38, 78; Terrell, Mary Church, 25; United Nations charter invitation, 78–83; White, Walter, 3, 78, 80, 81–83, 85, 95 109
National Association of Colored Graduate Nurses, 39
National Association of Colored Women (NACW), 6, 22, 23, 24–31, 39, 44, 123; Colored Women's League of Washington, DC (CWL), 24; Fifteenth Biennial Convention, 29; Good Will and Investigation Tour to Europe, 30; Harper, Frances, 24; Harriet Tubman Club of Boston, 24; Hunton, Addie, 28; Lifting as We Climb, 24, 30, 103, 123; National Council of German Women, 137; National Federation of Afro-American Women (NFAAW), 24; National Notes, 25; Peace and Foreign Relations Department, 28; Semper Fidelis Club, Birmingham, Alabama, 24; Talbert, Mary, 29, 32, 38; Terrell, Mary Church, 25; Thirteenth Biennial Convention, 28; Tuskegee Women's Clubs, 24; Wells, Ida B., 24; Woman's Musical and Literary Club, Springfield, Missouri, 24; Yates, Josephine Silone, 24

National Baptist Convention, Women's Auxiliary, 39
National Citizens Committee, 131
National Conference of Negro Leaders, 84
National Council of German Women, 137
National Council of Negro Women, 5, 9, 28, 129; Advisory Council for the Women's Interests Section, 70; *Aframerican Woman's Journal,* 7, 37, 43, 45, 46, 47–50; Alexander, Sadie T., 42; Ashburn, Eudora, 39; Bahamas, 4; Barbados, 8, 88; Barry, Marion, 138; Belgium, 137; Boys' Towns of Italy, 137; British Guiana, 8, 88, 91; Brown, Charlotte Hawkins, 39; Brown, Jeanetta Welch, 53, 79, 136; Carmichael, Stokely, 138; Coasey (Mrs.) John, 91; Cook, Mercer, 91; Cuba, 4, 37, 38, 44, 50, 51, 89; Daniel, Constance, 99, 105; Davis, Mamie, 80; Dickerson, Addie W., 32, 35, 40; European Tour with a Purpose, 130, 136; Ferebee, Dorothy, 80, 129–132, 138, 136; Five Year Plan, 47; Founding of, 7; Haiti, 4, 98–101, 131; Harris, Ethel Ramos, 48, 131; Headquarters (DC), 29, 90; Height, Dorothy, 130, 131, 133, 135–138; Higgins, Mame Mason, 92, 93; Howard University, 8, 89–90, 91; Hunton, Addie, 4, 28, 39, 42; Hunton, Eunice, 41, 42, 80, 131; International Night, 90, 91; International Program of Negro Women, 48; International Relations Committee, 8, 89, 90, 98, 133; Jamaica, 8, 88; Junior Council members, 131; Lampkin, Daisy, 39; Liberia, 4; Logan, Rayford, 52, 84, 133; Mallory, Arenia, 42; Mason, Vivian Carter, 90, 130, 131, 132–135, 136, 138; Maxwell, Irene E., 39; McCrorey, Mary L., 49; Mississippi Health Project, 131; National Citizens' Committee, 131; National Association for the Advancement of Colored People, 79, 129, 131, 133, 136; National Council of German Women, 137; National Council of Women, 12, 39, 114, 124; Nine Point Program, 131; Non-Governmental organization member, 85; Pan American Day, 133; Pandit, Vijaya, 4, 5, 7, 85, 89; Ponder, Fannye Ayre, 99; Riddle, Estelle M., 91, 92; Rocabruna, Angel Suarez, 91; Roosevelt, Eleanor, 41, 42; Seminar of Goodwill to Cuba, 49; Simmons, Virginia, 48; Slowe, Lucy Diggs, 40, 90; Smith, Christine, 39; Staupers, Mabel Keaton, 39; Tate, Merze, 8; *Telefact,* 95; Terrell, Mary Church, 4, 27, 37, 39, 40, 109; Thurman, Sue Bailey, 4, 37, 43–52, 80; Trinidad, 8, 88, 91, 92, 123; United Nations Charter denied, 79; United Nations Commission on the Status of Women, 130; United Nations Day, 129, 131, 133, 136; United States Agency for International Development (USAID)—African Bureau, 138; Welcome, Verda, 91, 131; Wesley, Dorothy Porter, 7, 8, 49, 70, 133; White, Walter, 78; Williamson, Florence K., 40; Women United to Help Understand and Help Peoples of Africa, 133; World Community Night, 85; World Health Day, 133; World Security Month, 79; World War II, 7; Young Women's Christian Association (YWCA), 38

National Council of Women, 12, 39, 114, 124
National Council of Women of Liberia, 114
National Federation of Afro-American Women (NFAAW), 24
National League of Women's Voters, 79
National Negro Youth Congress, 73
National Notes, 25
National Youth Administration, 37, 42, 73, 90, 102, 108; Black Cabinet, 40; Division of Negro Affairs, 7, 40–41, 106, 111
Negro History Week, 33; Omega Psi Phi Fraternity, 33; Woodson, Carter G., 38, 109
Negro World, 49, 94
Nehru, Jawaharlal, 98; Independent India, 95–96
New Africa, 72
New Deal, 40
New England Baptist Convention, 75
New Negro, 17, 51
New York Herald Tribune, 76
New York Times, 76, 140
Nigeria, 93, 94, 120, 130, 140, 142; Azikiwe, Flora, 134; Azikiwe, Nnamdi, 134
Nine Point Program, 131
Nineteenth Amendment, 1, 9, 19
Nineteenth Street Baptist Church, 24
Njakar, Austin A., 86
Njoku, Raphael Chijioke, 113
Nkrumah, F. Nwia Kofi, 72

Nkrumah, Kwame, 74, 110; Convention People's Party, 120
Non-Alignment movement, 97
North Carolina, 15, 27

Oberlin College, 25
Obiora, Ekekwe, 93
Okeke, Chukwuemeka, 86
Omega Psi Phi Fraternity, 33
Order of the Star of Africa Commander Cross (Star of Africa), 115; Brooks, W. Sampson, 115; Cole, Henry B., 115; Davis Sr., Benjamin O., 115
Oriole, Paulette, 103
Orizu, Nwafor, 85, 87; American Council on African Education, 86
Ortiz, Fernando, 50
Ostend Manifesto, 119

Palmer Memorial Institute, 39
Pan African Conference, San Francisco, 2, 3
Pan African Congress, 3
Pan-Africanism, 1, 3, 4, 9, 17, 22, 72, 87, 94, 104, 141, 142
Pan-Africanism definition, 2
Pan-Africanist, 1, 2, 10, 17, 104, 117, 141
Pan American Day, 133
Panama, Junta Femenine de Beneficencia, 109
Pandit, Vijaya Lakshmi, 4, 5, 7, 85, 89, 94–97, 109
Partido Revolucionario Cubano, 119
Paterson, Mary Jane, 24
Pearl Harbor, 67
Perry, Walter, 126
Philippines, 7, 23, 33, 49, 54, 78
Pickens, William, 51
Pilgrimage of Friendship, 43
Pinto, Angel C., 46
Pittsburgh Courier, 67, 68
Planos, Celia, 111–112
Platt Amendment, Cuba, 120
Plessy v. Ferguson, 10
Plummer, Brenda Gayle, 82
Ponder, Fannye Ayre, 99
Porter, Dorothy, *See* Wesley, Dorothy Porter
Portuondo, Pedro, 110
Powell, A. Clayton, Jr., 53; National Conference of Negro Leaders, 84

Presbyterian Board of Missions, 16
Prince Edward Hotel, Canada, 126
Puerto Rico, 49, 132
Puwaiah, Svati, 95

Queen Mother Elizabeth, 137
Quill, Michael, Transport Workers Union, 75
Quinquennial International Peace Conference, Zurich, 26

Rao, Lakshmi, 95
Red Scare, 76–77
Red Summer, 68
Refuge Home for Orphan Children, 105
Respected Grandma, 96
Retirement, 8, 107–128
Rice cultivation, 14
Riddle, Estelle M., 91, 92
Rief, Michelle, 34
Robeson, Eslanda, 73, 82
Robeson, Paul, 3, 53, 66, 77; Council on African Affairs, 72–76
Rocabruna, Angel Suarez, 91
Rogers, Edith Nourse, 69; Hobby, Oveta Culp, 69; Roundtree, Dovey Johnson, 69, 70; Women's Army Auxiliary Corps (WAAC), 69, 70; World War II, 69
Roosevelt, Eleanor, 41, 42, 69, 77, 82, 97, 126, 131; My Day, 93
Roosevelt, Franklin D., 6, 40, 45, 48, 52, 53, 69, 74; Division of Negro Affairs, 7
Ross, Robert Arthur, 123
Roundtree, Dovey Johnson, 69, 70
Ruffin, Josephine St. Pierre, 24

Saint Mary's Home for Blind Girls and Women, 92
Sampson, Edith, 133
San Francisco Conference, 3, 65, 66, 78–83, 94, 107, 140, 141
Sands, Stafford, 123
Sandwich First Baptist Church, 126
Sanger, Margaret, 37
Scarborough, Ellen Mills, 134
Schomburg Center for Research in Black Culture, 6
School Republique of Venezuela, 102
Scotia Seminary, 16, 21

Scott, Emmett J., 52
Selassie, Haile, 53, 72
Selassie, Tenagnework, 54; Women's Work Association, 53
Seminar of Goodwill to Cuba, 49
Semper Fidelis Club, Birmingham, Alabama, 24
Senegal, 14
Serro, Consuela, 44
Sierra Leone, 17, 29
Simmons, Virginia, 48
Simpson, Clarence L., 140
Simpson, Sarah, 107, 114
Sims, R. P., Bluefield Institute, 50
Singh, Rana S., 96
Slave Voyage Database, 14
Slowe, Lucy Diggs, 40, 90
Smallwood, Irene, *See* Bowen, Irene
Smith, Christine, 39
Smith, Ferdinand D., 72, 74
Smith, Thomas E., 13
Smith College, 49
Society of Afro-Cuban Studies, 37–38, 51, 142; Ortiz, Fernando, 50
Sojourner Truth Club, 27
South Africa, 17, 23, 33, 74, 76, 119, 130; Gandha, Mahatma, 43, 118; Help Africa Day, 74; Msezane, Edith Nono, 134
South America, 78, 95
South Carolina, 1, 3, 14, 15, 17; Kendall Institute, 19; Mayesville, 6, 10, 13, 14, 99, 141
Southeastern Federation of Colored Women's Clubs, 27
Southern Christian Leadership Conference (SCLC), 135
Soviet Union, 116
Spain, 109
Spingarn, Arthur, 74
Spingarn Medal, 38, 78
Spotlight on Africa, *See* New Africa
Sri Lanka (Ceylon), 32, 43
SS *Harriet Tubman*, 70, 71, 129
Star of Africa, 115
State Archives of Florida, 6
Statuary Hall, 5
Statue, 5, 138
Staupers, Mabel Keaton, 39
Sterne, Emma Gelders, 12

Stettinius, Edward R., 79, 80
Stewart, Maria W., 31
Stewart Missionary Foundation for Africa, and First African Christian Church Conference, 13
Stimson, Henry, 51, 69, 70
Stokes, Anson Phelps, 53
Stowell, James S., 112
Student Von-Violent Coordinating Committee, 138
Subversive organizations, 77
Sunshine Orphanage, 102
Symonette, Georgiana, 123

Talbert, Mary B., 29; International Council of Women of the Darker Races, 32, 38; Spingarn Medal, 38
Tarbell, Ida M., 37
Tate, Merze, 8, 90
Telefast, 95
Tennessee, 27
Terrell, Mary Church, 4, 5, 6, 22, 24, 25–27, 29, 31, 32, 37, 39, 40, 84, 109; International Congress of Women Congress, Berlin, Germany, 26; International Council of Women of the Darker Races, 32, 34; National Association for the Advancement of Colored People, 25; National Association of Colored Women, 25–27; National Conference of Negro Leaders, 84; Oberlin College, 25; Quinquennial International Peace Conference, Zurich, 26
Tesemma, Getahoun, 53, 54
Thompson, James G., 67–68
Thompson, John, 68
Thurman, Howard, 5, 94; Howard University Rankin Chapel, 43
Thurman, Lucy, 29
Thurman, Sue Bailey, 4, 29, 43–52, 89; *Aframerican Woman's Journal*, 7, 43 48; Cuba, 44; Gandhi, Mahatma, 43; International Program of Negro Women, 48; National Council of Negro Women, 4, 7, 37, 80; Pilgrimage of Friendship, 43; World Fellowship Committee, 43; Young Women's Christian Association, 43
Tiscornia Detention Center, 50
Tobias, Channing H., 52, 84, 109
Tolbert, William R., 113

200 · Index

Toote, Thaddeus, 123
Transport Workers Union, 75
Trinidad, 8, 88, 91, 92, 123; Port-au-Prince, 99, 101, 104
Trinity Presbyterian Mission School, 11
Truman, Harry S., 75, 81, 82, 100, 108, 112; India Emergency Food Aid Act, 98
Tubman, Antoinette, 113
Tubman William V. S., 52, 53, 93, 115, 116; Inauguration, 112–114; Papers, 6
Tucker, Nora R., 110
Turner, Henry McNeal, 17–18
Turner, Lorenzo Dow, 15
Tuskegee Women's Clubs, 24
Tuuri, Rebecca, 136

Underground Railroad monuments, Canada, 126
United Beauty School Owners and Teachers Association, 121
United Nations, 66, 75, 76, 78, 80, 87, 88, 109, 121, 129, 131, 132, 138, 141; American Association for the United Nations, 140; American Association of University Women, 79; Charter, 7, 65, 74, 79, 84; Declaration on the Granting of Independence to Colonial Countries and Peoples, 84; Eichelberger, Clark M., 140; Founding of, 2, 3, 13, 66, 80, 129; General Federation of Women's Clubs, 79; Hunton, Eunice, 74; National Association for the Advancement of Colored People, 78–83, 129, 130, 131, 133, 136; National League of Women's Voters, 79; Pan African Congress in San Francisco, 1, 3, 65, 66, 78–83, 94, 107, 140, 141; Women's Action Committee for Victory and Lasting Peace, 79
United Nations Commission on the Status of Women, 130, 133, 136
United Nations Conference on International Organization (UNCIO), 84
United Nations Day, 129, 133, 136; National Citizens' Committee, 131
United Nations Week, 132
United Negro Improvement Association (UNIA), 2, 28
United States, Department of State, 75, 78, 95, 117

United States Agency for International Development (USAID), African Bureau, 138
University of Liberia, 117
University of Madras, 95
University of Massachusetts Amherst Libraries, 6
University of Windsor Archive and Special Collections, 6
Urrutia, Gustavo, 51

Verna, Chantalle F., 103
Vesey, Denmark, 99
Vieux, Andre, 102
Virgin Islands, 49
Virginia, 27
Voting rights, 2, 19
Voyages: The Trans-Atlantic Slave Trade Database, 14

Walker, Mabel, 123
Walker, Madame C. J., 121
War Bonds, 71, 129
Washington, Booker T., 3, 24, 25, 32, 34, 52, 70
Washington, Margaret Murray, 23, 29; death, 35; International Council of Women of the Darker Races, 32–35; National Federation of Afro American women, 24; as Tuskegee Dean of Women, 24
Weaver, George, 95
Welcome, Verda, 91; National Council of Negro Women, 131
Wells, Ida B., 24
Wesley, Dorothy Porter, 7, 8, 49, 70, 90, 133
West, John, 117
West Africa, 14, 15, 17
West Indies, 78, 90
Western Bloc, 97
Western Reserve University, 86
White, Walter, 3, 78, 95, 80–83, 85, 95, 97, 109; United Nations Charter, 7, 79
White House, 37, 41, 53; Alexander, Sadie T. M., 42; Hunton, Addie, 42; Hunton, Eunice, 41; Mallory, Arenia, 42
Wilberforce University, 86
Wilkins, Roy, 95
Williams, A. Wilberforce, 31
Williams, Fannie Barrier, 1
Williams, Henry Sylvester, 2

Williams, Mary Lou, 75
Williamson, Florence K., 40
Wilson, Woodrow, 52
Windsor Emancipation Day, Canada, 125
Windsor Star, 140
Wobil, Joe Columbus, 93
Woman Development Club, 27
Woman's Musical and Literary Club, Springfield, Missouri, 24
Women United to Understand and Help Peoples of Africa, 133
Women's Action Committee for Victory and Lasting Peace, 79
Women's Army Auxiliary Corps (WAAC), 70; Hobby, Oveta Culp, 69; Roundtree, Dovey Johnson, 69
Women's Auxiliary of the National Baptist Convention, 39
Women's International League for Peace and Freedom (WILPF), 35
Women's Literary Art and Social Club, 27
Women's National Press Club, 49
Women's suffrage, 1, 8, 101, 142
Women's Work Association, Ethiopia, 53
Woodson, Carter G., 38, 109; Negro History Week, 33; Omega Psi Phi Fraternity, 33
The Worker, 77
World Columbian Exposition, 107
World Fellowship Committee, 43
World Health Day, 133

World Security Conference, 81
World Security Month, 79
World War I, 28, 42, 68, 80
World War II, 1, 7, 54, 66, 67, 70, 78, 81, 87, 97, 129, 137; Black women in, 3, 7, 69, 71, 88, 107; Double V campaign, 68, 71; Espionage and Smith Acts, 68; Hobby, Oveta Culp, 69, 70; Pearl Harbor, 67; Rogers, Edith Nourse, 69; Roundtree, Dovey Johnson, 69; Stimson, Henry, 69; Thompson, James G., 67–68; Women's Army Auxiliary Corps (WAAC), 69
Wormly, Margaret Just, 8, 90
Wright, Richard, 33
Wynn, Walter C., 114, 117

Yale University, 86
Yates, Josephine Silone, 24, 29
Yergan, Max, 53; Council on Africa Affairs (CAA), 72–77, 84
Young, (Mrs.) Charles S., 114
Young Men's Christian Association (YMCA): Hunton, Sr., William Alphaeus, 42; Yergan, Max, 73
Young Women's Christian Association (YWCA), 38, 43

Zebhiri, Mauclair, 133
Zeh, Feliz U., 94

Dr. Ashley Robertson Preston is an author, curator, and assistant professor of history at Howard University. She has served as director of the Mary McLeod Bethune Foundation National Historic Landmark at Bethune-Cookman University and as an archives technician for the National Archives for Black Women's History at the Mary McLeod Bethune Council House National Historic Site. She is the author of *Mary McLeod Bethune in Florida: Bringing Social Justice to the Sunshine State*. She has published articles in the *Journal of Negro Education, Journal of Black Studies, and Journal of African American History*. Dr. Preston's research interests focus on the activism of Black women during the early twentieth century and the ways in which they uplifted their communities, created institutions, and stood against systemic racism. In addition to her work as a historian she is the founder of the nonprofit Carter G. Cares. Inspired by her son, who was born prematurely at twenty-eight weeks, the organization raises awareness and provides support for NICU families and high-risk mothers.

www.ingramcontent.com/pod-product-compliance
Lightning Source LLC
Chambersburg PA
CBHW030623230426
43661CB00053B/2115